PRAISE FOR
WALTER SEMKIW'S
PRIOR BOOK

RETURN OF THE REVOLUTIONARIES:
The Case for Reincarnation and Soul Groups Reunited

"It looks fascinating!"

Bill Clinton
Former President, USA

"For the survival of humanity, this is the most significant book written in one thousand years. When research reveals scores of correlations, 'coincidence' becomes synchronicity, which is the foundation for many new scientific discoveries."

C. Norman Shealy,
M.D., Ph.D., Neurosurgeon,
Medical inventor, and author of 22 books.

"Dr. Semkiw's book, *Return of the Revolutionaries*, is perhaps the best-documented case study of human reincarnation in the Western world. This book is vitally important since, for the first time in western literature the true idea of reincarnation is introduced."

Wayne Peterson,
Author of *Extraordinary Times,*
Extraordinary Beings.

Born Again

Reincarnation Cases Involving International Celebrities, India's Political Legends and Film Stars

WALTER SEMKIW, MD

First Published in 2006 by
Ritana Books
81, Defence Colony Flyover Market,
New Delhi-110024, India
Phone : 011-24617278
Fax : 011-24636063
Email : ritana@vsnl.com
Website : www.ritanabooks.com

Walter Semkiw asserts the moral right to be identified as the author
of this work

ISBN : 81-85250-37-5

Published by Rock Furtado for Ritana Books
and Printed at IPP Ltd. New Delhi

MISSION STATEMENT

To make violence obsolete,
To make our oneness known
To help create a civilization
We return to with Joy,
On Planet Earth,
Our terrestrial home.

ACKNOWLEDGEMENTS

I thank Sunny Satin and Rock Furtado for
making this book possible.

I also applaud Sunny Satin,
a kind and gentle soul,
for his tireless efforts in bringing
Past Life Regression Therapy
to students around the world.

DEDICATION

I dedicate *Born Again* to all the Souls
who appear within as reincarnation cases.

Note to the Reader

Born Again is a study of past-life cases based on published sources and my own research, analysis, and commentary. The book is my own independent work, and no affiliation, endorsement, or sponsorship by the individuals mentioned in the text is claimed or implied, except where such endorsements are specifically given. The fact that I discern evidence of the past lives of various living individuals is not meant to suggest that these individuals share my beliefs or validate my findings. The commentary and conclusions set forth in *Born Again* are my own.

Every effort has been made to locate and secure the permission of copyright-holders when making use of copyrighted materials beyond the scope of Fair Use under the law of copyright. However, despite my best efforts, I was unable to determine the copyright status of a limited number of images, and I invite the copyright-holders of such images to contact the publisher so that proper credit can be afforded in future printings.

TABLE OF CONTENTS

Section Three :
Reincarnation Cases Involving Political Legends of India and Film Stars

REINCARNATION CASE LIST

Section One:
Independently Researched Reincarnation Cases

Section Two:
Cases Solved Through Kevin Ryerson and Ahtun Re

Section Three:
Reincarnation Cases Involving Luminaries of India

Born Again

SECTION ONE

Independently Researched Reincarnation Cases

1

Evidence of Reincarnation and Its Impact on Society and Religion

At about the turn of the millennium, multiple independently researched reincarnation cases have emerged, which reveal that from lifetime to lifetime, people have the same facial features, personality traits, passions, talents and even linguistic writing style. The most compelling cases involve those in which children have spontaneous memories of a past lifetime that can be factually verified. Recently, in the United States, such as case was featured on national television. In 2005, a reincarnation case involving a little boy named James Leininger, who remembered dying as a fighter aircraft pilot in World War II was aired on ABC Primetime, a popular television news program.

The parents had called on Carol Bowman, a reincarnation researcher who specializes in cases involving children, to help with their son, who had recurring nightmares regarding the crash. Through information given to his parents, Bruce and Andrea Leininger, his father was able to validate his son's past lifetime as US aircraft carrier pilot James Huston, Jr., and when little James was reunited with Huston's surviving sister, based on knowledge only James Huston could have known, the sister accepted little James as the reincarnation of her deceased brother.

Another case that Carol Bowman, author of *Children's Past Lives*, involves a little boy in India named Titu Singh, who had clear memories of a past lifetime in Agra, in which his name was Suresh Verma. He recalled that he had a wife name Uma and two children. When he was reunited with his past life family, he could identify family members, knew details of Suresh Verma's life that were validated and Titu was accepted by the Verma family as the reincarnation of Suresh. This case was broadcast on *Forty Minutes*, a BBC program in 1990 and was recently features in *Reincarnation International*, published in London.

Another case that involves childhood memories is that of Barbro Karlen, who since she was a little girl, remembered that her name was Anne Frank. The Frank/Karlen case has enormous significance from a sociological point of view, as Anne Frank was persecuted as a Jew, while Barbro was born into a Christian family. This case will be presented in detail later on.

This book is divided into three sections. The first involves independently researched reincarnation cases, which all demonstrate common principles of reincarnation, such as the observation that facial features stay the same from one incarnation to another, which were described above.

The second sections involves Western cases solved in my work with Kevin Ryerson, a world famous trance medium who is featured in three of Shirley MacLaine's books. A trance medium works by going into a meditative state, or trance, which allows spirit beings to speak through him. In doing reincarnation research, I found that Kevin channels an Egyptian spirit guide named Ahtun Re, who demonstrates the ability to make what I assess to be accurate past life identifications. This is a rare ability and when I found that Ahtun Re could be used as a resource in this capacity, I began working with Kevin on a regular basis. At the time of the publication of *Born Again*, I have worked with Kevin for over five years and have had over seventy sessions with him. Having such extensive experience with Kevin's spirit guide, I have learned to have confidences in Ahtun Re's abilities in establishing accurate matches in reincarnation cases. As such, I have used Ahtun Re as a "Gold Standard," to determine whether past life matches are accurate. All reincarnation cases found in *Born Again* and my earlier work, *Return of the Revolutionaries*, were confirmed to be accurate and valid by Ahtun Re.

The third section involves Indian reincarnation cases primarily derived through my work with Kevin Ryerson, though as we shall see, a soul can incarnate in India in one lifetime, and the United States or Pakistan in another. That last chapter features the Indian spiritual teacher Siva Baba, who supports my reincarnation research, and who independently has known of several of his own past lives.

Objective evidence of reincarnation, based on spontaneous memories of past lives both in childhood and adulthood, will inevitably grow. With the advent of the Internet, communication regarding these cases on a world wide basis will result in a large database of reincarnation cases. Indeed, I with Kevin Ryreson and others, have founded the Institute for the Integration of Science, Intuition and Spirit, (IISIS), that is dedicated to the scientific research of reincarnation, human or soul evolution and related matters. At this point, I would like to review some of the societal changes that objective evidence of reincarnation will bring,

- *One of the most beneficial and needed effects that an understanding of reincarnation will induce is a mitigation of violence between people belonging to different races, religions and ethnic backgrounds. This change is vitally needed, given events such as the destruction of the World Trade Center and the daily ration of violence and killing that we observe between people of contrasting cultures. The evidence presented in this book shows that people change religious, ethnic and racial affiliations from lifetime to lifetime.*

Once people realize that religious affiliation constitutes a temporary belief system, that one can be Christian in one lifetime and Jewish, Islamic, Hindu or Buddhist in another, then conflicts based on these affiliations will be seen as self-defeating. Indeed, we all must stop thinking of ourselves exclusively as Christians, Jews, Muslims or Hindus, for in the span of lifetimes, we become all of these, and more. The nice thing about this understanding is that no religion is negated, no religion is deemed wrong. Rather, we come to understand that from lifetime to lifetime, we have the opportunity to enjoy and learn from various religious doctrines. The key is not to get too attached to one particular belief system, for in the end, this only leads to division and conflict.

I believe that knowledge of the mechanism of reincarnation will help humanity evolve from a tribal mentality, in which we identify with one particular religious, ethnic, racial or nationalistic group, to the stage of the Universal Human. As a Universal Human, one understands and respects many cultures, but does not align one's self with any one denomination. In the United States, writers such as Gary Zukav and Barbara Marx Hubbard are forwarding the concept of the Universal Human. The information provided in this book will provide a greater foundation for their ideas.

As we move from tribal human to Universal Human, racism and religious prejudice will come to an end. Nationalism and ethnic pride will also be put in perspective, as we realize that we can be born in different countries and to parents of various ethnic backgrounds, from one lifetime to another. When people realize that one can be white in one lifetime and black or Asian in another, racial prejudices will also dissolve.

•   Diverse religions will adopt a more universal set of teachings, as spirituality becomes more scientific in nature, based on observation and objective data. Indeed, spirituality will inevitably move from the domain of belief to the realm of science. Religious organizations will still remain important, as we need places to congregate and worship God collectively.

•   Just as collective conflicts and wars will be diminished, individual violent behavior and crime will be curtailed. This premise is based on two principles. One is

*that people will understand karma as a reality. We will
know that what we do to others will return to us in time.
This will create a change in behavior in those who have
been atheists, as well as those who belong to organized
religions. Currently, religious doctrines teach that wrong
action can be absolved or forgiven by one's particular
religious authorities and one's particular God. This reduces
the motivation to behave in a proper manner.*

*Evidence of reincarnation will bring the realization that
we are responsible for our actions and that in a subsequent
lifetime, we will be subject to the same actions that we
create in this lifetime. If we scorn someone in this lifetime,
we will be the object of scorn in another. If we kill someone,
in another lifetime, we will have to experience the suffering
that our action caused. If we express tolerance and
compassion, these things will come back to us too. With
this understanding, every action that has the potential to
harm others, will be more carefully weighed. Some will say
that in cultures that embrace reincarnation, crime still exists.
I counter this with the argument that there is a big difference
in believing in reincarnation and knowing that reincarnation
is the way the human soul evolves. When you absolutely
know that reincarnation and karma are real, then committing
a crime is like purposely placing your hand into a roaring
furnace..*

*A second reason why violence will be curtailed is that
people will realize that they can bring with them, in future
lifetimes, knowledge and skills earned in this lifetime. This
is especially important for those born in poverty or other
disadvantage. For those born with little, for those who feel
shortchanged in life, crime may seem like the only way out.
This is particularly true in American culture, where
materialism runs rampant, and the discrepancy between*

those who have and those who have not is greater than ever. Given a situation of inequity, those who perpetrate crimes may see their actions as retribution for being placed in unfair circumstances and as a remedy for hopelessness.

Evidence presented in this book shows that from lifetime to lifetime, we pick up where we have left off, that we bring with us skills and abilities that we have earned in previous lifetimes. We will see that individuals can return to life to complete a job or to bring to fruition a goal which was initiated in a prior lifetime. This can bring hope to those caught in unfortunate circumstances. Someone who finds opportunities blocked in this lifetime can plan and invest for a subsequent lifetime. One can begin studying, learning, and practicing in this incarnation in preparation for the next.

For example, if you want to become a great musician, then put that desire into practice today. In a future incarnation, you will be able to bring forth talent earned in the past. If you want to be wealthy, study finance and investment today, and you will bring business acumen with you in another lifetime. If you want to be a great musician, practice your instrument and study composition today, so that talent can emerge on another morrow. Knowing that effort expended in this lifetime will be rewarded in another will bring hope to those in despair.

• *Combating world hunger and poverty will become a more pressing concern for each individual on the planet. This will occur due to two realizations. First of all, we will comprehend that we return to a world that we helped create. We are responsible for the conditions that we will live under in future incarnations. From the point of view of self-interest, the knowledge that we may be reborn someday in an impoverished land will motivate those in developed countries* to share resources with poorer countries. Citizens of developed countries will feel a greater need to help poor nations in implementing infrastructure and economic policies that will ensure that basic needs of the population are met. Our attitudes towards Third World debt will change, as we become more concerned about the plight of the poor.

Secondly, from a spiritual perspective, people will realize that the amount in one's bank account at the time of death means nothing in the eyes of God. Rather, good karma is based on what we have done during our lifetime to help our fellow man. With a better understanding of karma, the rich will care more about alleviating the suffering of those who have not.

Collectively, we will invest more of our time, energy, money and creativity on devising ways to make the world a better place for those born in unfortunate circumstances. We will be less motivated to put our resources in bigger houses, fancier cars, jewelry and trinkets, sports teams and violent games. Instead, we will have a desire to improve conditions of life for the collective. Knowledge of reincarnation will change what we value, and a desire will emerge to pursue those things that count from a spiritual point of view.

- Protecting the environment will become a more pressing concern as people realize that they will have to return to planet Earth, our terrestrial home, many times in the future. People will realize that in subsequent lifetimes, they themselves will have to deal with environmental problems created today. Profit will no longer take precedence over protecting the environment, for people will realize that everything they do is taken into account and that crimes against Earth have a karmic toll, too.

- *Relationships between family members, friends, and even foes, will be enhanced, as people realize that we return to life in groups, that we return to Earth with those we have known before. Those with whom we have conflicts in one lifetime we will meet again in another. Our bitterest enemy may come back to us as a family member or coworker, so that we may have another opportunity to truly know the other person and have a chance for resolution of conflicts to occur. As such, a greater effort will be made to understand one another in our present incarnations. We will learn to have tolerance for those with opposing views and differing values in life. Loving relationships will be recognized as a more precious commodity than money or gold.*

ORGANIZED RELIGION AND THE ACCEPTANCE OF REINCARNATION

It will be interesting to see how organized religions respond to the mounting evidence of reincarnation that is streaming into the world. Religious authorities will have two options: to integrate reincarnation into their doctrines or to reject it. If religious authorities reject evidence of reincarnation, they will maintain the status quo and guarantee their short-term security, but they will also propagate continuing religious conflicts, which could eventually grow into nuclear disaster.

If religious authorities embrace the information regarding reincarnation, they will help create a more peaceful world. Their religions will endure, as the wonderful and beautiful teachings of their prophets will not be diminished. Further, people will always need religions, as people need to congregate and worship God collectively. Fortunately, there are references in the doctrines of many of our major religions that seem to support the existence of reincarnation, which may make it easier to integrate reincarnation into traditional belief systems. Though I am no religious scholar or authority in these matters, let share with you passages in religious texts that seem to allude to reincarnation. I focus on Christianity, Judaism and Islam, as reincarnation has traditionally not been emphasized in these religions.

REINCARNATION AND CHRISTIANITY

Leaders of the Christian, Jewish, and Islamic faiths may have an easier time accepting this new technology if they recognize that teachings on reincarnation were once part of the doctrines of their prophets. As such, the information presented in this book is not new technology at all. Rather, teachings regarding reincarnation in major religions have been ignored and at times, purposely hidden. Let us take Christianity as an example.

In the New Testament, Jews are depicted as expecting the reincarnation of their great prophets. Indeed, these prophets were already thought to have reincarnated in times past. For example, the Jewish sect called the Samarians believed Adam reincarnated as Noah, then as Abraham, then Moses.[2] Reincarnation of the old prophets was also on the minds of Jews at the time of Jesus. In fact, followers of Jesus thought that he was a reincarnated prophet. Let us reflect on the following passage from the Gospel of Matthew: "When Jesus came into coasts of Cesarea Philippi, he asked disciples, saying, 'Whom do men say I, the Son of man, am?' And they said, 'Some say that thou art John the Baptist, some, Elias; and others, Jeremias, or one of the prophets.'" (Matthew 16:13–4)

Herod, who was in command of Jerusalem under the Romans, also speculated on who Jesus may have previously been. Herod also thought Jesus might have been one of the old prophets, or even John the Baptist, whom he had recently had beheaded.

When Jesus announced that he was the Jewish Messiah, his followers became confused, as the scriptures stated the prophet Elias (or Elijah in Greek) would return and precede the coming of the Messiah. The disciples put this apparent discrepancy to Jesus. The disciples pointed out: "Why then say the scribes that Elias must come first. And Jesus answered and said unto them, Elias truly shall first come, and restore all things. But I say unto you, That Elias is come already, and they knew him not. . . . Then the disciples understood that he spake unto them of John the Baptist." (Matthew 17:9–13)

In another section of the New Testament, Jesus unequivocally states that John the Baptist is the reincarnation of the prophet Elias: "Among them that are born of women there hath not risen a greater than John the Baptist. . . . And if ye will receive it, this is Elias. . . . He that hath ears to hear, let him hear." (Matthew 11:11–15)

Reincarnation is alluded to in a section of the New Testament in which the disciples ask Jesus why a man was born blind. The disciples asked, "Which did sin, this man or his parents?" (John 9:34) This passage implies that the blind man had a previous incarnation where he had the opportunity to commit a sin that would result in the karmic consequence of blindness. Without the premise of reincarnation, how could the blind man commit a sin responsible for his handicap, as the man was blind from birth? Jesus didn't dispute the reasoning of the disciples, though he stated that the blindness was due to other factors.

In addition to these citations from the New Testament, evidence shows that reincarnation was part of the Church's early doctrine and was promoted by Church Fathers, writers who established Christian doctrine prior to the eighth century and whose works were used to disseminate Christian ideas to populations of the Roman Empire. To be considered a Church Father one had to meet the following criteria. One had to lead a holy life;, one's writings had do be free of doctrinal error; one's interpretation of Christian doctrine was deemed to be exemplary; and one's writings had to have approval of the Church. A number of Christian Church Fathers believed in and wrote about reincarnation: St. Justin Martyr (100–165 A.D.) expressly stated that the soul inhabits more than one human body. Origen (185–254 A.D.), who was considered by St. Jerome as "the greatest teacher of the Church after the Apostles," defended the idea that the soul exists before the body, fundamental to the concept of reincarnation.

Another Church Father, St. Gregory, Bishop of Nyssa (257–332 A.D.), wrote: "It is absolutely necessary that the soul should be healed and purified, and if this does not take place during its life on earth it must be accomplished in future lives. . . . The soul . . . is immaterial and invisible in nature, it at one time puts off one body . . . and exchanges it for a second." St. Gregory also wrote: "Every soul comes into this world strengthened by the victories or weakened by the defeats of its previous life." St. Augustine (354–430 A.D.), one of the greatest theologians of the Christian church, speculated that philosopher Plotinus was the reincarnation of Plato. St. Augustine wrote: "The message of Plato . . . now shines forth mainly in Plotinus, a Platonist so like his master that one would think . . . that Plato is born again in Plotinus." Other Church Fathers who demonstrated a belief in reincarnation included Synesius (the Bishop of Ptolemais), St. Ambrose, Pope Gregory I, Jerome, St. Athanasius, St. Basil, St. John Chrysostom, St. Gregory of Nazianzus, and Clement of Alexandria.[3]

If the belief in the pre-existence of souls and reincarnation was prominent in the early Christian Church, why is it not present in contemporary doctrine? The reason is that a Roman Emperor named Justinian made arrangements for reincarnation to be removed from official Church doctrine in 553 A.D. In the early centuries of the Christian Church, disputes over doctrine were settled by bishops of the Church, through meetings called Ecumenical Councils. These Councils were major gatherings, which occurred infrequently, sometimes once in a hundred years. To understand the story of reincarnation and the Christian Church, we must go back in time to the year 330 A.D.

In that year, Constantine the Great moved the capital of the Roman Empire from Rome to Constantinople, a city which today is called Istanbul.

As a result, two centers of the Christian Church developed, the Western Church in Rome and the Eastern Church in Constantinople. The emperors of Constantinople controlled the Eastern Church and dictated policy as they pleased. As an example, Emperor Leo III prohibited images and portraits from being kept in churches, so icons, which today are so admired for their beauty, had to be removed from places of worship. Similarly, Justinian determined Church policy regarding reincarnation.

In the sixth century, the Church was divided over the issue of reincarnation. Western bishops in Rome believed in pre-existence of the soul while Eastern bishops were opposed to it. Emperor Justinian of Constantinople, who controlled the Eastern Church, was against the doctrine of reincarnation. As an example of his interference in Church matters, Justinian excommunicated the Church Father Origen who openly supported the idea of reincarnation. To further his agenda, Justinian convened the Fifth Ecumenical Council in 553 A.D., with only six bishops of the Western Church in attendance. On the other hand, 159 bishops of the Eastern Church, which Justinian controlled, were present. It was at this meeting that pre-existence of the soul was voted out of Church doctrine. Emperor Justinian manipulated Church doctrine by stacking the voting deck in his favor.

Pope Vigilius protested this turn of events and demanded equal representation between Eastern and Western bishops. Though the Pope was present in Constantinople at the time of the Fifth Ecumenical Council, he boycotted the Council in protest. Justinian not only ignored Pope Vigilius, but persecuted him.

The *Catholic Encyclopedia* states that the conflict between the emperor and the Pope was so extreme that the Pope suffered many indignities at the hands of the emperor and was almost killed. Can you conceive today that a politician or head of state could dictate policy to the Pope? That the Pope would boycott the biggest meeting at the Vatican in a hundred years? Yet this is what happened as the Fourth Ecumenical Council was convened in 451 A.D. and the Sixth Ecumenical Council was held in 680 A.D. As a result, the *Catholic Encyclopedia* states, the Council called by Justinian was not a true Ecumenical Council, so the removal of pre-existence of the soul as a Church doctrine should not be considered an actual decree of the Ecumenical Council.[4,5]

The rift between the Eastern and Western Church increased in 1054 when the two branches of the Christian Church excommunicated each other. When Christian Crusaders from the Western Church were on their way to capture Jerusalem from the Muslims, they made a point to raze the Christian city of Constantinople. Following that episode, a permanent split occurred and the Western Church became the Roman Catholic Church, while the Eastern Orthodox Church went its own way. Even today, members of the Eastern Christian Church do not consider the Pope in Rome as their leader. So we see that the political fragmentation within the Eastern and Western branches of the Christian Church is as real today as it was in the time of Emperor Justinian and Pope Vigilius.

In addition to Christian leaders fighting among themselves, there are disturbing examples of Christians fighting with those opposed to their doctrines. The

Inquisition was established by a series of Papal decrees between 1227 and 1235 to confront dissident religious movements. In this effort, Pope Innocent IV authorized the use of torture in 1252. Later, the persecution of presumed witches in Europe between 1450 and 1700 arose as orthodox Christianity went through its existential anxieties resulting from Martin Luther's Reformation and the emerging scientific paradigm. The Papal decree *Summis Desiderantes*, issued by Pope Innocent VIII in 1484, stimulated another wave of torture and executions. This Papal dissertation was anti-feminine and condemned witches. Thousands of innocent women were executed based on confessions obtained through torture.

The last outbreak of this persecution occurred in Salem, Massachusetts, in 1692. Twenty women were executed after a group of young girls became emotional or hysterical while playing at magic. In reality, some of those considered witches in the past were most likely girls who had psychic gifts but who were perceived as dangerous by those who were not similarly talented. Today, many women who participate in classes designed to stimulate intuition and psychic abilities remember past lives in which they were persecuted and burned at the stake. It can be dangerous to be an evolved being in a relatively primitive world.

REINCARNATION AND JUDAISM

As mentioned, reincarnation was part of Jewish thought at the time of Jesus. The Jewish historian, Flavius Josephus (37–100 A.D.), wrote that there were three sects of Jews during that era, the Sadducees,

Essenes, and Pharisees. Josephus wrote that two of the sects, the Essenes (of Dead Sea Scroll fame) and the Pharisees both believed in reincarnation. Josephus wrote, "The Pharisees believe that souls have an immortal vigour in them and that the virtuous shall have power to revive and live again: on account of which doctrines they are able greatly to persuade the body of people."[6]

Josephus himself, who served as a soldier, once rallied his men to fight by citing the doctrine of reincarnation. Josephus said to his men, "Do ye not remember that all pure Spirits when they depart out of this life obtain a most holy place in heaven, from whence, in the revolutions of ages, they are again sent into pure bodies."[7]

Reincarnation is also a part of the Zohar, a classic Kabalistic text, thought to be written by Rabbi Simeon ben Jochai, in AD 80, with contributions made by medieval Hebrew scholars. The Kabalistic movement focused on hidden wisdom of the Jewish faith. The Zohar was edited and first published by Rabbi Moses de Leon, in 1280. Here are sample passages from the Zohar, regarding reincarnation:

All souls are subject to the trials of transmigration (reincarnation); and men do not know the designs of the Most High with regard to them; they know not how they are being at all times judged, both before coming into this world and when they leave it. They do not know how many transmigrations and mysterious trials they must undergo.

Souls must reenter the absolute substance whence they have emerged. But to accomplish this end they must develop all the perfections, the germ of which is planted in them; and if they have not fulfilled this condition during one life, they must commence another, a third, and so forth, until they have acquired the condition which fits them for reunion with God.[8]

Another prominent Jewish theologian who believed in reincarnation was Rabbi Manasseh ben Israel (1604-1657). It was this rabbi who convinced Oliver Cromwell to remove the Crown's prohibition of Jews from residing in England, a policy that had existed for 150 years, since the time of Edward I. In his book *Nishmath Hayem*, Rabbi Manasseh ben Israel wrote:

The belief or the doctrine of the transmigration of souls is a firm and infallible dogma accepted by the whole assemblage of our church with one accord, so that there is none to be found who would dare to deny it. . . . Indeed, there are a great number of sages in Israel who hold firm to this doctrine so that they make it a dogma, a fundamental point of our religion. We are therefore in duty bound to obey and to accept this dogma with acclamation . . . as the truth of it has been incontestably demonstrated by the Zohar, and all books of the Kabalists.[9]

REINCARNATION AND ISLAM

Reincarnation is also included in the teachings of Islam, a religion founded by the Prophet Mohammed. Mohammed was born in 570 A.D. into a prominent family that served as caretakers of the holy site of Mecca, which tradition holds was built by Abraham. Mohammed married his employer, a businesswoman named Khaadija; Mohammed was 25 and Khaadija 40. Islam's holy text is the Quran (or Koran), which means the "Recital" or "Reading." In essence, the Quran is a channeled work, transmitted from God through Mohammed.

Mohammed's first revelation occurred when he was 40 years old in 610 A.D. He then began recording verses which, over time, became the Quran. As this spiritual movement grew, Mohammed and his followers became the subjects of persecution and they had to flee Mecca in 622 A.D., taking refuge in Medina. Mohammed was a warrior as well as prophet and led his people into battle many times. Eventually Mohammed brought his followers back to Mecca, today's shrine of Islam.

There are several references in the Quran that refer to reincarnation. Let us review a few of these passages.

And when his body falleth off altogether, as an old fish-shell, his soul doeth well by releasing, and formeth a new one instead...The person of man is only a mask which the soul putteth on for a season; it weareth its proper time and then is cast off, and another is worn in its stead.[10]

God generates beings, and sends them back over and over again, til they return to him.[11]

How can you make denial of Allah, who made you live again when you died, will make you dead again, and then alive again, until you finally return to him?[12]

God is the one who created you all, then provided you sustenance, then will cause you to die, then will bring you to life.[13]

Surely it is God who splits the seed and the stone, bringing the living from the dead; and it is God who brings the dead from living.[14]

I tell you, of a truth, that the spirits which now have

affinity shall be kindred together, although they all meet in new persons and names.[15]

This last verse is one of my favorites, as it alludes to the existence of soul groups. People who are connected, emotionally and by karma, return to life with those they have known before. This is an observation I have made in my research. In addition to passages on reincarnation, the Koran also references karma:

God does not compel a soul to do what is beyond its capacity: it gets what it has earned, and is responsible for what it deserves.[16]

Every soul will be brought face to face with the good that it has done and with the evil it has done.[17]

And We will set up the scales of justice for the day of reckoning. And no soul shall be wronged in anything. And be it the weight of a mustard seed, We will bring it forth: and We are well able to take account.[18]

For We give life to the dead, and We record what they sent before and what they left after them: and We have taken account of all things.[19]

The Quran has wonderful passages that make one think in terms of the Universal Human; religious affiliation is minimized and one's benevolence is deemed most important. Consider the following verse: "Indeed, be they Muslims, Jews, Sabians, or Christians, those who believe in God and the final day and who do good have nothing to fear, and they will not grieve."[20]

Mohammed cautioned against exclusionary religious practices, which in his day was aimed at the Christian Church. Mohammed's point was that God should be the central theme in a person's life, not the messengers or prophets who convey God's words.

The "Book" in this passage refers to the Bible. "People of the Book, do not go to excess in your religion, do not say of God anything but truth. The Messiah, Jesus son of Mary, was only an Envoy of God and a Word of God bestowed on Mary, and a spirit of God."[21]

Jalaluddin Rumi (1207-1273), was a great Islamic and Sufi poet. Sufis are considered the esoteric holders of Islamic wisdom, much as the Kabalists are regarded as holders of the hidden wisdom of Judaism. Rumi wrote:

Like grass I have grown over and over again. I passed out of mineral form and lived as a plant. From plant I was lifted up to be an animal. Then I put away the animal form and took on a human shape. Why should I fear that if I died I shall be lost? For passing human form I shall attain the flowing locks and shining wings of angels. And then I shall become what no mind has ever conceived. O let me cease to exist! For non-existence only means that I shall return to Him.[22]

It is interesting to note that a Christian Church Father mused similarly about the pathway of human evolution, as did Rumi. This view suggests that the plant and animal kingdoms can serve as a stepping stone for a soul's advancement to the stage of human development. Let us contemplate the following quotation from the Christian Church Father Synesius, Bishop of Ptolemais (370–430 A.D.), from his *Treatise on Dreams*: *"Philosophy speaks of souls being prepared by a course of transmigrations. . . . When first it comes down to earth, it (the soul) embarks on this animal spirit as on a boat, and through it is brought into contact with matter."*[23]

In these passages of the Islamic poet Rumi and the Christian Father Synesius, the common theme of human evolution through repeated incarnations is hypothesized and voiced.

GALILEO AND A DIALOGUE ON NEW WORLD SYSTEMS

It will be interesting to see how organized religion reacts to the evidence of reincarnation that is coming into the world today. Religious authorities have the options of refuting the information or being open to the possibility that there may be some validity to the reincarnation cases that are emerging. In this context, I would like to raise another historical example, that of the scientist and astronomer, Galileo.

Galileo was interested in the motion of tides and found that tidal motion fit best with the theories of Nicolaus Copernicus (1473–1543). Copernicus proposed that the Earth orbited the sun. This view was in opposition to the belief that the Earth was the center of the universe, which was the cosmology sanctioned by the Roman Catholic Church. Galileo's studies of the motion of the oceans indicated that Copernicus was correct and that the old understanding of reality was flawed. In 1624, Galileo wrote *Dialogue of the Tides*, which the censors of the Roman Catholic Church licensed, though they changed the title to *Dialogue on the Two Chief World Systems*.

Though *Dialogue on the Two Chief World Systems* was published in 1632 with the approval of church censors, Galileo was ordered to appear in Rome to stand trial for "grave suspicion of heresy." The Roman

Catholic Church, it turned out, didn't like the worldview proposed by Copernicus and Galileo, which placed the sun in the center of our solar system, with Earth orbiting the sun. The Church forced Galileo to recant his theory that the sun stood at the center of the solar system and sentenced him to life imprisonment. To further humiliate him and to maintain control of belief systems, the Roman Catholic Church ordered that Galileo's prison sentence be announced in every university and that his *Dialogue on the Two Chief World Systems* be burned.

Interestingly, the late Pope John Paul II reopened Galileo's case in 1979. Thirteen years later, in October 1992, centuries after the scientific world accepted Galileo's conclusions, the Roman Catholic Church admitted the Vatican's error in 1632. In 1992, 360 years after Galileo published his paper, the church officially accepted that the Earth revolves around the sun, and not the other way around. It is to the credit of Pope John II that he righted this wrong. It is also meaningful that as part of his millennium address, Pope John II asked God for forgiveness for sins committed throughout history in the Church's name.

Another episode in history that demonstrates that Church authorities can make mistakes involves the leader of the Reformation, Martin Luther. Prior to Luther's time, the Bible was only available in Latin. As such, the only people who had access to the scriptures were priests, who were trained in Latin. Martin Luther translated the Bible into German, so that the common person could read the Bible. Church authorities were vehemently opposed to Luther's translation, as it took the scriptures out of their exclusive domain. The Church ordered Martin Luther to cease distribution of his Bible. When Luther refused, he was forced into exile.

Reflect on how many people, over the centuries, have received comfort from reading the scriptures. Reflect also on how unbelievable it seems today that the Christian Church was opposed to giving people access to Christianity's holy text.

In conclusion, I hope that the leaders of organized religions, as well as of political regimes, will embrace the mounting evidence of reincarnation. Acceptance of this evidence, which demonstrates that can people change religious and ethnic affiliation from lifetime to lifetime, is the only lasting way to curtail violence between diverse groups. It will take courage, though, to reevaluate entrenched ways of thinking. I know without doubt that the evidence supporting reincarnation will only grow in time. Just as Galileo's truth prevailed, the truth about reincarnation will also prevail.

2

Principles of Reincarnation and the Work of Ian Stevenson, MD

In this chapter, two cases researched by Ian Stevenson, MD of the University of Virginia will be presented, which demonstrate that facial features remain consistent from one incarnation to another. In chapters that follow, independently researched cases will show that personality traits, talents and linguistic writing style stay consistent. In the reincarnation cases of Paul Gauguin and Picasso, we will observe that artistic development is replicated from one incarnation to another, though at an earlier age, demonstrating that we do indeed build upon accomplishments of past lifetimes. In the case of the reincarnated Laurel and Hardy, we even see that comedic development is replicated. Prior to presenting two key Stevenson cases, I would like to elaborate on principles of reincarnation derived from cases featured in this book, which can be summarized as follows:

1. *Physical Appearance*

Facial architecture, the shape and proportions of the face, appears to be consistent from lifetime to lifetime. Physical habits, such as postures, hand gestures and the type of jewelry worn, can also be consistent from lifetime to lifetime. Even poses struck in portraits and photographs are often uncannily similar from one lifetime to another.

Body types can be consistent from lifetime to lifetime, though the size of the body can vary. An individual can have a slight physique in one lifetime and a powerful one in the next. One can be short in one incarnation and tall in another, though facial features, postures and gestures, appear to remain the same.

I would like to comment on the subject of beauty. It is my contention that any particular facial architecture can be perceived as beautiful or handsome. The perception of beauty largely depends on factors such as complexion and physique. For example, a woman in one incarnation may be tall, thin, have wonderful skin, a perfect smile and a toned body. Due to these factors and their effect on her appearance, this woman may become a celebrated fashion model or beauty queen. In another incarnation, this same woman, with identical facial architecture, may be born with a coarse complexion, a stout body and crooked teeth. This woman would now be considered ordinary appearing, by observers.

In fact, a case that recently has been researched that demonstrates this point involves the American actress and beauty Angelina Jolie. A past lifetime has been identified for her in France, in the time of Louis XIV, in which she was described as being unattractive as her forehead was too high for her face, her teeth were crooked, her complexion coarse and she walked with a limp as one leg was shorter than the other. She had the same facial architecture and in a portrait looks likes she does now, but cosmetic factors made her appear unappealing. Of note, in that era, Jolie had a big heart, as she does now, and took in poor families under her wing.

The point is that any facial architecture may be perceived as beautiful or unattractive, based on these variables. I believe that we can alternate being attractive and ordinary, from lifetime to lifetime, based on the lessons we are to learn in a particular incarnation.

Of note, my reincarnation research shows that in approximately 10 to 20 percent of cases, a soul changes gender. Even in these cases, facial architecture still remains consistent. Overall, most people (80 to 90%) maintain the same gender from one lifetime to another, and it seems that our essence has an innate masculine or feminine quality. Those who are innately masculine tend to reincarnate as males. Those who are innately feminine prefer to return in a female body. I think, though, that we all switch gender periodically, to learn what it is like to be a different gender.

2. *Personality*

Personality traits appear to persist from lifetime to lifetime. One's way of approaching life and the way that others perceive you remains consistent. Some of our personality traits are positive and we carry them with us to our benefit. Other personality traits can be detrimental and can cause suffering from one lifetime to another. It appears that part of our evolution is to smooth out the rough spots in our dispositions.

As an example, consider a person who is an extremely aggressive by nature. A benefit of being aggressive is that the person accomplishes his goals. A negative aspect is that other people may be hurt by an aggressive approach. The goal for an aggressive person over the period of one lifetime or more would be to take in consideration the feelings of others.

Though personality traits remain consistent, I have observed that physical and mental illnesses do not persist from one lifetime to another. Individuals who are chemically dependent or have a psychiatric illness in a previous lifetime do not appear to carry these disorders over to subsequent ones.

Spiritually and intellectually, we seem to pick up where we have left off. Our hard earned achievements in spiritual and intellectual pursuits are retained—they are a part of us. As such, efforts in advancing ourselves are never wasted and we build upon our endeavors from lifetime to lifetime. Similarly, talents can come through from one lifetime to another, but conversely, if the soul needs to take a different path in a particular lifetime, talents may at times be blocked.

Though we seem to have a similar level of spiritual maturity and intellectual advancement across lifetimes, we can trade off being poor and rich, famous and unknown. We take turns being placed in and out of the spotlight. Our status in life seems to be determined by the karma we have created in past lifetimes, as well as by the lessons our souls have set for ourselves to learn. Still, there is the pattern that powerful souls come back as powerful souls, great artists come back as great artists and those who have made an impact in the past do so again in subsequent lifetimes.

As discussed at length in the Prologue, religious affiliation and ethnic background change from lifetime to lifetime. A soul can be Christian in one lifetime and Jewish or Islamic in the next. This casts new insight regarding conflicts based on religious or ethnic differences.

As a correlate to personality similarities, I have noticed that many times there will be a similarity in the way that a person chooses to identify themselves by name, from one lifetime to another. More specifically, the cadence and inflections of one's chosen name are often similar from one lifetime to another. Of course, our parents give us our name at birth, but as we mature, we choose what version of our given name we wish to be known by. Some choose to use a middle name rather than the first name, others prefer a nickname or to use initials. We tend to choose a variant of our name that reflects an internal rhythm, an energy pattern or energy signature.

3. *Writing Style*

Just as personality traits remain consistent from lifetime to lifetime, a person's manner of expression seems to be similar from one lifetime to another. In the case of John B. Gordon/Jeff Keene, a formal linguistic analysis by a university professor was done which indeed demonstrated that writing structure can remain the same from one incarnation to another. Some variation in writing style, of course, will be observed due to differing customs of various eras. Still, consistencies in modes of expression and in content are observed. Just as portraits allow us to see how one's appearance is the same from lifetime to lifetime, historical documents, diaries and other available documentation allow us to study writing style across incarnations. Two reincarnation cases featured in this book, those of William Shakespeare and of the British playwright, Tom Taylor, will provide a wealth of material for the analysis of the composition of dramas across incarnations.

4. *Karmic Soul Groups*

People appear to come into life in groups, based on shared karma and emotional attachments. Couples often come back together and entire family units can recur. When an individual reincarnates, other members of that person's karmic group will be present. Identifying members of the person's karmic group is another important criterion in establishing a past-life match.

How do we connect with our karmic groups? The answer, I believe, is destiny. In analyzing past-life cases, I have observed that we all have a predetermined destiny or life itinerary which brings us to the people we are supposed to spend time with. To better understand how destiny works, I use the analogy of a journey. Think of your life as an extended vacation that you plan in advance. You decide who you want and need to see, where you want to go, and what activities you would like to participate in. You coordinate your itinerary with the people you are to rendezvous with. You, your karmic friends, and loved ones all agree to the plan before you are born. Once you come into life, destiny ensures that you meet up with your karmic soul group. The settings for karmic affiliations can be our families, work life, and recreational pursuits. These settings are stages on which we play out the karmic dramas of our lives. This casts a new light on Shakespeare's phrase, *"All of life is but a stage."*

We meet up with different karmic groups at different points in life. When we get the urge to take a new job, travel to a new city, or take up a new recreational pursuit, many times this is a part of our destiny being played out. New venues bring us to karmic groups we need to be with.

If this is true, one must question whether we have free will. My belief is that though we all have a predetermined itinerary that we are committed to honor, we have free will in what we do along the way. Indeed, growth and human evolution could not occur without free will. Some people may have a more structured itinerary that limits diversionary treks, while

others may have a less structured game plan. Either
way, we have free will along our destined paths.
Karmic groups provide insights regarding déjà vu
experiences. If we meet up with people we have known
in past lives, it is not surprising that we may have a
spark of recognition when we meet. Since people have
consistent patterns of behavior, we may recognize these
traits and idiosyncratic reactions when situations recur.
Finally, déjà vu may occur if we recognize an event
that is part of our itinerary. We may become aware of
a road mark along our predetermined path.

5. *Past-Life Symbols, Synchronistic Events, and*
Anniversary Phenomena

A common feature in past-life research is that
symbols from a prior lifetime are found in the person's
contemporary incarnation and synchronistic events
occur which seem to reinforce past life connections.
In my own case, many "coincidental" events occurred
which seemed to correlate to a past lifetime of mine as
John Adams, a leader of the American Revolution in
Boston. For example, the first time I spoke in public
about my past lifetime was in at the "Publick House"
in Massachusetts, built in 1771, in a room filled with
Revolutionary paraphernalia. The graphics pertaining
to the reincarnation cases of Bill Clinton, George W.
Bush, Al Gore and myself were hand delivered to
President Clinton, then in office, at the White House
on John Adams birthday, almost magically. Without
realizing it, I also signed my book contract for *Return*
of the Revolutionaries on John Adams birthday, not

becoming aware the synchronistic signing until the following day.

6. *Attraction to Specific Geographic Locations*

Individuals are often attracted to geographic settings of past lives. In many cases, people are observed to gravitate to places where they have lived before. Individuals may reside in these areas or visit old haunts on vacation. In some cases, it appears that the soul is simply nostalgic for familiar settings. In other cases, the soul may direct the individual to a specific place to trigger a remembrance of the past lifetime or to facilitate a spiritual awakening. The cases of Robert Snow and Jeffrey Keene illustrate how guidance to geographic locations can lead to revelations regarding past lives.

7. *Memories*

Memories of past lives can have a profound effect on the individual who has experienced them. Memories can occur spontaneously or through past-life regressions. In a regression, a therapist guides a person into a state of deep relaxation. The subject is coached to go back in time until former lives are experienced or remembered. Memories, whether spontaneous or experienced through regression, are subjective. Alone, these memories provide only weak evidence of reincarnation to those who have not experienced them. Memories, though, when supported by objective facts obtained through historical research and corroboration, provide compelling evidence of reincarnation.

Ian Stevenson, M.D., a psychiatrist at the University of Virginia, has compiled and studied thousands of cases involving children who remember past lives in detail. Dr. Stevenson travels to the scenes of the contemporary and past lifetimes and attempts to verify the details provided in the past-life accounts. Two key cases that Dr. Stevenson has researched, which demonstrate that facial features remain consistent from one incarnation to another, are presented below. Before we review these cases, I would like to address two very common questions that are raised regarding reincarnation.

IF REINCARNATION IS REAL, THEN HOW CAN THE POPULATION BE SO MUCH LARGER NOW?

If reincarnation is true, how can there be so many people on the planet today than in the past? The easiest was to address this issue is simply frequency of incarnation. In the past, when the population on earth was much smaller, then perhaps souls could only incarnated once in a few hundred years. With today's population, souls can incarnate much more frequently, almost continually.

WHY IS EVERYONE FAMOUS IN A PAST LIFETIME?

The second question often raised is why is everyone famous in past lifetime? In truth, most people were not famous individuals in prior lifetimes, though famous people do have to reincarnate like everyone else. It is true that souls who have made a great impact in a prior lifetime do tend to make significant impacts in subsequent lifetimes, as these souls bring earned skills with them from one incarnation to another. This is demonstrated by the reincarnation cases involving Picasso, APJ Abdul Kalam, Vikram Sarabhai, Shah Rukh Khan, Rekha and Amitabh and Jaya Bachchan.

Individuals can mistakenly believe that they were someone famous in a past lifetime for two reasons. One, they may have known a famous person in a past lifetime and in trying to ascertain a past life identity, one confuses the famous person for one's true past life identity. For example, instead of being Cleopatra, one may have been Cleopatra's advisor or friend. I call this type of mistaken matches "landmark cases," in that the famous person acts as a landmark for a person's incarnation in place and time.

Mistakes can also be made because a famous person may be acting as a guide to a person. We all have spirit guides that try to help us in our lives. Deceased relatives and people who we have had close relationships with in past lives can serve as spirit guides. Sometimes, people can confuse a spirit guide for one's own past incarnation. For example, a person may have been an assistant to Leonardo da Vinci in his art studio and in a contemporary incarnation, Leonardo serves as this person as a spirit guide. This person pursues a career in art and at times gets inspiration from Leonardo, who is coaching the person from the other side. The person then starts to believe that they indeed were Leonardo da Vinci in a past lifetime, though in reality, Leonardo is serving as a spirit guide.

With these issues clarified, let us now examine reincarnation cases that involve spontaneous memories in childhood.

THE REINCARNATION RESEARCH OF IAN STEVENSON, M.D.

Dr. Stevenson, recently retired, in his career served as chairman of the department of psychiatry at the University of Virginia, School of Medicine and he was also honored as the Carlson Professor of Psychiatry at that institution. For forty years, Dr. Stevenson investigated children who remember past lives. Most of these cases come from Asia, India or other areas where the doctrine of reincarnation is accepted. In locations were reincarnation is not an accepted belief system, it is thought that parents inhibit a child's expression of past-life memories. The childhood cases studied by Ian Stevenson have a common pattern, marked by the following features:

• As soon as the child can communicate, the child starts to describe a previous lifetime. Often, the child declares that his or her name is different than the name given to the child by its biologic parents. The child insists that the current family is not its true family, but that his or her real family lives in a different village or town. The child typically remembers the names of various family members from the past lifetime. Physical features of the house and neighborhood in which the child lived during the prior lifetime may be recalled.

• The child remembers details of its death in the prior lifetime. In approximately 50 percent of Dr. Stevenson's childhood reincarnation cases, a violent or premature death occurred in the previous lifetime. Dr. Stevenson has found that individuals who died of traumatic wounds, such as bullet or knife wounds, often are born in a subsequent incarnation with scars that mirror the wounds incurred in the previous lifetime. In the contemporary lifetime, the child often has a phobia related to the cause of death in the prior lifetime.

• The child's family from the prior incarnation is eventually identified. When the child meets this family for the first time, the child is able to identify family members by name or by relationship. The child often knows family secrets that only members of the prior family would know. As a result, the family from the prior lifetime often accepts the child as the reincarnation of their deceased relative. The biologic parents of the child in the current incarnation often fear that the child will leave them for the family from the prior lifetime, as the mutual bond between the child and prior family becomes so strong. This fear turns out to be unwarranted, as the bond between the child and the contemporary parents endures. A long-term relationship, though, typically ensues between the child and family from the prior lifetime.

• Personality traits, personal preferences, and habits often persist from one incarnation to another.

• Physical appearance is reported to be similar in a number of cases. In 95 percent of Dr. Stevenson's cases, the child returns assuming the same sex as in the prior lifetime. Thus, in five percent of cases, gender is reversed from one lifetime to another.

In 1998, Dr. Stevenson revisited cases he first investigated twenty years ago. In two of these cases, photographs of the individuals from the prior lifetime were available. These images show that in maturity, physical appearance is consistent from lifetime to lifetime. Let us review these two cases, which happen to have originated in Lebanon and are summarized in a book about Dr. Stevenson called *Old Souls* by Tom Shroder.

THE CASE OF HANAN MONSOUR/SUZANNE GHANEM

Hanan was born in Lebanon, in the mid-1930s. When she was twenty, Hanan married Farouk Mansour, a member of a well to do Lebanese family. The couple had two daughters, named Leila and Galareh. Hanan had a brother named Nabih, who became prominent in Lebanese society, but died as a young man in a plane crash.

After having her second daughter, Hanan developed a heart problem and her doctors advised her not to have any more children. Not heeding the warning, Hanan had a third child, a son, in 1962. In 1963, shortly after the death of her brother Nabih, Hanan's health started to deteriorate. Hanan then started to talk about dying. Farouk, Hanan's husband, said that Hanan told him that "she was going to be reincarnated and have lots to say about her previous life."[1] This was two years before her death. At age of thirty-six, Hanan traveled to Richmond, Virginia, to have heart surgery. Hanan tried to telephone her daughter Leila before the operation, but couldn't get through. Hanan died of complications the day after surgery.

Ten days after Hanan died, Suzanne Ghanem was born. Suzanne's mother told Ian Stevenson that shortly before Suzanne's birth, "I dreamed I was going to have a baby girl. I met a woman and I kissed and hugged her. She said, 'I am going to come to you.' The woman was about forty. Later, when I saw Hanan's picture, I thought it looked like the woman in my dream."[2] In other words, Suzanne Ghanem's mother had a dream that she would have a child that had the appearance of Hanan Monsour, and this dream became a reality.

At 16 months of age, Suzanne pulled the phone off the hook as if she was trying to talk into it and said, over and over, "Hello, Leila?" The family didn't know who Leila was. When she got older, Suzanne explained that Leila was one of her children and that she was not Suzanne, but Hanan. The family asked, "Hanan what?" Suzanne replied, "My head is still small. Wait until it is bigger, and I might tell you."[3] By the time she was two, she had mentioned the names of her other children, her husband, Farouk, and the names of her parents and her brothers from the previous lifetime—thirteen names in all.

In trying to locate Suzanne's past life family, acquaintances of the Ghanems made inquiries in the town where the Monsours lived. When they heard about the case, the Monsours visited Suzanne. The Monsours were initially skeptical about the girl's claims. They became believers when Suzanne identified all of Hanan's relatives, picking them out and naming them accurately. Suzanne also knew that Hanan had given her jewels to her brother Hercule in Virginia, prior to her heart surgery, and that Hanan instructed her brother to divide the jewelry among her daughters. No one outside of the Monsour family knew about the jewels.

Before she could read or write, Suzanne scribbled a phone number on a piece of paper. Later, when the family went to the Monsour's home, they found that the phone number matched the Monsour's number, except that the last two digits were transposed. As a child, Suzanne could recite the oration spoken at the funeral of Hanan's brother, Nabih. Suzanne's family taped the recitation, though the tape was eventually lost.

At five years of age, Suzanne would call Farouk three times a day. When Suzanne visited Farouk, she would sit on his lap and rest her head against his chest. At 25 years of age, Suzanne still telephones Farouk. Farouk, a career policeman, has accepted Suzanne as the reincarnation of his deceased wife, Hanan. To support this conclusion, Farouk points out that from photographs, Suzanne accurately picked out scores of people they had been acquainted with, and knew other information that only Hanan would have known.

THE CASE OF RASHID KHADDEGE/DANIEL JURDI

Rashid Khaddege was an auto mechanic who lived in a town named Kfarmatta (pronounced "fur mat ta"), in Lebanon. Rashid was born in 1943. When he was 25, a friend named Ibrahim picked him up to go on a car ride. Ibrahim sped towards the Mediterranean Sea and at a place called Military Beach, lost control of the car. Rashid was thrown from the vehicle, incurred head trauma, and was instantly killed.

Over a year later, Daniel Jurdi was born. Daniel's earliest word was "Ibrahim." At the age of two, he told his mother Latifeh, "I want to go home." At two and one half, Daniel made the statements, "This is not my house. You are not my mother. I don't have a father. My father died." Daniel's mother recalled, "He would not call Yusuf daddy." "He called him by name." Further, Daniel said, "My father was Naim." Naim was Rashid Khaddege's father.[4]

At two and a half years of age, at a family picnic, a relative tried to pronounce the name of the town Kfarmatta. Daniel intervened and correctly pronounced the name of the town. When his father asked how he knew the name of the town, Daniel replied, "I am from Kfarmatta."[5]

When Daniel and his mother were driving in Beirut, they passed a place on the sea called Military Beach. Daniel shut his eyes, hiding them with his hands, and started crying. He then screamed, "This is where I died."[6] Daniel also related that in his prior lifetime, he was mechanic. Regarding the accident, Daniel said that Ibrahim was speeding and lost control of the car. Daniel said "I flew out of the car and landed on my head." When help came to assist the injured, Daniel said that he heard someone say, "Leave this one, he's dead."[7]

In nursery school, Daniel told teachers his name was Rashid Khaddege. In another incident at the nursery school, little Daniel pinched an attractive young teacher and made a suggestive remark. Eventually, Daniel's father sent an acquaintance to Kfarmatta, to inquire about someone fitting Daniel's description of a mechanic who died in an auto accident at Military Beach. The Khaddeges heard about the story and visited Daniel.

When Ian Stevenson interviewed the two families in 1979, both said that upon their initial meeting, Daniel instantly recognized Rashid's sister, Najla, and called her by name. When the families met, Daniel told his mother to bring bananas for the guests. Rashid loved bananas and his mother and sister stopped eating bananas after his death, because bananas reminded them of their loss of Rashid. Later on, during a visit to Kfarmatta, Daniel also spontaneously recognized Ibrahim, as well as Jijad, Rashid's hunting buddy.

Rashid's family has accepted Daniel as their son from a previous lifetime. They have a picture of him at their home and keep a bed for Daniel, who visits one to two times a month. Daniel has married and works as an accountant. Daniel has a phobia of racing cars, which apparently reflects the psychological trauma incurred by Rashid in the crash at Military Beach.

Dr. Stevenson has studied almost 3000 cases in which children are reported to remember past lives. Dr. Stevenson has stringent criteria for considering cases valid and of the 3000 cases that he has examined, a thousand meet his criteria for being authentic. Though Dr. Stevenson did not focus on physical resemblance in the early years of his research, the cases of Suzanne Ghanem, Daniel Jurdi, and others have made him revise his approach. Hanan Monsour and Suzanne Ghanem have the same facial architecture, the same facial features. Rashid Kaddege and Daniel Jurdi also share the same facial features. An image comparing Kaddege and Jurdi is provided at the end of this chapter. To view the facial architecture shared by Hanan Monsour and Suzanne Ghanem, please refer to *Old Souls* by Tom Shroder. In his book, *Where Biology and Reincarnation Intersect*, Dr. Stevenson recommends that future researchers systematically study "facial resemblances between subjects and previous personalities."[8]

Dr. Stevenson is a pioneer in the scientific research of reincarnation. His work, *Twenty Cases Suggestive of Reincarnation*, first published in 1966, is a classic. In fact, I submit that anyone who reads *Twenty Cases* with an open mind will develop a belief in reincarnation.

Daniel Jurdi holds image of Rasid Khaddege. Since childhood, Jurdi has had memories of being Khaddege in a past lifetime.

Photo Credit : Daniel Jurdi, Courtesy of Tom Shroder

3

The Reincarnation of Anne Frank

One of the most culturally significant reincarnation cases involves Barbro Karlen, who I have had the honor of doing joint presentations with over the years. I first met Barbro in 2000 and I now consider her a good friend. I have heard her story many times and I would like to share it with you at this time.

Anne Frank died in the Belson Bergen Concentration Camp in 1945. Less than ten years later, in 1954, Barbro Karlen was born to Christian parents in Sweden. When she was less than three years old, Barbro told her parents that her name was not Barbro, but Anne Frank. Barbro's parents had no idea of who Anne Frank was, as the book, *Anne Frank: Diary of a Young Girl,* also known as *The Diary of Anne Frank,* had not yet been published in Sweden.

Barbro relates that they wanted her to call them "Ma and Pa," but Barbro knew that they were not her real parents. Barbro even told her mother that her real parents would soon come to get her and take her

home. During her childhood, Barbro told her parents
details of her life as Anne, which her parents thought
were fantasies. Barbro also had nightmares as a child,
in which men ran up the stairs and kicking in the
door to the family's attic hiding place. Barbro had a
fear of men in uniform, an aversion to beans, which
the Frank family existed on for nearly two years, and
she would only take baths, not showers.

Barbro's memories concerned her parents and at
one point, they had her evaluated by a psychiatrist.
Barbro, though, had by this time learned that it was
not wise to talk about the other world she lived in, the
world of Anne Frank, as she noticed that everyone
"got tense" when she described her memories to them.
When she saw the psychiatrist, she made no mention
of her memories of being Anne and was deemed a
perfectly normal little girl.

When Barbro was a little older, she became
confused when her schoolteacher began talking about
Anne Frank in class. How could her teacher know
about Anne Frank? Further, Barbro began to realize
that Anne Frank was a well known person. How could
that be? As Barbro related later at life, for her as a
child, "all this didn't work for me." Imagine how
hard it must have been for Barbro to have these
spontaneous memories and have no one to talk to
about them, no one, like Carol Bowman, who could
help her with her confusion and nightmares.

Barbro received her first validation of being Anne
Frank when she was ten years old, which she describes
in her book, *And the Wolves Howled*. I will paraphrase
the scene. When she was ten, Barbro's parents took
her on a tour of the major cities in Europe. One

destination was Amsterdam, the city where the Frank family lived. During World War II, Otto Frank and his family had to go into hiding in the attic of the building where Otto had his business, for the Nazi's had invaded the Netherlands and were persecuting Jews. The Frank family hid in this attic for about two years, until they were discovered by the Nazis, arrested and sent to concentration camps. The only survivor was the father, Otto Frank, who subsequently found the diary of this daughter, Anne, which he later had published. After the war, the hiding place was made into a museum, which is called the Anne Frank House.

By the time Barbro was ten, the *Diary of Anne Frank* had been published and while in Amsterdam, her father wanted to visit the Frank House. At their hotel, he took the phone off the hook and asked for a taxi to take them there. Barbro suddenly exclaimed: "We don't need a taxi, it's not far to walk from here." Barbro was so dead certain that it didn't occur to her parents to object, they just meekly followed her as she walked off.

"We'll soon be there, it's just round the next corner," Barbro said. She herself wasn't at all surprised when they arrived at the Anne Frank House after a ten minute walk through the winding streets of Amsterdam, but her parents stood there speechless and just looked at one another.

"That's strange," Barbro said, when they stood in front of the steps up to the house. "It didn't look like this before." She looked wonderingly and her parents didn't know what to say. They entered the house and went up the long narrow staircase. Barbro, who had been so carefree when showing them the way, suddenly went quite white in the face. She broke out in a cold sweat and reached for her mother's hand. Her mother was quite horrified when she felt Barbro's hand, which was as cold as ice.

When they entered the hiding place the same irrational terrors overcame Barbro as she had experienced so many times in her dreams. She found it hard to breathe and panic spread through her body. When they went into one of the smaller rooms, she suddenly stood still and brightened up a little. Barbro looked at the wall in front of her exclaimed, "Look, the pictures of the film stars are still there!" The pictures of the movie stars that Anne had clipped and affixed to the wall, which Barbro saw at that moment, made her feel happy, almost as if she had come home.

Her mother stared at the blank wall and couldn't understand this at all. "What pictures? The wall is bare?" Barbro looked again she saw that this was true. The wall was bare! Her mother was so confounded that she felt driven to ask one of the guides whether she knew if there had been pictures on the wall at one time. "Oh yes," one guide replied, "they had only been taken down temporarily to be mounted under glass so that they wouldn't be destroyed or stolen." Barbro's mother didn't know what to say.

"How in the world could you find your way here first of all, then insist that the steps outside were different and then see the pictures on the wall when they weren't there?" Sara's mother was full of questions and really quite irritated. But Barbro was quite incapable of saying even a single word. She just wanted to get out of there, she couldn't stand it a moment longer.

Her legs felt like jelly as she went down the stairs. She had never before in her life felt so wretched. The tears ran unrestrainedly down her face, and her legs would not carry her. When she reached the bottom step her legs folded under her and she fell.

In these passages taken from *And the Wolves Howled*, Barbro relates the incidents that finally made her parents believe that she is the reincarnation of Anne Frank. After all, how else could she know how to get to the Anne Frank House, on the family's first trip to Amsterdam and without directions? How could she know that the stairs had been modified or that pictures of movie stars that Anne Frank had affixed should be found on a wall, when the pictures had been removed for mounting? Barbro's mother responded by becoming very spiritual and a believer in reincarnation. Barbro's father, on the other hand, seemed annoyed. Barbro relates that her father responded by saying: "I can't deny that you have somehow been here before. Perhaps you have lived before and have reincarnated, but you are the only one!" Barbro understood that being faced with the possible reality of reincarnation, the happenings of the day upset her father's Christian world view, where "everything was set right." Barbro was much happier, though, from this point on, as she could now talk to her mother about her lifetime as Anne Frank and she had her mother's support.

Like Anne Frank, Barbro Karlen was a childhood writing prodigy. Barbro relates that learning to write was a great gift, as when she could not speak to anyone about her past life memories, once she learned to scribe, she could have discourses with her writing tablet. One day, when she was eleven or so, a family friend read her notes to herself and realized that this was worthy prose. Barbro was asked if her casual writings could be compiled, which she agreed to, and at the age of twelve, her first book of prose was published. This book, *Man on Earth*, became the best selling prose/poetry book in Swedish history. Barbro became a little celebrity, debating theology with ministers and theologians on television programs.

After her adolescence passed, her past life memories began to fade, which was a relief to Barbro, as now she could finally lead a normal life. It was not until she was in her forties that memories began to emerge again, as described in her book. Barbro never thought that she would write about her memories of being Anne Frank until this time, but as Barbro wistfully once commented in an interview, "never say never." After her book came out, she received a great deal of attention in Europe. On an intuition and a whim, she decided to move to California, where I was fortunate to meet this great soul. When I first received a phone call in 1999 or 2000, in which I was told that a woman who claims to be the reincarnation of Anne Frank, I was dubious. I met her though, with her husband Stephan, and I came to realize that I had truly met that reincarnation of Anne Frank. In her book and presentations, she never once mentions that she has the same appearance as Anne Frank, as her memories are what are most meaningful to her, not appearance. Upon meeting her, though, I realized that Barbro has the same facial architecture as Anne, and the images that are provided in this book are the first to compare the facial features of Barbro Karlen and Anne Frank.

In addition to facial features and postures, there are many personality similarities between Barbro and Anne Frank. These include:

A. Spirituality and a love of nature

Lawrence L. Langer, in *Anne Frank, Reflections on Her Life and Legacy*, writes the following regarding Anne.

"Spiritual insight rarely falls from the lips of a thirteen or fourteen year old girl. Indeed, as many of the new entries in the diary will show, Anne Frank was essentially a physical being, a lover of nature, intrigued with her own sexuality."

These traits are reflected in Barbro Karlen, who at sixteen years of age moved to a cottage in the woods, along with her horse, two dogs, two cats, a sheep and a flock of hens and chicks. Barbro especially loved her horse and horseback riding, which eventually lead to her pursuing a career as a mounted policewoman. Her sexuality is evidence by an early marriage and pregnancy by age 18. Indeed, many of Anne's desires seem to have come to fruition early in the life of Barbro Karlen.

Barbro's spirituality is linked to nature. In her book, she describes a childhood encounter with God while contemplating footprints on a sandy beach. The name she gave God at that moment was the "Wanderer." Barbro demonstrates, as did Anne, the qualities of an old soul at a young age.

B. Natural literary skills

Despite her lack of training, Anne Frank has been recognized as a gifted writer. Similarly, Barbro Karlen has been a childhood literary prodigy. Her first book was published at 12 years of age and became the all time best selling poetry book in Sweden. Between ages 12 to 17, nine books written by Barbro were published. It is interesting to note that Anne Frank always hoped to be a published writer. On May 11, 1944, Anne wrote that her "greatest wish" was to become a journalist, "and later on, a famous writer." Once again, it appears the Anne's desires were fulfilled early in the life of Barbro.

Similar themes are found in the writings of Frank and Karlen. Though one may argue that these similarities are intentional, but Barbro Karlen maintains that she has not studied Anne Frank's works. Anne Frank, due to the persecution of the Jews by the Nazis, reflected extensively on issues of good and evil. She also had a tendency to personify human qualities, as seen in the quotation cited below regarding "Lies." Anne's legacy is based on her ability to maintain hope in the face of dismal circumstances. Despite the persecution and suffering endured, Anne Frank's most famous quote affirms the basic goodness of man.

Barbro Karlen also writes of good and evil in her book, *And the Wolves Howled*, partly due to her memories of the Frank lifetime and partly due to persecution experienced in this lifetime. She also has a tendency to personify human qualities. Let us compare passages written by Frank and Karlen regarding evil:

Anne Frank-On Evil

"There's in people simply an urge to destroy, an urge to kill, to murder and rage."

"I get frightened myself when I think of close friends who are now at the mercy of the cruelest monsters ever to stalk the earth. And all because we are Jews."

"Yesterday evening, before I fell asleep, who should suddenly appear before my eyes but Lies! I saw her in front of me, clothed in rags...Her eyes were very big and she looked so sadly and reproachfully at me that I could read in her eyes: Oh Anne, why have you deserted me? Help, oh help me, rescue me from this hell!"

Barbro Karlen-On Evil

"If only she could write about how important, even vital it is never to give up in the face of evil, regardless of how dark and wretched everything may seem. Evil was present on the earth and would probably always be there. It would always try to conquer Good."

Anne Frank-On Good

"In spite of everything, I still really believe that people are really good at heart."

Barbro Karlen-On Good

"But the more people there were who believed in Good, and in the Good Force within themselves, the greater the possibility of keeping evil under control. If only they could believe in Good, and in the presence of the inner Force, many unhappy people would be able to fight their way up from the darkness."

"Most people on earth were not yet aware that they could find the Good Force within themselves and that it could help them if they only sought it out."

In closing, Anne Frank believed in goodness in the face of evil and persecution. In the persona of Barbro Karlen, we hear the voice of Anne in a wiser form. Barbro has had to integrate Anne's death at Bergen-Belson concentration camp. If we accept Barbro as the reincarnation of Anne, then Anne returns with a poignant message. That evil cannot kill spirit and that spirit has no particular religious, ethnic or racial ties.

Barbro was raised as a Christian in this lifetime, whereas Anne was persecuted as a Jew. Reflect that if only a few decades ago, the German people knew that a person could be born Jewish in one lifetime and Christian in another, that the Holocaust could never have happened. Those who may object to Barbro's story because it is thought to diminish the horror of the Holocaust miss the more important point—that spirit does not die and by the grace of God, the soul so loved and commemorated walks once again on earth. Let us not dismiss this glory.

In addition, let us acknowledge that the knowledge that Anne Frank has reincarnated into a different religion, that one can change religious, racial and ethnic affiliation from lifetime to lifetime, can prevent future Holocausts to come.

I will cite one last quotation from Anne Frank's diary, which refers to the perseverance of the Jewish faith and people. It also has a poetic ring of truth regarding reincarnation, perhaps not intended by Anne, yet beautiful all the same.

"Who has inflicted this upon us?
Who has made us Jews different from all other people?
Who has allowed us to suffer so terribly up till now?
It is God who had made us who we are,
but it will be God, too,
who will raise us up again."

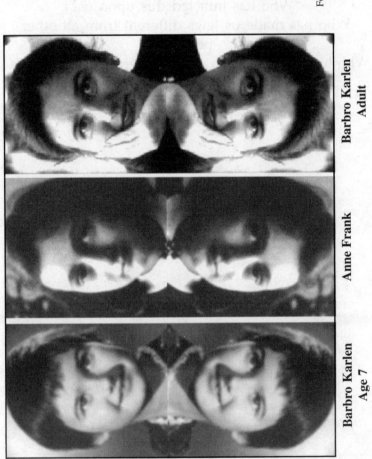

**Barbro Karlen
Age 7**

Anne Frank

**Barbro Karlen
Adult**

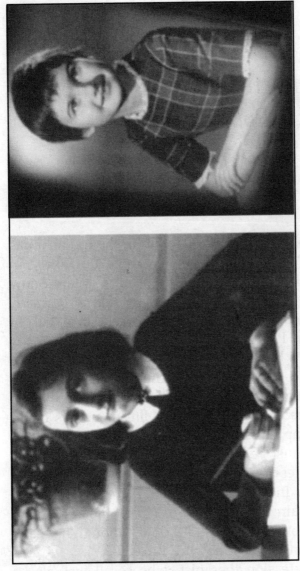

Anne Frank   **Barbro Karlen**

Note Similar Postures

Photo Credit Anne Frank : Courtesy ANNE FRANK-Fonds Basel CH/Anne Frank Stichting Amsterdam NL
and Portrait of Barbro Karlen : Courtesy of Barbro Karlen

4

The Portrait Painter and the Police Captain

Robert Snow is a Captain in the Indianapolis Police Department who is currently in charge of Organized Crime. Captain Snow has written a book called *Looking for Carroll Beckwith*, which documents his reincarnation case in detail. In this chapter, I will provide a synopsis.

The story begins at a party, where a fellow police officer, who conducted past life regressions as an avocation, was describing how she would guide clients into a relaxed state so that past life memories could emerge. Captain Snow thought that these so called memories must be fabricated and he discounted past life memories as fantasies and told the regression therapist so. Incensed, the past life regression therapist dared Captain Snow to have a past life regression himself. Snow said, "Sure, I'll do it," though he really had no intention of following through.

The regression therapist, who recall was also a fellow police officer, kept hounding Snow and even accused him of being "scared." That did it and reluctantly, Captain Snow got a referral for a different regression therapist and scheduled an appointment, only so it wouldn't look like he had "welshed on the dare." Captain Snow did not believe in reincarnation and did not expect to have a meaningful experience during the session.

A delightful aspect of Captain Snow's book is the high level of skepticism and a mischievous sense of humor that infuses the narrative. Let us share in Captain Snow's experiences through the following passages from *Looking for Carroll Beckwith*. We start with the regression therapist, Dr. Mariellen Griffith, guiding the regression. Dr. Griffith begins by instructing Captain Snow to imagine that he is relaxing comfortably in his den at home. The narrative from Captain Snow's book follows:

"Now, picture your higher self coming into the room to greet you," Dr Griffith said.

I did that, too, though as I sat on the couch with my eyes closed, I couldn't help but wonder what the hell I was doing there, particularly when she asked me what my higher self was wearing. How the hell would I know? This was her daydream. But I decided to give it a try.

"White," I answered, "A long white gown. Wasn't that what all spirits wore?"

"Your higher self is standing there and asking if you're ready to go on a trip. It is telling you that it will guide you and protect you on your trip."

Oh Lord, I thought, as I tried to maintain a facial expression of seriousness, I can't believe I'm doing this.[1]

Eventually and much to his shock, Captain Snow experienced powerful and very clear past-life memories during the regression. Captain Snow has related that his perception of the past-life events was as clear as waking consciousness. He recalled several different lifetimes, but the one that was most prominent was as a portrait painter in what seemed to be the 19th century. Captain Snow remembered 28 specific details regarding this lifetime. One involved painting a portrait of a hunchback woman. Captain Snow vividly remembered the experience, including his questioning of why someone with a pronounced deformity would want a portrait of themselves.

The regression had such a profound effect on Captain Snow that he became obsessed with trying to determine whether it was authentic. Captain Snow himself still did not believe in reincarnation and operated under the assumption that he had learned about the portrait painter in the past, through a book, in school or at a museum, and that the regression experience represented a forgotten memory that had surfaced. Snow investigated the regression experience as he would a police case. He methodically examined art books, visited art galleries, and contacted art dealers, searching for the portrait of the hunchback woman he had seen in the regression, or to find some other clue. Captain Snow was unable, though, to identify any historical artist consistent with the regression persona.

Snow is an experienced researcher, having written six books on police management and other topics. He is also highly intelligent; he scored straight A's in college and earned a full scholarship for a doctorate program in psychology. Nonetheless, after a year of research, he came to a dead end. He concluded that it was unlikely that he would ever be able to identify the artist seen during his regression. At that point in time, Captain Snow's wife, Melanie, suggested that they take a vacation trip to New Orleans.

Once there, in an art gallery in the French Quarter, Captain Snow had another profound experience. This incident demonstrates how people can be guided, apparently by spiritual sources, in reincarnation research. This art gallery into which Captain Snow had wandered by apparent "chance," he spotted the portrait of the hunchbacked woman. Captain Snow describes the scene:

Whirling around, I stared open-mouthed at the portrait, reliving an experience I'd had once when I grabbed onto a live wire without knowing it, the current freezing me in my tracks as huge voltage surged up and down my arms and legs . . .

For the next several minutes, I didn't move from in front of the portrait, but instead continued closing my eyes to see again and again the scene of me painting this very portrait in my studio, and then opening my eyes to see the actual finished portrait. The situation began to feel surreal, more like a very vivid dream that you wake up sweating from, a dream that you have to keep telling yourself over and over again was only a dream. It wasn't real.

Finally, even though I knew with absolute certainty that this was the same painting I had seen while under hypnosis, I convinced myself that stumbling onto it by accident like this was simply too bizarre to be true. I toyed with the idea for a few moments that perhaps I'd had some kind of stroke and just thought I stood in front of this portrait, when in actuality I was in a hospital bed somewhere or maybe even in a nursing home. After giving this possibility a few moment's consideration, I realized how very desperate I had become to find a rational answer for what was happening. But desperate or not, things like this just didn't happen in real life. What were the chances, after all the months of systematic searching, that I would just happen onto the painting like this? What were the chances that Melanie would just happen to want to go to New Orleans, and that we would just happen to visit this gallery, just when they happened to have this painting for sale? . . .

During my 30 years as a police officer, I have always searched for the truth. Sometimes the truth didn't turn out to be what I expected, but still, the truth was what I had always searched for. And now, here I was seeming to be facing the truth I had been looking for, but at the same time trying to deny it, trying to find any way to deny the truth of what I had found. . . . Supernatural things didn't happen to real people. Maybe they did in the movies, but not in real life.[2]

These passages from Captain Snow's book show that supernatural things do happen in people's lives. From the portrait of the hunchback woman, Captain Snow learned that the name of the artist in his past-life regression was Carroll Beckwith. Captain Snow researched Beckwith's life through an extensive diary that Beckwith had left behind, as well as through other sources. Of the 28 specific memories that Snow had documented from the regression, such as the painting of the hunchback woman, 26 were verified through this research. Though initially reluctant to accept reincarnation as the basis for his regression experience, Captain Snow finally came to the conclusion that he had been Carroll Beckwith in a prior lifetime. He states that the evidence he compiled would stand up in court and that no plea-bargaining would be entertained.

Interestingly, Captain Snow was not aware of a physical resemblance between himself and Carroll Beckwith. When I met Captain Snow at a meeting of the International Association of Regression Research and Therapies (IARRT) in September 2000, I offered to take his picture and compare it with Beckwith's. I knew from experience that these comparisons are best done by lining up images side by side. At this point, please refer to the comparison of Beckwith and Snow provided in this book. You will notice that though Captain Snow is heavier in the photograph than Beckwith was at the time of the portrait, facial architecture is very similar between the two.

Captain Snow's case demonstrates a characteristic phenomenon that occurs when one becomes concretely aware of a specific past lifetime. The past-life information often triggers a traumatic reaction in a person, followed by a period of integration. When one faces the reality of reincarnation, a reevaluation of how one views the world is required. Over a lifetime, we all develop a unique way of understanding the world.

That belief system may involve a spiritual aspect to life, or an atheistic view may be held. Regardless of what one's belief system is, concrete evidence of reincarnation demands an alteration of one's belief system. Even if one believes in reincarnation, the shift from a belief in past lives to observing objective evidence of reincarnation can be a shock.

Recall that Captain Snow did not believe in reincarnation at the time of his regression and that following his past-life experience, he tried to find a logical explanation for his memories. Even after stumbling into the portrait of the hunchback woman in the art gallery, Captain Snow still explored the possibility that Beckwith's work had been displayed in a museum and that at some point in his lifetime he had viewed it. Snow was falling back on the theory that his regression experience represented repressed memories from his current lifetime. Let us rejoin Captain Snow and the New Orleans gallery worker, who was still trying to sell the Beckwith painting to Snow, and share in Captain Snow's reaction to the turn of events.

"No," the man said, giving his head a slight shake, "you haven't seen this work before. This portrait's been in a private collection for years. And besides, let me be honest with you, I don't think there has been an exhibition of Beckwith's work in the last seventy-five years. He wasn't that famous. So I can let this go very reasonably."

As the gallery worker's answer dashed my seemingly logical explanation for what had happened, the vertigo returned. My whole belief system was not only teetering. It was falling. Everything around me had such a surrealistic feeling to it that I could have been in a Kafka novel. And so I simply stood there open-mouthed, feeling numb and detached from reality. As I discovered in 1978, when things that can't happen do happen, when the impossible becomes reality, your mind seems to detach itself from your body.[3]

Just as Captain Snow went through a period of shock and disbelief when confronted with evidence of reincarnation, society as a whole will undergo the same reaction. This is especially true for those cultures where reincarnation is not the cultural norm. We will collectively need to adjust our belief systems as objective evidence of reincarnation comes into the world. Overall, the news is good, but it takes some getting used to.

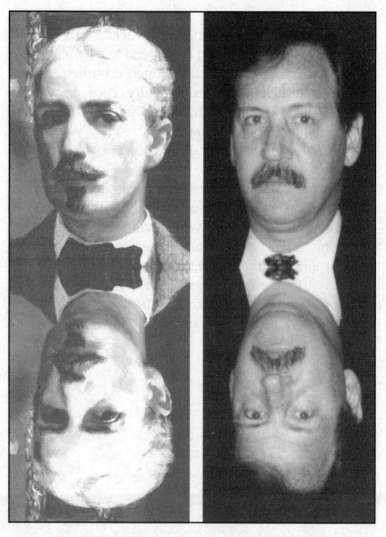

Carroll Beckwith   **Robert Snow**

Photo by Walter Semkiw

Detail Carroll Beckwith, Self Portrait, 1898 James Carroll Beckwith, Gift of the
Artist, Photograph ©1999 The Detroit Institute of Arts

5

The Confederate General and the Connecticut Yankee

Jeffrey Keene is a retired decorated fire fighter and an Assistant Fire Chief in Westport, Connecticut. Following the destruction of the World Trade Center in 2001, Keene received a special tour of "Ground Zero." A relationship has existed between the two fire departments, as Westport's firefighters have had a tradition of "riding along" with Rescue #1 of the Fire Department of the City of New York. Eleven members of this elite unit, Rescue #1 lost their lives on the morning of September 11, 2001.

Like Captain Robert Snow, Mr. Keene is a highly responsible member of his community who, unexpectedly, found himself researching a past-life identity. In this pursuit, significant information came to him through synchronistic events and in time, Keene came to the conclusion that he was being guided in his research efforts. Let me quote from the forward of his book, *Someone Else's Yesterday:*

Like most people, I was stumbling through life minding my own business when all at once the world started having its way with me. Suddenly, the extraordinary became ordinary and strange occurrences throughout my life started to make sense. I found that I had been a friend to some very famous people, people that I was not even aware that I had met. I was being given insights that answered some of life's greatest questions. Before too long I found myself on the front page of a state wide newspaper and featured in an Arts and Entertainment Network documentary titled, Beyond Death. Getting to the point were the word "coincidence" was worn very thin, I decided to accept the fact that I was being guided and opened myself to what life wanted to show me. Long after I had been convinced of a past life, unusual events kept reinforcing my conclusions, so much so that the only reason I could come up with for such revelations was that I was to share them with others.[1]

Mr. Keene has related to me that the element of guidance in his past-life research has been so strong that he has felt like the spiritual world has been pushing him around "like a shopping cart." Jeff's story began in May 1991, when he was on vacation with his wife, Anna. They were looking for antiques and stopped in Sharpsburg, Maryland, which was where the Civil War battle of Antietam was fought. Though Jeff had never read a book on the Civil War or had any affinity for that era, he felt compelled to visit the battlefield.

At a portion of the field called Sunken Road, Jeff listened to an audio taped narration of events that took place in 1862. The battle involved a regiment called the Sixth Alabama, which was commanded by a Colonel John B. Gordon. After listening to the tape, as he walked along the old farm lane, Jeff unknowingly strolled into the area that had been occupied by Gordon and his men. At this location, Jeff Keene had the following reaction:

A wave of grief, sadness and anger washed over me. Without warning I was suddenly consumed by sensations. Burning tears ran down my cheeks. It became difficult to breathe. I gasped for air, as I stood transfixed in the old roadbed. To this day I cannot tell you how much time transpired, but as these feelings, this emotional overload passed, I found myself exhausted as if I had run a marathon. Crawling up the steep embankment to get out of the road, I turned and looked back. I was a bit shaken to say the least and wondered at what had just taken place. It was difficult getting back to the car because I felt so weak. I had regained most of my normal composure on the way back and said nothing to Anna about what had just happened. What could I say? How could I explain it to her? I did not have any answers, just questions.[2]

Before leaving Sharpsburg, Jeff and Anna visited a gift shop. A magazine, *Civil War Quarterly (Special Edition, Antietam)*, caught Jeff's eye and he purchased it, along with a souvenir bullet found in the area. At home, Jeff placed the magazine in a drawer that held the family's phone books, though he did not look at the journal until a year and a half later.

In October 1992, Jeff and Anna attended a

Halloween party. A clairvoyant named Barbara Camwell had been hired to give readings at the party. When it was Jeff's turn, his experience at Sunken Road came up. Barbara told Jeff that he was a soldier then and that he had been shot full of holes at that battlefield. He then had floated above his body, which was lying, apparently lifeless, on the bloodied ground. Barbara then said, "When you were hovering over your body looking down, you were very angry and yelled no!" Jeff relates that there was a pause at that moment. Jeff corrected Barbara, for reasons unknown to him, and exclaimed: "Not yet!"

The next day, Jeff decided it was time to read the souvenir magazine regarding the battle at Antietam that he had purchased in May 1991. Jeff reflected again that it was the first Civil War magazine that he had ever purchased. Jeff opened the journal to a page that had a picture of Sunken Road, the spot were Jeff had experienced the strange flood of emotions. As he scanned the text, he saw a quote: "Not Yet." The hair stood up on the back of his neck.

Reading on, Jeff learned that "Not Yet" was an order given by Colonel John B. Gordon to the Sixth Alabama. Yankee troops were approaching and the men of the Sixth Alabama were anxious to fire. The order to fire was not given until the Union troops were less than one hundred yards away. Gordon himself was quoted, regarding the encounter. "A huge volume of musketry spewed out from the sunken road. My rifles flamed and roared in the Federals faces like a blinding blaze of lightning. The effect was appalling." As he read Gordon's passage, Jeff started to experience the same emotions that he had felt at Sunken Road, and tears came to his eyes.

The article then described the wounding of Gordon. "John B. Gordon of the Sixth Alabama was hit in the left arm, the right shoulder and twice in the right leg before passing out from loss of blood after receiving a wound in the face." Jeff himself writes of what happened next. "I turned back to the page with the picture of the Sunken Road, and on the page across from it was another picture. This time a chill ran through me and the hair on the back of my neck stood up again. The picture was of Brigadier General John B. Gordon. The face was not unknown to me, I knew it well, I shave it every morning."[3] Jeff noted that in the caption Gordon was identified as a general, whereas in the article Gordon was identified as a colonel at the time of his wounding. Gordon apparently had survived the battle at Antietam.

In his book, Jeff describes how he later retrieved memories of his lifetime as John B. Gordon. Jeff also describes habits and traits he has in common with Gordon. These include a preference to stand with arms crossed, similar clothing tastes and scars on his face and body that reflect Gordon's battle wounds.

He recounts two symbolic events. One involved orders written by General Lee on September 9, 1862, which defined the Confederate Army's plans to invade the North. Nine copies of the orders were made; one copy was lost in transit and recovered by Union soldiers. This information gave the Union Army detailed information regarding the position of Confederate troops and led to the battle of Antietam.

In sum, orders written on September 9 resulted in the Civil War conflict in which John B. Gordon was severely wounded and almost died. The symbolic event in contemporary times is Jeff Keene's birthday, which is September 9.

Another symbolic event involving the date September 9 occurred on Jeff Keene's 30th birthday. On that day, Jeff was taken to the emergency room to be treated for facial and neck pain. Doctors could find no physical cause for Jeff's pain syndrome. The location of his pain corresponded to the facial and neck wounds incurred by John B. Gordon at Antietam. Gordon was 30 at the time of his injuries; Jeff's facial pain occurred on September 9, 1977, his thirtieth birthday. This incident appears to represent an anniversary phenomenon related to Gordon's wounding. Keep in mind that Jeff's emergency room visit occurred in 1977, which was 15 years before Jeff became aware of his connection to Gordon.

In his book, Jeff includes documents that show similarities in writing style. In his later years, General Gordon wrote a book called *Reminiscences of the Civil War*, which provided material for Jeff's analysis. Let us compare two passages, one from Gordon's book, describing the efforts of his men to put out a fire in Wrightsville, Pennsylvania, and one from Keene regarding his fire department's response to an emergency incident. My observation is that the two documents seem to be written in the same "voice." At my request, Miriam Petruck, Ph.D., a linguistics professor at the University of California, Berkeley, conducted a linguistic analysis of these documents, which is provided as an addendum to this chapter.

This analysis confirmed that the two passages have definite structural similarities.

John Gordon (from *Reminiscences of the Civil War*):

With great energy my men labored to save the bridge. I called on the citizens of Wrightsville for buckets and pails, but none were to be found. There was no lack of buckets and pails a little while later, when the town was on fire...My men labored as earnestly and bravely to save the town as they did to save the bridge. In the absence of fire-engines or other appliances, the only chance to arrest the progress of the flames was to form my men around the burning district, with the flank resting on the river's edge, and pass rapidly from hand to hand the pails of water. Thus, and thus only, was the advancing, raging fire met, and at a late hour of the night checked and conquered.[4]

Assistant Chief Jeffrey Keene (from a letter to the Fire Chief):

With my radio restored, man power and apparatus were brought in and put under the guidance of Acting Lieutenant Christopher Ackley. While setting up a plan of action, Lieutenant Ackley displayed good common sense, knowledge, training and a deep concern for the safety of firefighters under his command. A large amount of gas entered the structure by way of a open window. Though we tried to remove all possible sources of ignition, we were able to remove all but two. The owner informed us that the house contained an oil-fired furnace and a hot water heater. There was no way to shut them off from the inside or outside. Using metering devices,

a positive pressure fan and opening and closing windows,
the hazard was removed.[5]

I stated earlier that people reincarnate in groups,
based on shared karma, emotional attachments, and
joint projects. Due to the premise of group incarnations,
both Jeff and I suspected that his fellow firefighters in
the Westport, Connecticut, Fire Department were likely
military acquaintances of John B. Gordon during the
Civil War. Subsequently, Jeff has established several
matches between colleagues in his firehouse and
officers that fought with Gordon. One of these
proposed past life pairings, which demonstrates a
striking similarity in physical resemblance, involves
Confederate General Cadmus Wilcox and Firefighter
Wayne R. Zaleta. Images comparing General Wilcox
and Zaleta can be viewed next to images of General
Gordon and Jeffrey Keene.

In terms of past-life memories, Jeff describes three
kinds. First, through a series of meditations, Jeff was
able to visualize or remember details of his life as
Gordon. Jeff purposely conducted these meditations
before he read *Remembrances of the Civil War*. He
documented these experiences and later was able to
confirm many details through Gordon's book and other
sources.

A second type of memory involves spontaneously
knowing details of Gordon's life without having
learned the information from any other source. As an
example, Jeff toured a visitor's center where artifacts
of a Confederate surrender ceremony were housed.
Gordon had participated in this specific ceremony. An

image depicted the setting of the ceremony, complete with the flag used by Gordon and his fellow Confederate officers in surrendering. Jeff *knew* that the flag in the display was not the flag actually used in the ceremony. Jeff recognized the correct flag from an assortment displayed at the visitor's center. Upon questioning the staff, he verified the flag in the display was indeed from a later era and that Jeff had identified the authentic flag used in the ceremony.

A third type of memory Jeff has experienced can be called emotional memory, as described in the incident at Sunken Road, in which Jeff had the intense emotional reaction when revisiting the scene of a past-life trauma.

Jeff Keene has reflected that during the Civil War, he was a general in the South's Confederate Army, yet in this lifetime, he lives in the North. Jeff has noted that an ancestor of his fought with the Union Army and as such, when he was John B. Gordon, he may have gone to battle against his own ancestor from his current Connecticut lifetime. Reincarnation gives us a different perspective on war, one that lets us see how wasteful war is in terms of lives and resources.

I would like to bring this chapter to a close with a section taken from Jeff Keene's book, *Someone Else's Yesterday*. It has great import for our times, given the amount of conflict we observe on our planet today. Note that the passage comes from someone who was, in a past lifetime, one of the greatest battlefield generals that the United States has ever produced. Reflect on how an understanding of reincarnation mollifies the character of even battlefield heroes.

Pause for a moment and contemplate what the world would be like if reincarnation were proven to be a fact of life. How would we then treat others? When dealing with family, friends or acquaintances, we would need to ask ourselves some questions like: Who are these souls? What is their relationship to me? Am I to learn something from them or am I to be their Teacher? The possibilities are endless. We all live in the same house and that house grows smaller everyday. This planet has become a "Global Village." No longer does it take the written word to tell of events on the other side of the earth. With the flick of a switch we can sit and watch events unfold. Every country effects all others with their finances, pollution problems and petty hostilities. Now more than ever everyone needs to change his way of thinking. No more I, but US. No more Them, but We. We leave a mark on ourselves and those around us, so let us strive to use a gentle touch.[5]

John B. Gordon

Photo Courtesy of Jeffrey Keene

Jeff Keene

Photo by George Cordorzo

Cadmus Wilcox   **Wayne Zaleta**

Gordon and Wilcox fought together in the Confederate Army.
They reincarnated as Keene and Zaleta, who worked in the same
firehouse in the Westport, Connecticut Fire Department.

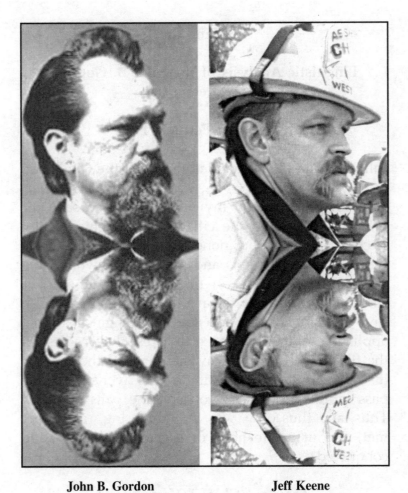

John B. Gordon

Courtesy of the Library of Congress

Jeff Keene

Courtesy of Jeffery Keene

Addendum

Linguistic Analysis of the John B. Gordon/
Jeffrey Keene Case

by Miriam Petruck, Ph.D

John Gordon (from Remembrances of the Civil War)

With great energy my men labored to save the
bridge. I called on the citizens of Wrightsville for
buckets and pails, but none were to be found. There
was no lack of buckets and pails a little while later,
when the town was on fire...My men labored as
earnestly and bravely to save the town as they did to
save the bridge. In the absence of fire-engines or other
appliances, the only chance to arrest the progress of
the flames was to form my men around the burning
district, with the flank resting on the river's edge, and
pass rapidly from hand to hand the pails of water.
Thus, and thus only, was the advancing, raging fire
met, and at a late hour of the night checked and
conquered.

Assistant Chief Jeffrey Keene
(from a letter to his Fire Chief)

With my radio restored, man power and apparatus
were brought in and put under the guidance of Acting
Lieutenant Christopher Ackley. While setting up a plan
of action, Lieutenant Ackley displayed good common
sense, knowledge, training and a deep concern for the
safety of firefighters under his command. A large

amount of gas entered the structure by way of a open window. Though we tried to remove all possible sources of ignition, we were able to remove all but two. The owner informed us that the house contained an oil-fired furnace and a hot water heater. There was no way to shut them off from the inside or outside. Using metering devices, a positive pressure fan and opening and closing windows, the hazard was removed.

Summary of Linguistic Analysis performed by Miriam Petruck, Ph.D.

- Close in average number of words per sentence: Gordon¾21; Keene¾18
- Use of compound sentences: Gordon¾"the only chance to arrest the progress of flames was to form my men around the burning district, with the flank resting on the river's edge, and pass rapidly from hand to hand the pails of water." Keene¾"While setting up a plan of action, Lieutenant Ackley displayed good common sense, knowledge, training and a deep concern for the safety of firefighters under his command."
- Use of preposed clauses in complex sentences: Gordon¾"In the absence of fire engines"; Keene¾"While setting up a plan of action."
- Use of existential-there sentences with negation: Gordon¾"There was no lack of buckets." Keene¾"There was no way to shut them off."
- Adverbial clauses at beginning of sentence: Gordon—"With great energy," "In the absence of fire-engines"; Keene—"With my radio restored."

- Most of text is in active voice except at the end. In both passages, paragraphs end in passive voice, as if the success came about without the intervention of those involved. Excitement is achieved by altering expected word order, separating two parts of the verb. Gordon¾"was the advancing, raging fire met, and at a late hour of the night checked and conquered." Keene¾"Using metering devices . . . the hazard was removed."

Note from Dr. Petruck:

Given the similarities already noted, we must, nevertheless, include a disclaimer about authorship. More specifically, because the texts are very small and the analysis is (necessarily) limited to major structural features, any claim about authorship is, at best, tentative. Further analysis is required to make a stronger claim in this regard.

Larger sample texts that have not been preselected would facilitate a variety of frequency tests on different subsets of words. In addition, it would be instructive to examine such text to answer other questions about the substylistic features of the texts. For example, do they use distinctive vocabularies? Do the texts employ rare collocations (combinations) of common words? Is there any irregular spelling or hyphenation of words, or more generally, punctuation of sentences?

6

Neurosurgeon Norm Shealy as the Reincarnation of Dr. John Elliotson; Charles Dickens Reborn as J.K. Rowling

Norm Shealy is a world famous neurosurgeon, inventor, writer and specialist in pain management. Norm is the inventor of the TENS Unit, a devise that discharges an electrical current thought the skin which blocks pain. He also the inventor of the Dorsal Column Stimulator, a subcutaneous device that has wires that are implanted next to the spinal cord, which discharge an electrical current to block pain impulses in cases that involve severe and intractable back pain. Dr. Shealy also is the inventor of the Facet Rhizotomy, a surgical procedure in which nerve fibers are cut to reduce pain coming from the joints of the back. Dr. Shealy is also considered the father of modern

comprehensive pain programs, which involve
multidisciplinary approach, utilizing psychologists as
well as physicians. For all these reasons, Norm Shealy
is known in the medical community around the world.
Norm Shealy has learned about a past lifetime of his
in which he was John Elliotson, a 19th century physician
in Britain who was also a medical innovator and pain
specialist. In his own words, Dr. Shealy explains how
he came to learn about this past incarnation. In the
text provided below, Snowmass refers to a ski resort
in Colorado.

In January 1972, I was sitting in a lecture at the
Neuroelectric Society in Snowmass at Aspen
waiting for Dr. William Kroger to finish his lecture.
I was a bit annoyed because he was trying to
convince us that acupuncture was hypnosis and he
suddenly said, "In the last century a British
physician demonstrated that you could operate on
patients who were mesmerized. His name was John
Elliotson." When he said that, I felt as if someone
had thrust an iceberg down my back and I said to
myself, "My God, that's me."

I was neutral about reincarnation at that time.
I asked my medical librarian if she could get me
any information on John Elliotson and she could
not. So in the June of that year, I went to London.
I got in a cab and asked the cab driver to take me
to the Royal College of Surgeons, assuming that
John Elliotson must have been a surgeon. As we
turned down one corner to the right, I was sitting
in the back of the cab and suddenly was picked up
physically and turned in the opposite direction,

again feeling as if there were an iceberg down my back. A block down to the left, instead of the right, was University College Hospital of London, where my office had been as John Elliotson. I walked in the building and felt at home.

It turns out that John Elliotson was the first Professor of Medicine at the University College Hospital. He made his reputation in the 1830s giving public lectures on various aspects of medicine. James Wakeley, editor of the *Lancet* at that time, often published his lectures. During his career as an internist, John introduced the stethoscope and the use of narcotics, both from France where he had studied. He also introduced mesmerism and began to put on public displays of mesmerism in the amphitheater. He was a bosom buddy of Charles Dickens and William Thackery. The taught Dickens how to use mesmerism on his hypochondriacal wife. Elliotson was the first physician in London to give up wearing knickers. He had striking black curly hair and walked with a congenital limp.

He also demonstrated that some of his patients who were placed in a mesmeric trace became clairvoyant and easily made diagnoses. Elliotson also inspired James Esdaile to do a large number of operations upon mesmerized patients. Esdaile later wrote a book called *Natural and Mesmeric Clairvoyance* and mentioned Elliotson's use of hypnotic mesmerism for inducing clairvoyance. Eventually, Elliotson was asked by the Board of Trustees to stop putting on public displays of mesmerism. Elliotson became angry and resigned.

For twelve years he continued publishing *The Zoist*, in which he recounted many aspects of mesmerism, including well over 300 patients who were operated on by another surgeon when Elliotson put the patient into a trance. Eventually he was invited by the Royal College of Physicians to give the annual Haverian Lecture because of his contributions to medicine. He gave his lecture on the hypocrisy of science in accepting new thoughts.

Now to similarities in my own life. At age 9, everyone wore knickers but me. My mother tried to get me to wear knickers and I would have temper tantrums and tear them apart. As a young child, perhaps 4 or 5, I wanted black curly hair so badly that I once went up to an aunt of mine and cut a lock of her black hair. When I was sixteen and just leaving to go to college, I dyed my hair black but I never did it more than once. It was just too much trouble. John was also a Latin scholar and I won the Latin medal two years in high school. When I was 9 years old I had a small stress fracture of the right tibial plateau. It became infected with an abscess. This was before antibiotics and I was told that I would always walk with a limp.

Although from the age four I said was going to be a physician, by age sixteen I always thought I was going to be a neurosurgeon. Between my junior and senior years in medical school, I took a three-month trip to visit various and sundry surgical internship possibilities. I went back to Duke and decided to take an internship in internal medicine instead of surgery, even though I still pursued neurosurgery after the internship.

Charles Dickens was one of my favorite authors as a child. In 1974, I visited Olga Worrall, the great healer. In a hypnotic trance, I saw her walk across her living room, pick up a book on a table, and put it back down. I later called Olga and asked her what was the book lying on the table in her living room. She said it was *Pendennis* by William Thackery. Thackery dedicated his novel, *Pendennis* (1850), to Dr. Elliotson and modeled his character, Dr. Goodenough, in that novel, after Elliotson.

I have spent much of this life getting people off narcotics rather than putting them on them. Six months before I heard Elliotson's name, I published anonymously a novel based on the hypocrisy of medicine in accepting new ideas. I used many of the examples that Elliotson did in his Harverian lecture. In 1973, again a month before I heard John Elliotson's name, I received a $50,000 grant from a Fortune 500 company, which had asked to remain anonymous, to study psychic diagnosis.

In 1973, I visited seventy-five individuals who were said to be excellent clairvoyants, and I did a test of medical intuition, or the ability of really untrained psychics or intuitives to do medical diagnosis. We found five who were between 70 and 75% accurate. When I told the seventy-five intuitives I visited that I had this personal feeling that I had been John Elliotson, all seventy five concurred. For some seven years in by life, I published a newsletter, *Holos Practice Reports*, on alternative approaches to medicine.

In summary, I have never had any question that I was John Elliotson in my last life. John Elliotson

was born October 24, 1791. At age 19 he graduated
from medical school. Interestingly, I entered medical
school at age 19. He died July 29, 1868. Incidentally,
John founded the Phrenology Society in London
and it is interesting that I went into neurosurgery,
which certainly has a lot to do with the skull.

Let us briefly review the key features of the
Elliotson/Shealy case. When Dr. Shealy first heard John
Elliotson's name, he knew viscerally that he was
Elliotson in a past lifetime. This occurred even though
Dr. Shealy was neutral about reincarnation, at that
point in time. Dr. Shealy had this inner knowing, which
was accompanied by a dramatic sensation of an
"iceberg" going down his back, before studying
Elliotson's life and without seeing an image of
Elliotson. When Dr. Shealy went to London to research
Elliotson, he intuitively found Elliotson's office. This
event also was accompanied by the "iceberg" sensation.
Dr. Shealy then learned that he and Elliotson had much
in common. Both share the trait of being medical
innovators, in that Elliotson introduced the use of the
stethoscope in England and Norm Shealy has invented
the TENS unit and the Dorsal Column Stimulator.
    Both have demonstrated an interest in the
management of pain. Elliotson introduced the use of
narcotics in England, while Dr. Shealy has become a
world expert on pain management. In his
contemporary career, Dr. Shealy has labored to find
ways to manage pain so that people can get off
narcotics. Elliotson was an internist, who later founded
phrenology, which involves study of the skull. Dr.

Shealy first choose to go into internal medicine, then switched fields and became a neurosurgeon.

Elliotson was interested in mesmerism or hypnosis, an interest shared by Dr. Shealy. Elliotson was interested in the observation that hypnosis could stimulate clairvoyance. Dr. Shealy has worked with clairvoyants and medical intuitives, including Caroline Myss. Both have been ridiculed by conservative elements in the medical community for their innovative approaches. Elliotson gave his detractors a piece of his mind when in a Harverian Lecture, he delivered a speech on the hypocrisy of science in accepting new ideas. Dr. Shealy published a novel with the identical message and utilized the same examples that Elliotson used in his Harverian Lecture. Elliotson had striking black hair which Dr. Shealy, in his youth, tried to recreate. Elliotson gave up wearing knickers, which were pants that went down just below the knee. Dr. Shealy had a tantrum when his mom tried to get him to wear the same dreaded piece of clothing.

It is significant that when I first contacted Dr. Shealy in 2002, he was unaware that facial features remain consistent from lifetime to lifetime. When I asked him whether he looked like John Elliotson, Norm responded, "I don't' know!" Norm agreed to send me images of Elliotson and himself as a medical student, which he thought might bear some resemblance. The images, which are presented at the end of this chapter, clearly demonstrate matching facial architecture. Much as in the case of Robert Snow, the fact that Norm Shealy derived his own past life case in a compelling manner, believed without doubt that he is the reincarnation of Elliotson and did not even focus on common appearance, reinforces that the consistency of facial features from one incarnation to another is indeed a valid phenomenon.

Two interesting additional past life matches have evolved from Norman Shealy's case. One involves Anton Mesmer, who significantly influenced John Elliotson. Mesmer was an Austrian physician, who lived from 1734 to 1815. He developed a form of hypnosis, which came to be known as "mesmerism." Mesmer found that certain patients received beneficial effects from this meditative, trance state. Other physicians in the medical community, such as John Elliotson/Norm Shealy, supported Mesmer's work. In 1785, the French Government created a committee, which included Benjamin Franklin, to investigate Mesmer's work. The committee's report was unfavorable to Mesmer and as a result, he was relegated as a charlatan. Posterity, though, has vindicated Mesmer, as hypnosis and its sister, meditation, were later found to be helpful for a number of medical conditions.

In contemporary times, Anton Mesmer has been identified as Jon Kabat-Zinn, Ph.D., who has brought "Mindfulness Meditation" to the medical community in the United States. Mindfulness Meditation is used to alleviate conditions aggravated by stress, and it can be seen as a contemporary version of mesmerism. A wonderful aspect of this story is that in today's world, Anton Mesmer has been acclaimed for his work, rather than being ridiculed. The match between Mesmer and Kabat-Zinn, by the way, has been confirmed by Ahtun Re, the spirit guide channeled through Kevin Ryerson, who has demonstrated an ability to make accurate past life matches.

Mindfulness Meditation is taught in many medical institutions, In this lifetime, Dr. Kabat-Zinn has been a member of medical academia, as he is a retired Professor of Medicine at the University of Massachusetts, Medical School. I love this story as it demonstrates that individuals, who are condemned by those with closed minds in one lifetime, do receive their just rewards in the end.

The other past life case that emerged, in relation to Norm Shealy, involves Charles Dickens, who was noted to be a good friend of John Elliotson. In a session with Kevin Ryerson, I asked Ahtun Re whether Dickens was incarnate today, and I was told that he is. I was surprised to learn who Dickens is in contemporary times, though on further reflection, it made perfect sense. Charles Dickens has reincarnated as J. K. Rowling, the author of the *Harry Potter* series. Ahtun Re pointed out that in this lifetime, as in the last, Dickens/Rowling is bringing magic into children's lives through written works. The physical resemblance between Dickens and Rowling is impressive.

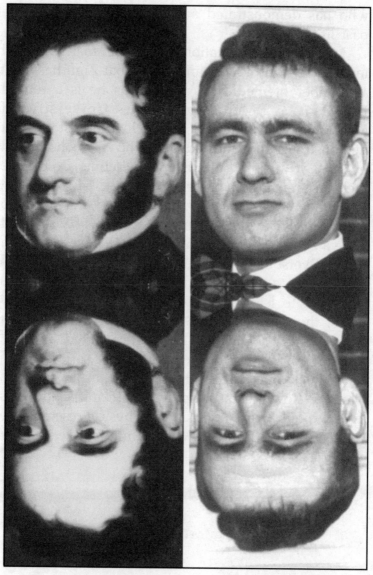

Doctor John Elliotson

© The Royal Society

Doctor Norm Shealy

Courtesy of Norm Shealy

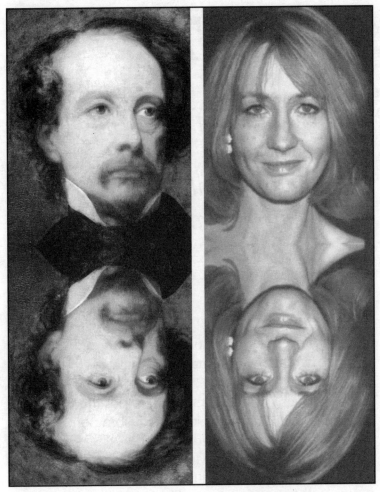

Charles Dickens   **J.K. Rowling**

J.K. Rowling is the author of the *Harry Potter* book series.

Detail © Bettman/CORBIS   Detail © Mitchell Gerber/CORBIS

7

Past Lives of US Diplomat Wayne Peterson and his Relationships with Maitreya and Sai Baba

Wayne Peterson is a recently retired career US Diplomat who served the United States for 32 years. For the last 17 years of his career, Mr. Peterson directed the Fulbright Scholarship Program, based in Washington, DC, but which is administered though US embassies throughout the world. Most recently, as part of his work at Fulbright, Mr. Peterson worked directly with Senator John Kerry on a humanitarian project in Vietnam.

Mr. Peterson started his international service in the Peace Corps, where he founded the extremely successful S.O.S program in Brazil, a privately funded venture which provided aid to the very poorest citizens of that country. Melvin Laird, who later became

Secretary of Defense under Richard M. Nixon, was a direct supporter of Mr. Peterson's project. At the end of his Peace Corps tour of duty, Peterson was approached by the American ambassador in Brazil, who asked him to become a career diplomat and to serve in the embassy in Rio de Janeiro. Mr. Peterson passed the qualifying examinations and was accepted into the U.S. Foreign Service before his Peace Corps term was over. For the next 13 years, he served in various diplomatic capacities in Latin America, Southeast Asia and, finally, Africa.

Mr. Peterson returned to Washington where he was awarded the directorship of the Fulbright Scholarship Program, a position he held for 17 years. In the course of his career, Mr. Peterson has had Thanksgiving dinner with Robert F. Kennedy and his wife Ethyl, he had a private meeting with President Richard M. Nixon, and he met Presidents John F. Kennedy and Lyndon Baines Johnson.

In addition to being a retired US Diplomat of distinction, Mr. Peterson is also a very spiritually evolved human being. He has led Transmission Meditation groups for many years and is the author of the book, *Extraordinary Times, Extraordinary Beings*, in which Mr. Peterson describes his direct encounters with spiritual masters such as Maitreya, a spirit being working to help humanity evolve. Maitreya, by the way, does not have a physical body in the sense that you or I have bodies. Rather, Maitreya is a spirit being, like Ahtun Re, who is able to manifest himself in a "light body," which appears very real to those who see him. The British author and artist, Benjamin Crème, has written several volumes on Maitreya and it was Crème who initiated the Transmission Mediation program, where energies from masters on the spiritual planes are "transmitted" to participants.

Interestingly, Ahtun Re, the spirit being channeled through Kevin Ryerson, who has solved many reincarnation cases presented in *Born Again* and *Return of the Revolutionaries*, is familiar and respectful of Maitreya. Ahtun Re has explained that all great spiritual beings, such as Mohammed, Buddha, Moses, Jesus, Hindu masters and Maitreya, all work together with a common purpose, to help humanity evolve spiritually. We will now examine three past lives of Mr. Peterson's, which were discovered on his own, with a little help from his spiritual master, Maitreya.

THE REINCARNATION CASE OF FRANCESCO FOSCARI/ WAYNE PETERSON

Wayne grew up in the 40s, in rural Wisconsin, outside of Green Bay. As a child, he began having subtle memories of past lives, so subtle, that he didn't realize that reincarnation was the basis for these memories. For example, as a small boy, when people asked him what his name was, Wayne would refuse to tell them, since he strongly believed that he had a better name which identified "the real me." Regarding the situation, Wayne explains:

> *This was a battle of wills between my parents and me for years. When they would say, 'His name is Wayne,' I would immediately say that it is not. My mother would often challenge me to provide another*

name, but I could never remember what my name should be, although I knew that I had another name. It was not until I was twelve years old that I decided that my real name was Francesco Foscari. This was not a name fetched from thin air. For several years the name Foscari floated around in my head as a word. Eventually I put it together with Francesco because it sounded right. I had a deep emotional attachment to the name. As a young teenager, I was determined that when I became an adult, I would officially change my name to Francesco Foscari.

All teens at some point probably think about changing their names to imitate a movie star or to a more romantic sounding name. With me, however, it was a name I had never heard or seen written anywhere. In fact, Italian names did not exist in our community in Wisconsin; so it was odd that I should find an Italian name so magnetic.

Note how similar young Wayne's experience was to that of Barbro Karlen, who as a young girl told her parents that her name was not Barbro, but Anne Frank. The difference is that Wayne didn't realize that his attraction to the name Francesco Foscari was related to a past incarnation, for Wayne didn't have visual memories of that lifetime. In contrast, Barbro Karlen did have clear memories of being Anne Frank.

Mr. Peterson relates that the years went by and after he joined the US diplomatic service, he traveled to Venice, where he experienced distinct feelings of déjà vu, feelings that he had been there before. Though he had never taken art classes, in adulthood, he found that he could paint with great skill. He found he was particularly good at depicting the architecture of classic buildings, though for some reason, he chose to only paint scenes of Venice. When friends asked why all of his artwork involved Venetian scenes, Mr. Peterson could not provide an explanation.

A breakthrough came in 1990, when Mr. Peterson, almost 50 years after his initial attraction to the Italian name Foscari, experienced vivid memories of a lifetime in Venice. Mr. Peterson relates that he distinctly saw the interior of a house that he had lived in. Mr. Peterson realized that he was the man who owned the house and he started experiencing the emotions that the man was feeling. He saw himself wearing a long red brocade robe, which he later learned was the official attire of a Venetian senator.

Mr. Peterson then looked out a window of the building and saw that he was on the second floor of a huge house that ran alongside a small, funnel shaped canal, which emptied into a very large waterway, presumably the Grand Canal of Venice. Mr. Peterson then moved down a hallway and looked out a window that had a view of the rear of the property. He saw that a wall separated his house from a small street, which connected to a distinctive white arched bridge that crossed another small canal. Mr. Peterson also heard a woman speaking to him from the lower level of the house. He realized that she was speaking Italian and that he understood her, though in his contemporary lifetime, Mr. Peterson doesn't speak Italian.

This experience, which Mr. Peterson states was facilitated by Maitreya, allowed him to understand his lifelong attachment to the name Francesco Foscari.

After experiencing what appeared to be past lifetime in Venice, Mr. Peterson bought books on houses of Venice, focusing in particular on buildings located on the Grand Canal. After much searching, Mr. Peterson found the house next to a funnel shaped canal, which opened into the Grand Canal, which had a white arched bridge in the back. The house was exactly as Mr. Peterson had seen it in his past life memory. Mr. Peterson was most amazed when he found that the house was built by Francesco Foscari, a politician and leader of the Venetian Republic, who lived from 1373-1457.

In a subsequent visit to Venice, Wayne Peterson tried to find the burial place of Francesco Foscari. Since Foscari was a Doge, a leader of the state, Mr. Peterson reasoned that Foscari would be entombed in the cathedral where other Doges were buried. Foscari's tomb, though, was not there. Later, when he was walking through the streets of Venice, Mr. Peterson had the intuition to enter a smaller place of worship. He walked up to front of the church, up to the alter, which was cordoned off from the main hall of the church. A sign indicated that entry past this point was prohibited. Mr. Peterson, though, was inwardly guided to trespass beyond it. There, behind the alter, Mr. Peterson found the tomb of Doge Francesco Foscari.

THE REINCARNATION CASE OF LOUISE VANDERBILT/ WAYNE PETERSON

Wayne Peterson also experienced memories of a past lifetime in which he was Louise Vanderbilt, wife

of Frederick Vanderbilt, a member of the American
Vanderbilt dynasty. In contrast to the childhood
remembrances regarding the Foscari lifetime, his
memories of the Vanderbilt lifetime were more direct
and visual. Let us let Mr. Peterson narrate the turn of
events:

*My earliest memories in childhood included detailed
images of a time when women wore long billowing
gowns and people still used horse drawn carriages. I
remembered specifically a large sandstone house, a man
named Fred, friends arriving for social gatherings, a
large reception area with a high ceiling and floors of
white stone. Central to all this I remembered most a
woman that was the center of all related activity. The
mystery lady was the center of several scenes that were
repeated again and again during my earliest years and
continued even to this day. I used to wonder who these
people were and wondered why they appeared so real to
me.*

*As a young child I believed these people were part
of my current life. Why they never visited our home I
could never explain. I actually believed they would arrive
one day and they would remember me and
unexplainably, I would be very happy. I assumed that
in my earlier years as an infant I had perhaps experienced
these people with my parents and had now forgotten
most of those intimate experiences. It was the only way
I had as a child to explain the vividness of these people
I visited in my dreams. However, these people never did
appear in this current life and I remained at a loss to
explain their appearance in my mind. I had no knowledge
of reincarnation at that early pre-school stage of my life.*

Mr. Peterson reflects that these memories were especially odd since in the 1940's, there was no television, nor were there motion pictures, to fuel his imagination. He reflects that nothing in his real time experience of a small town in central Wisconsin correlated to his visions. Clothing, houses and social manners were entirely different in Wisconsin than what he experienced in his memories. Yet a man named Fred, women in billowing gowns transported in horse drawn carriages and the large sandstone house, were very real to little Wayne. Perplexed, Wayne asked his mother about these people and the house that he remembered. He asked if he had been ever taken to such a place as an infant. The answer was always no. Though he could not explain the source of his memories, these memories continued to be a source of comfort, and he maintained a nostalgic emotion for a person named Fred.

As a young adult, as described above, Wayne Peterson joined the Peace Corps and was on route to Brazil. His flight to Rio de Janeiro was via New York City. Since Wayne had never been to the big city before, he arranged to have a few days in NYC, to take in the sights of the Big Apple.   On his second day in NYC, at noon, Wayne was walking down Fifth Avenue. He was impressed by the crush of people. Let us now allow Wayne to narrate the scene, as he stood on the sidewalk of Fifth Avenue:

Suddenly a woman with hat and white gloves across the wide sidewalk waved her hands in my direction and shouted, 'Louise, Louise, over here, it's me.' She kept shouting Louise and I froze. I instantly believed she was calling me. For whatever reason, I suddenly believed I was Louise.

All my attention focused on this strange woman moving in my direction through the crowd. In my mind I was someone else, someone named Louise. I believed the woman moving toward me was an old friend, but the face did not look familiar. Nevertheless, there was a great relief within my mind, I thought that finally someone recognized the real me. Not the young man from Wisconsin, but a woman named Louise. It was as if I had been a victim of amnesia and suddenly someone shocked me into reality. Unfortunately, the moment of intense excitement passed when the woman in the hat and gloves brushed past me andgrabbed the elderly woman standing directly behind me.

Instantly, my mind was on overload and I could not move or think. I was still having a moment as Louise and I looked at these two women and thought, you fools, why don't you remember me? I am the real Louis, I thought. How long I stood and stared at these two women enjoying their renewed acquaintance I do not know, but eventually my logical mind returned and I was forced to question my actions and thinking. Embarrassed and bewildered, I returned to my hotel room.

In the hotel I relaxed on the bed and for some hours pondered what had just happened. Why, I kept wondering, did I think I was Louise? Why was it so real to me and so important that I be Louise? I pondered this strange experience during my entire stay in New York, but found no answer until years later...Nonetheless, I was content that I was Louise in a past life about the turn of the century and that Fred was my husband.

What I knew of Louise and Fred was not only a few visions of past lives, but I could feel emotions that were from Louise. I intuitively knew she was often frustrated with Frederick at social events. Louise would be in the huge reception area of the house greeting guests. She wore several dresses that I could remember in great detail. I always envisioned Fred in white tie and jacket with tails. He appeared to be perfectly comfortable dressed in that attire but whenever possible he escaped to the small office/library. I can vividly remember the library door, inside it would be quiet and Fred would be seated in the high backed sofa that hid him from the view from anyone at the doorway exit...Eventually, Louse grew tired of making excuses to the guests about Fred's absence.

In these past life reminiscences experienced when he was a very young man, Wayne Peterson still did not know who Fred and Louise were specifically. Decades later, in the 1990's, a hint came when Mr. Peterson was visiting an upper class friend in New York City, whose name was Mary. This upper class friend insisted that Wayne join her on a vacation at her Irish house on the South coast of Ireland. Mary said that they would have a wonderful time and added that her friend Gloria would be joining them also. Wayne asked, "Gloria who." Mary replied, "It's my friend Gloria Vanderbilt." Let us allow Mr. Peterson describe his reaction to this statement regarding Gloria Vanderbilt:

Instantly my logical mind was again paralyzed just as it had been years before when in New York City that elderly woman shouted the name Louise. Another personality or another identity took over my consciousness and I said, "Great, Gloria and I can chat and gossip about our family relatives."

There was a silence from my friend Mary and I began to realize what I had said. Mary asked what I meant by common family relatives, and I babbled nervously about something while trying to think up any good excuse for my ridiculous statement. Eventually, I explained that I thought Gloria had an interesting family tree. After terminating that conversation I realized that for a few moments I was transported into another life. It was so total that I really believed I was a relative of Gloria Vanderbilt and we could indeed gossip about family members. Why, I kept wondering again, why did I say such a stupid thing with such conviction?

In the days that followed my conversation with Mary I began to wonder if there ever could have been a Frederick and Louise Vanderbilt. No, I reasoned the odds against it were simply too remote to even bother to explore. Nevertheless, some weeks later while wandering in my favorite bookstore, my attention was attracted to a book on the wealthy families of the 1800's and early 1900's. I noticed the book only because it was on the lowest shelf and protruding into the aisle by some 4 to 5 inches.

Although I pushed the book into its proper alignment several times with my foot, the book continued to spring forward multiple times before I finally picked it up and read its cover. I even explored on hands and knees what was in the shelf which forced the book out into the isle. Naturally, there was nothing but an empty space behind the book.

Curious, I briefly looked at the price of the book and immediately wanted to place it back on the shelf. For whatever reasons, I could not give up the book although my mind wanted to place it back on the shelf. Even after paying for the book I was angry with myself for having no self-control over purchasing a book I did not want. I took the book home and placed it on my own bookshelf thinking that this is one book that I will probably never read, and therefore it was a total waste of money.

However, later that night I had a dream that I must read this new book. Unable to sleep because of this nagging notion, I went downstairs and opened the book. At first nothing captured my imagination but soon I opened a page that totally took me by surprise. There in full color was a photo of the very room I had always envisioned as a child. The distinctive ceiling, the fireplace and white marble floor and the very same sofas I so clearly remembered. It was all there as if only yesterday I had stepped out of that room.

The next page was even more revealing. Again, in a color photo, was the library/office I knew so well. The pale green sofa that Fred would hide in during social events and the two beautiful desks were part of a his and hers arrangement. Transfixed in wonderment, I thought about the strange attachment I had to this scene and what I might learn from this extraordinary experience.

I began to read the article that went with the photos. The house, it said, was built by Frederick Vanderbilt at Hyde-Park New York in the late 1800's. Wouldn't it be a strange coincidence, I thought, if this Fred Vanderbilt had a wife named Louise?...As I read down the page, I was overwhelmed when I read that Frederick was *married to Louise H. Anthony. The following pages were most revealing, especially when I saw the color photos that followed...The photos brought to life the rooms that I remembered from my earliest memories as a child. I realized that I had opened a book that revealed all the secrets of a past life.*

Mr. Peterson also read that though their Hyde-Park house was their favorite, their main home was on Fifth Avenue, in New York City. The fact that Louise Vanderbilt lived on Fifth Avenue sheds further light on young Wayne's experience on Fifth Avenue, when the elderly woman in white gloves called out "Louise," and Wayne was transported to his past incarnation as Louise. Not only did the name "Louise" trigger his past life recall, but Wayne later found out that during that incident, he had actually been standing in front of the very spot where Fred and Louise Vanderbilt had their house in NYC on Fifth Avenue. This phenomenon of a geographic setting triggering past life experiences was also demonstrated in the case of John B. Gordon/ Jeff Keene.

Mr. Peterson also learned that Louise and Frederick were very interested in metaphysics, as Mr. Peterson is in contemporary times. Louise was also a great fan of the grand ladies of 18th century France, especially Marie Antoinette. Louise Vanderbilt had even filled her bedroom with French reproduction furniture. Mr. Peterson also learned that Frederick, with encouragement from Louise, used his money to found Vanderbilt University, and great sums were also given to Yale and Columbia. Louise died in 1926, in Paris, which was one of her favorite cities. Frederick lived out his remaining years largely in seclusion, passing away in 1938. Frederick, by the way, has also been identified in contemporary times. Fred turns out to be a friend who Wayne Peterson has known for years, who shares with Wayne an interest in metaphysics and Maitreya. Though Wayne has known this person for a period of time, his identity as Frederick Vanderbilt was not determined until the year 2004. At that time, Frederick and Louise Vanderbilt were consciously reunited, 78 years after they were separated by death.

THE REINCARNATION CASE OF CLAUDE LEDOUX/WAYNE PETERSON

There was a reason that Louise Vanderbilt had a fascination with Marie Antoinette and French furniture, for Wayne Peterson had a past lifetime in that era. This reincarnation case is unique, as it was solved through the combined efforts of two spirit beings, Ahtun Re and Maitreaya. Since Wayne had become a good friend, I assumed that I knew him in a past lifetime. In session with Kevin Ryerson, I asked whether Wayne had been incarnate during the American Revolution. Ahtun Re, the spirit guide that I have been working with through Kevin Ryerson, who has demonstrated an ability to make accurate past life matches, told me that Wayne was incarnate during that era, but that he was in France and was affiliated with the French Court. Upon questioning, Ahtun Re told me that Wayne's name in that lifetime was "Ledoux."

With that information, I tried to find this Ledoux historically, but was unsuccessful. I passed this information on to Wayne and left the issue alone. Fortunately, the spirit being Maitreya came to our assistance, who gave Mr. Peterson clues telepathically. Amusingly, Wayne tends to get these telepathic messages while he performs his morning shaves. One routine day, while Wayne was tending to his whiskers, he received the telepathic message, "If you want to find Ledoux, look in this magazine." In his mind, Wayne then saw a clear image of the cover of a specific issue of *Architectural Digest*, complete with Volume and Number. Wayne later ordered this issue and when he received it, read it cover to cover, but he found nothing on a Ledoux. Time passed and while shaving, Wayne received another telepathic message, "If you want to find Ledoux, look in this chapter." Wayne then visually saw a specific article in the *Architectural Digest* issue he possessed, which consisted of only a few pages. Wayne read and reread the article multiple times, but no Ledoux. When he told a friend of this frustration in not being able to find Ledoux, she replied, "Perhaps you need to look closer. I gave you a magnifying glass as a gift, why don't you use it?"

Wayne initially thought this was a silly idea, but he followed her suggestion. He focused on a photo of a man, the subject of the article, who was seated in front of a bookcase. To his great excitement, in studying the volumes in the bookcase under magnification, he clearly saw a black book with gold lettering which had the title *Claude Ledoux*. Wayne went on the Internet and found that this book was readily available and he ordered it. When he received it, Wayne found that the completely related to this artist and architect, Claude Nicolas Ledoux, in that his art and architecture were consistent with the paintings that Wayne had been doing for years. The talent for architectural painting came from the Ledoux lifetime, though the Venetian scenes that he chose to paint derived from his incarnation as Francesco Foscari.

Wayne also noted that that he had replicated specific designs in contemporary times from the Ledoux lifetime. For example, Ledoux had been commissioned by the King of France to design a village. Ledoux created an integrated community, stressing that beauty must be part of the environment for all inhabitants, not only for the aristocrats, but for the peasantry as well. Wayne recalled that as a child he would create the same utopian village out of mud in his back yard. Further, Wayne painted a mural on his garage wall years before he learned about the Ledoux lifetime, which replicated a piece done by Ledoux. In this mural, Wayne painted a landscape using the arch of a door to frame the scene. Under the arch is a curved eucalyptus tree and in the distance, buildings of a settlement were portrayed. Ledoux had created a similar design 200 years before, utilizing the arch of a bridge to frame a landscape. Under the arch, buildings of a city can be seen in the distance and the same curved, eucalyptus looking like tree is found in the foreground.

In addition to this example, in the reincarnation cases of Gauguin and Picasso, we shall see dramatic examples of how artistic development is unconsciously replicated, from one incarnation to another.

Sai Baba

I would like to close with two interesting tales regarding Wayne Peterson's relationship with Sai Baba, who is considered by some, to be a spiritual avatar incarnate in India. Wayne's first experience occurred back in the 1970's, when Wayne first went to see Benjamin Crème, who was giving a lecture in a nearby venue. Wayne was new to spiritual matters and when Benjamin Crème said that he was going to channel energy from Sai Baba, Wayne thought this was a silly claim and he didn't take it seriously. Wayne was sitting in the back of the auditorium and for some reason; Crème focused his gaze on Wayne and held up the palms of his hands, directing them in Wayne's direction. Wayne then felt a tremendous sensation of heat and suddenly, he and his chair were propelled backwards a distance of five feet. The energy was too strong and Wayne began feeling nauseated. He mentally formulated the message, "Sai Baba, if this is you, please make this stop." The energy flow then ceased. Wayne, stunned, walked out of the auditorium and ran to the washroom, as the nausea had become extreme and he had to vomit. Following that presentation, Wayne developed a keen interest in Maitreya, Sai Baba and spiritual matters.

Though Wayne has never met Sai Baba, there does seem to exist some type of connection between them. The following narrative involves the American actress Judith Light, who read Wayne's book and became a fan. The story goes like this. Mr. Peterson has a friend who went to visit Sai Baba in his ashram in India, in the 1990's. This friend was not a devotee of Sai Baba, but accompanied others who were devotees. Paradoxically, when Sai Baba cast his attention on this woman non-devotee, she had a profound spiritual experience and unexpectedly decided to stay at his ashram for six months. When she returned to the United States, this woman gave Mr. Peterson a photo of Sai Baba, blessed by him, which is considered a great gift. Mr. Peterson kept this photo for almost ten years.

When Mr. Peterson visited Judith Light over the 2003 Thanksgiving holiday, Mr. Peterson received a telepathic message that he should give this photo of Sai Baba to Ms. Light. When he gave it to Judith, she responded, "This is valuable to you, Wayne, are you sure you want to give it to me?" Mr. Peterson stated, "I insist." Judith Light then replied, "Maybe Sai Baba will be good and send you another one." Mr. Peterson gave the photo to Ms. Light on November 21, 2003.

In January 2004, almost two months after giving the Sai Baba photo to Judith Light, Mr. Peterson unexpectedly received a letter from Sai Baba's ashram in India. The letter contained a photo of Sai Baba with a note on the back. The note was dated November 21, 2003, the exact date that Wayne Peterson gave the photo of Sai Baba to Judith Light. On the back of this new photo was the inscription: "The secret of the soul is to see through the form." The image of Sai Baba that was sent to Mr. Peterson featured a parrot on the shoulder of Sai Baba. What is remarkable is that the eye and eyebrow of Sai Baba can be seen through the form of the parrot. How this image of Sai Baba was sent to Wayne on the same day that he gave a similar image away to Judith Light, on a day that Judith suggested that perhaps Sai Baba would be good and send Wayne another picture, remains a mystery.

Interestingly, on the Fourth of July holiday in 1968, Sai Baba gave a declaration, stating his purpose for incarnating at this time. It is my hope that the objective evidence of reincarnation that is being presented in this book with help bring into concrete existence, the sentiments that Sai Baba expressed on that day. On July 4, 1968, Sai Baba revealed:

> *I have come to light the Lamp of Love in your hearts, to see that it shines day by day with added luster. I have not come in behalf of any exclusive religion. I have not come on a mission of publicity for a sect or creed or cause, nor have I come to   collect followers for a doctrine. I have no plan to attract disciples of devotees into my fold or any fold. I have come to tell you of this unitary faith, this spiritual principle, this path of love, this duty of love, this obligation of love.*

Though objective evidence of reincarnation, we can understand that we are all spiritual beings here on earth for the purposes of developing and expressing ourselves. Let us fulfill our various missions and goals without conflict or division, but rather, let us tread, as Sai Baba says, on a "path of love."

Doge Francesco Foscari   **US Diplomat Wayne Peterson**

Courtesy of Wayne Peterson

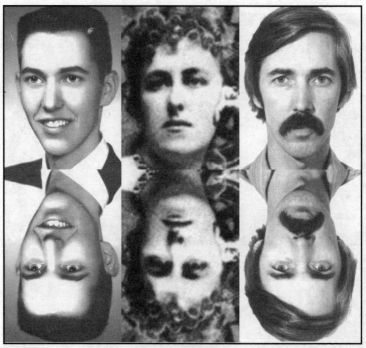

Wayne Peterson   **Louise Vanderbilt**   **Wayne Peterson**

Courtesy of Wayne Peterson

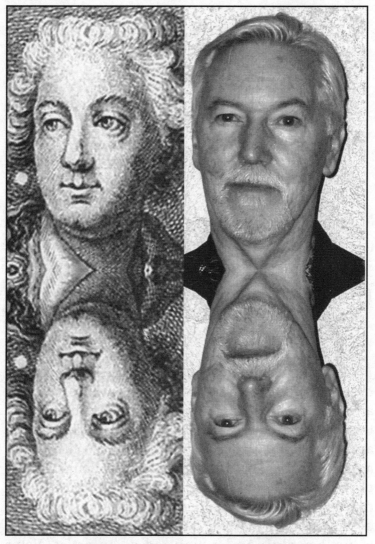

Claude Ledoux   **Wayne Peterson**

Courtesy of Wayne Peterson

8

The Reincarnation of
Paul Gauguin and Pablo Picasso

PETER TEEKAMP AS THE REINCARNATION OF PAUL GAUGUIN

Peter Teekamp's story begins in his childhood years, when the words "Go-Gone, Go-Gone," kept popping into his mind. It took several decades before Peter associated these words with the artist Paul Gauguin and even longer for him to accept that he is the reincarnation of Gauguin. Facial features and personality traits are consistent.. What is truly amazing is that analysis of sketches has demonstrated that Peter unconsciously replicated the artistic development of Gauguin, though at a younger age, demonstrating that we do indeed build upon past achievements. As he matured as an artist, Peter developed a style that has become more realistic and at times, surrealistic. When in 2005, Peter decided to do a series of paintings inspired by Gauguin; we find that the work of these two artists is almost indistinguishable.

Paul Gauguin was born in Paris on June 7, 1848. His father was a journalist and his mother originated from Peru. In 1849, Gauguin's father died during a sea passage to South America. Gauguin spent his early childhood years in Peru, later returning to France where he attended boarding schools. His mother died in 1867, when Paul was 19 years of age. As a young man, Gauguin became a sailor, traveling around the world with the French Merchant Marines, then serving with the French Navy. In 1872, when he was 24, Gauguin entered the business world as a stockbroker. During this period, Gauguin began painting in his spare time. He would continue to work in business, though, for over ten years before devoting his life to painting full time.

In 1873, at the age of 25, Paul married Mette Gad and the couple eventually had five children. Gauguin soon was befriended by the artists Pissaro and Cezanne. At the age of 28, a painting by Gauguin was accepted for the Salon d'Automne, a prestigious art exhibition in Paris. In 1884, Gauguin moved his family to Copenhagen, Denmark, his wife's country of origin. A year later, in 1885, at age 37, Gauguin separated from wife and returned to Paris, to become an artist on a full time basis. Upon his return to France, one his of first paintings was of a scene from the town of St. Cloud, just outside of Paris, entitled, "Paysage a Saint-Cloud," produced in 1885.

In 1887, Gauguin briefly worked for the Panama Canal project as a canal digger and then he traveled to Martinique. Returning to France, Gauguin became friends with Vincent Van Gogh, whom he painted with at Arles, in the south of France. Van Gogh and Gauguin shared a house and it was in this setting that on

December 23, 1888, Van Gogh cut off his ear, which he then presented to a prostitute. Why did Van Gogh cut off his ear? Ultimately, the reasons are unknown, other than that the act reflects Van Gogh's developing mental illness. Gauguin reported that Van Gogh had threatened him with a razor the day prior to the ear incident. The day after Van Gogh cut off his ear, Gauguin left Arles.

During his period at Arles, from February to December 1888, Gauguin developed the style that he is known for, using flat, pure colors, with black outlines. Subjects often involved Christian religious themes. Though the art world would come to revere Gauguin in the future, at this time, he was unrecognized and poor. In 1891, at age 43, Gauguin sold 30 paintings or so, to finance his passage to the South Pacific, where he settled in Tahiti. Gauguin was disgusted with Western civilization and with this move he sought a more simple way of life. For the next two years, Gauguin captured scenes from the South Pacific. It was in Tahiti where his most famous art works would be produced.

Gauguin, though, ran out of funds in Tahiti and had to travel back to France in 1893. Gauguin returned to Tahiti in 1895, at age 47, never to see Europe again. Gauguin's last five years were spent in continuing poverty and worsening health. Gauguin became severely depressed and even tried to commit suicide in 1897, when he was 49 years old. Gauguin survived. In 1901, debilitated and at odds with the French authorities in Tahiti, Gauguin moved to the Marquesas Islands. Gauguin died at the age of 55, on May 8. 1903, and was buried in the Calvary Cemetery.

In his waning years, Gauguin wrote, "For the majority, I shall always remain an enigma, I realize people will understand me less and less ... No matter what happens, I assure you that I shall achieve things of the first order. I can feel it and we shall see." Gauguin's prophecy was accurate. In 1906, three years after his death, his works were exhibited at Salon d'Automne, where his fame and popularity began.

Peter Teekamp was born in Holland, in the Netherlands, in 1950, 47 years after the death of Gauguin. Peter's father was Catholic, while his mother was Jewish. His parents had marital problems and separated when Peter was four. Peter was placed in a Catholic orphanage, where he became an altar boy and sang in the church choir. At age 9, Peter's mother remarried and Peter went to live with his mother and new stepfather.

When he was ten years old, two syllables kept popping into his mind, "Go-Gone, Go-Gone." Little Peter did not associate any particular meaning to these words, but he reveled in them. When he would play, Peter would shout, "Go-Gone, Go Gone," as a cheer. It wasn't until he was fifteen that he started to wonder what "Go-Gone" meant. He asked his school teachers, "What does Go-Gone mean?" His teachers, thinking that he was inquiring about a Dutch word, told him that they didn't know what the term meant.

It is proposed that Peter was actually remembering his name from a past lifetime, that "Go-Gone" was a phonetic pronunciation of Gauguin. This type of remembrance was also observed in the case of US Diplomat Wayne Peterson. Recall that as a small boy, Wayne wouldn't respond to his name when his parent's called him. In frustration, they asked, "So what do you want to be called?" Wayne declared, "My name is FrancescoFoscari," though he had no idea why he wanted to be called that particular name. As a teenager, Wayne was so emotionally attached to it he even considered legally changing his name. Decades passed before Wayne learned that in a past lifetime, he was Francesco Foscari, a Venetian senator and doge. Recall also that Barbro Karlen, as a young girl, told her parents that Anne Frank was her real name, and in the cases of Daniel Jurdi and Titu Singh, past life names were also recalled in childhood.

As a teenager, Peter began to draw. What is remarkable is that Peter's early drawings replicated sketches Gauguin had done almost a hundred years before, though Peter had no knowledge of these Gauguin sketches when he reproduced them. In fact, Peter Teekamp was not exposed to the Gauguin sketches, which are presented at the end of this chapter, until 2003, when Peter was 53 years old. With these pencil drawings, Peter was actually retrieving memories of his artwork from a past lifetime, the lifetime of Paul Gauguin. What is interesting is that Peter replicated Gauguin's artwork unconsciously at a much younger age than when Gauguin produced these sketches. As such, this phenomenon demonstrates how in each lifetime, we build upon accomplishments of a prior incarnation.

Peter attained a degree in business and like Gauguin, entered the business world as a career. Peter has worked as a manger of various retail operations over the years. Also like Gauguin, Peter became a world traveler, visiting places such as Varanasi, in India, Tel Aviv,

Portugal and Egypt, living in these locations for periods of time, paying his way by painting murals.

Eventually, Peter immigrated to the United States. In 1972, Peter settled in, of all places, St. Cloud, Minnesota, where he started to paint in a serious way at the age of 22. This is reminiscent of Gauguin moving back to France from Copenhagen, to become an artist full time. Recall that one of Gauguin's early paintings, upon his return to France, was "Paysage a Saint-Cloud." What is the connection between St. Cloud, France and St. Cloud, Minnesota? I believe that what happens is that an individual can subconsciously recognize that a place has symbolic meaning from a lifetime gone by. Though Peter didn't consciously know that St. Cloud had symbolic meaning for him from the Gauguin lifetime, I believe there was a subconscious recognition and attraction that derived from his soul, which influenced Peter's decision to live in St. Cloud.

In Minnesota, Peter got married to a woman named Angela and the couple had two children. Peter continued to manage retail stores and in addition, he pursued his career as a painter. He participated in art fairs, where he would sell his works. Several times, people came up to him spontaneously and told him about past lives. One told him he lived in France, another told him his name was Paul. Peter didn't know what to make of these comments, though he was open to reincarnation. Peter has related to me that when he was 19 years old, he read Siddhartha, by Herman Hesse. At that time, Peter came to the conclusion that reincarnation is the only spiritual philosophy that embodies "justice and fairness," that provides "an equal chance for everyone." Still, in the early 1970s, Peter did not have any idea of who he might have been in a past lifetime and the comments made by sidewalk psychics regarding a past lifetime of his in France, in which his name was Paul, simply amused him and meant nothing more.

Things changed in 1979, when Peter was 29 years old. His wife, Angela, started to undergo a drastic change in personality, in which she became deeply religious. Though Peter initially honored her need to be more spiritual, he became worried that her new devotional lifestyle was becoming excessive. One day, Peter walked into a room in their home and found his wife praying among lit candles. Angela rose and handed a book to Peter which fell open to a portrait of Paul Gauguin, surrounded by red hues. Angela told Peter, with deep conviction, "You are the reincarnation of Paul Gauguin," an assertion she repeated to him thereafter.

Angela's insistence that he was Gauguin reincarnated made Peter reflect on the words, "Go-Gone, Go-Gone," which echoed in his mind throughout childhood. Peter also noted that his facial features were similar to Gauguin's. Later, he found that Gauguin liked to place faces in the background of his paintings, sometimes overtly, sometimes hidden, a practice that Peter had also spontaneously developed. Still, it was too bizarre for him to conceive that he could be Gauguin.

Peter and Angela grew apart over the years and despite efforts to preserve their marital union, the couple eventually separated. Peter relocated to Apache Junction, Arizona, where he opened an art gallery. Peter was attracted to Native American culture of the Southwest, much like Gauguin was attracted to Tahitian life. Peter's paintings during this period featured Native American themes. Soon after moving to Apache

Junction, Peter met a woman who did past life regressions and Peter decided to give it a try. Peter had this regression in 1980, when he was 30. Peter accessed memories from a lifetime in which he was indeed a painter. He saw cobblestone streets in a village, or perhaps Paris. He saw himself climbing up a dark stairwell to a studio that was dark and filthy; it appeared that the room had not been cleaned in years. Peter observed dirty, neglected paint brushes and he experienced a terrible feeling of depression, such as he had never experienced before. He felt loneliness, rejection and a feeling that he was misunderstood.

Whether he tapped into the lifetime of Gauguin, Peter was not sure. But the regression experience was powerful and it made him study Gauguin ever more earnestly. What he found, though, he did not like. First of all, Peter did not like Gauguin's style of painting, which he found "cartoonish, primitive and unfinished." As mentioned, in this lifetime, Peter has developed a style that is more realistic. Indeed, in the Gauguin inspired art that Peter has created the colors and feel are the same as Gauguin's, but Peter's renditions have more definition. Paintings that demonstrate Peter's progression of style include Gauguin's portrait of his daughter, Aline, and Peter's portrait of Amanda, a girl who died in childbirth. Amanda's portrait is really an artist's depiction, since she perished as a newborn, so it is interesting to note the similarities in appearance between Aline and Amanda. The painting of Amanda, though, is much more realistic with many detailed objects placed in the background.

In addition to the fact that Peter didn't really admire Gauguin's art, there were other things that chagrined

Peter. For example, Peter didn't like how it was perceived that Gauguin had abandoned his wife and children to pursue a career in art. Lastly, Gauguin died of a venereal disease, which Peter did not find admirable. In short, Peter didn't like this guy, Gauguin.

Eight years went by before the issue of reincarnation was raised once again, when Peter was 38. In Apache Junction, in 1988, Peter was befriended by a chiropractor who was a large, burly man in his mid fifties. Over a period of two months, this chiropractor took Peter out to lunch or dinner two or three times a week. Though grateful for the man's kindness, Peter began to wonder what the motive was for the man's generosity. Peter is heterosexual, so he did not want the chiropractor to get any romantic hopes up. Peter decided to confront the issue at one of their meetings.

After Peter questioned the burly man regarding the reasons for his generosity, the chiropractor's face grew red and he stood up, grabbing Peter by his shirt. The man drew Peter's face to within five inches of his own and declared, "You are the reincarnation of Paul Gauguin." Peter was shocked, as he had not breathed a word to the chiropractor about Gauguin—the chiropractor simply had no way to know of Peter's past experiences regarding Gauguin! The chiropractor then let go of Peter and left. Peter never saw him again. Now Peter had been told by two people, his former wife and the chiropractor, who was nearly a stranger, that he was the reincarnation of Gauguin. The trouble was, Peter still did not want to be Gauguin.

Watershed events occurred a year later in 1989, when Peter was 39. Peter's art gallery landlord unexpectedly walked in and told Peter that he was being evicted. The landlord related that Peter had signed a lease that had a clause in it that allowed him to evict Peter without notice and the landlord was evicting him immediately, as he received a better offer. So Peter's business was about to be shut down. That same week, the woman he had been dating left and Peter was involved in a major auto accident in which his car was totaled. Suddenly, Peter felt that he had lost everything that he had in the world and he became acutely suicidal. Peter decided to kill himself in the desert. He bought a pistol and a bottle of whisky and headed out for the barren mountains. Fortunately, Peter is not a drinker and though he fired some shots into the desert air, Peter passed out from the alcohol before he could kill himself.

Note that Gauguin also tried to commit suicide. Why would this type of pattern be repeated? In my observation, we have the same energies, the same approach to life from lifetime to lifetime. As such, we also have the tendency to get into the same types of problems and conflicts; we also react to challenges in the same way. Gauguin and Teekamp both lived stable lives when they were engaged in traditional business and enjoyed financial success, but they both gave up security to pursue the dreams of an artist. Both, in response to loss and financial crisis became acutely depressed and suicidal, though both were unsuccessful in their attempts.

We all have modus operandi that characterize us, both positive and maladaptive, and these ways of being stay consistent across lifetimes. Maladaptive responses get us into trouble, though hopefully over a lifetime, we modify these traits to our advantage. A great promise of understanding reincarnation is that once we know about a past lifetime and we are able to study our personality patterns from before, we can grow more consciously and effectively in our current incarnation.

One last observation that I would like to make is that biologic mental disorders, such as schizophrenia, do not appear to persist from lifetime to lifetime. These severe disorders come with the body that one incarnates into, just like diabetes or a thyroid disorder, and they do not typify the soul across lifetimes. In other words, one can be schizophrenic in one lifetime and normal in another.

When Peter woke up the next morning on the desert floor, he was hung over and had a grand headache. Peter resolved that he needed to make a new start and decided that he should move to California. Peter also reflected that he had been in denial regarding the Gauguin lifetime and that he would examine the possible past life connection with greater openness. When Peter got back to town, he called his former supervisor, an owner of a retail chain, and was pleased to hear that his old boss not only had a job for him in Atascadero, California, but that the boss was going to send a truck to pick him up. Peter reflects that since he decided to look at the Gauguin lifetime sincerely, at age 39, things seemed to go more smoothly and effortlessly for him; Peter states that life "flowered" for him.

Peter did well managing the retail store in Atascadero and was promoted to managing an entire shopping center, as well as a retail store, in Hollister, California. There, in 1991, he met Michelle Moshay, who worked for a local newspaper selling advertising space. Peter, representing the store and shopping center, became a customer of Michelle's, placing ads in the paper she worked for. In 1997, Peter decided to become a newspaper layout artist himself, in an attempt to better integrate his vocation and avocation. In this capacity, Michelle became his mentor in regards to the newspaper trade. It was at this time that Peter and Michelle felt a deep resonance towards each other and they became close friends.

Peter began sharing details of his life, including the stories regarding Gauguin. Michelle was not a believer in reincarnation at the time, but she was open. Michelle then shared with Peter a series of synchronistic events of her own involving Gauguin. In 1978, as a present, Michelle's father offered to fund a trip to wherever she wanted to go in the world. Michelle chose to go to Tahiti and when she was there, she visited the Gauguin Museum. The next year, on her twenty third birthday, Michelle went to Paris. Michelle went sightseeing on the Seine on a barge cruiser named the Wandering Wasp (Les Guepes Buissonniere). Interestingly, Gauguin edited a publication in Tahiti entitled, The Wasp. When in Paris, Michelle was 23 years old, the same age Mette was when she met and married Paul Gauguin.

Peter had been working on a journal, which included his contemplations on Gauguin, and Michelle offered to help Peter with editing of the journal. As such, in 1997, they became partners in researching Gauguin and writing an account of Peter's story. Shortly thereafter, they opened one of the first books Michelle bought on Gauguin. Peter looked at the image on the page and he exclaimed to Michelle, "Look, it's you!" Peter was looking at a picture of Gauguin's wife, Mette, and the resemblance to Michelle was undeniable.

Peter and Michelle continued to quietly ponder the possibility that they were Paul and Mette Gauguin and the years went by. In 1999, Peter departed for what would become a four year tour of the world, painting murals as he traveled. Peter kept in touch with Michelle, corresponding with her, much like Paul had corresponded with Mette when he was in Tahiti. Michelle, in the interim, moved to Washingtion State to be near her family and her childhood sweetheart. While Peter was traveling, it was Michelle who took it upon herself to research Gauguin extensively and it was she who found the pencil sketches. It was Michelle who first realized that Peter, in his youth, had unconsciously replicated Gauguin's drawings. When Peter returned to the US in 2003, Michelle's mother found a cottage apartment for him in nearby Bremerton and Peter moved in. It was then that Michelle showed him the sketch comparisons, which Peter found amazing. The comparison of Peter's and Gauguin's drawings added to the growing list of experiences that made Peter start believing that he was indeed the reincarnation of Paul Gauguin.

One day, as he was walking through Bremerton, a wall mural caught his eye. A restaurant, Chamorro's, was situated next to the mural and Peter went in for a cup of coffee. As he looked around the interior, Peter spotted what appeared to be a Gauguin charcoal of two women on a beach. Peter asked the proprietor where the sketch came from. The proprietor related that the sketch originally was in the possession of his great grandmother in Guam, who was given the sketch as a gift. He explained that the Chamorro, the native people of Guam, were displaced by the Japanese during World

War II. His great grandmother and her family hid in caves until the occupation ended. She took the sketch with her during their period of hiding.

After the war, his great grandmother stored the sketch in her attic for 33 years until she gave it to her daughter, the proprietor's mother, in 1978. The proprietor received it from his mother. When he immigrated to the United States in 1999, he brought the sketch with him and later hung it on the wall of his restaurant. The proprietor told Peter that when he removed the sketch from its protective container, he found charcoal on his hands. This made Peter realize that the print was not a copy at all, but an original charcoal sketch. If it was indeed an original Gauguin, which Peter believes it is, then the sketch would be worth millions.

The proprietor then shared that he was in financial straits and needed money to keep his business afloat. Rather than waiting for the sketch to be authenticated, the proprietor said he would sell the sketch for $5000 to the first person who would pay him that amount. Peter agreed to purchase the sketch and gave the proprietor $5000. Peter added a clause to the sales agreement that "if and when" the sketch was sold, Peter would split the proceeds with the proprietor. Authentication of the sketch is pending. In this way, Peter Teekamp came into possession of what appears to be an original Gauguin. Further, it is interesting that Peter found the Gauguin sketch in 2003, which is the 100 year anniversary of Gauguin's death.

Synchronicities and anniversary phenomena are ways that the spiritual world, including our own souls, can communicate with us. Recall that Michelle had the option of traveling anywhere in the world and that she elected to visit Tahiti and the Gauguin Museum, and that she visited Paris at the same age that Mette met Paul Gauguin. These synchronistic events are not accidental, rather, they are orchestrated by our spiritual guides and our own souls, though telepathic messages which are experienced as intuitions and desires. Indeed, Peter's rendezvousing with Michelle in California was also not accidental, but predetermined. We make agreements, contracts, to meet up with people we have known in prior lives. We make these agreements before we are even born.

In the same way, Peter's finding of what appears to be an original Gauguin on the 100 year anniversary of Gauguin's death was not an accidental event. Rather, I assert, it was an event orchestrated by beings in the spiritual world. This event had the purpose of reinforcing to Peter that he is the reincarnation of Gauguin. In my book, *Return of the Revolutionaries*, synchronistic events and anniversary phenomena abound. Through symbolic coincidences, the spiritual world sends messages to us.

At this point, as you can imagine, Peter and Michelle were ecstatic, not only because they had a sketch that could be worth millions, but because the possibility of Peter being the reincarnation of Paul Gauguin felt more real. Michelle began researching reincarnation on the Internet and she found my web site, **www.johnadams.net**, which features many reincarnation cases, such as are being presented in this book. Suddenly, Peter and Michelle were not alone regarding their reincarnation experiences; there were others who had also discovered past lives too.

Michelle contacted me and stated, "Dr. Semkiw, we have something we think you'll find of interest. I believe that my friend Peter Teekamp is the reincarnation of Paul Gauguin." Ironic as it may seem, I am always dubious when someone claims to be the reincarnation of a famous individual. I listened to their story and took notes. Then, in a subsequent session with Kevin Ryerson, Ahtun Re, the spirit guide that Kevin channels who has demonstrated an ability to make accurate past life matches, confirmed that Peter Teekamp and Michelle Moshay are indeed the reincarnation of Paul Gauguin and his wife Mette. In the fall of 2004, Peter, Michelle, Kevin Ryerson and I met in person and they told us their story. At that meeting, Kevin and I became convinced that the reincarnation cases of Peter Teekamp/Paul Gauguin and Michelle Moshay/Mette Gauguin were valid, given their history, which has now been presented in this narrative.

Peter Teekamp, from my observation, did not fully step into the shoes of Gauguin until the weekend of July 4, 2005, when he attended a gathering of individuals who had knowledge of their own past lives, many from the time of the American Revolution. The event was hosted by Norm Shealy at his farm in Missouri. Attendees included 6 MDs (including a university professor and researcher from the Human Genome Project), 6 PhDs, 6 published authors, 2 US Diplomats, 2 US military Captains, several clairvoyants and a television star, each with past lives identified. As each person told their stories, reincarnation became more of a reality to Peter and Michelle and it was only then that they took true ownership of being Paul and Mette Gauguin.

In fact, prior to July 4, 2005, Peter Teekamp never created artistic works in the style of Gauguin and in truth; it bothered me that the reincarnation of Gauguin didn't paint like Gauguin. After the July 4 meeting, I suggested to Peter that it wouldn't hurt if he did a few pieces reminiscent of Gauguin. A few pieces soon turned into a deluge, much to my delight. Accordingly, all the images presented at the end of this chapter, in which Peter has recreated the art of Gauguin, were painted between July 4 and December 2005.

In closing, Paul Gauguin, in 1903 at the age of 55, died in tragic circumstances. In 2003, one hundred years after Gauguin died, Peter Teekamp came into the possession of what appears to be an original Gauguin sketch. At the gathering held over the July 4 weekend in 2005, Peter Teekamp was 55 years old. As such, Peter reclaimed his identity as Paul Gauguin at the same age that Gauguin departed this earth.

ALEXANDRA NECHITA AS PABLO PICASSO REBORN

In addition to Paul Gauguin, I assert that another artist, who some deem to be the greatest artist of the 20th century, has reincarnated and is producing masterpieces once again. This case was brought to my attention in a casual way. Indeed, the reincarnation case of Pablo Picasso is so self-apparent, that it almost solved itself. Ahtun Re, the spirit guide channeled through Kevin Ryerson, has confirmed that Alexandra Nechita is the reincarnation of Pablo Picasso. Let me explain how the case of Picasso/Nechita evolved.

In the summer of 2004, I did a reincarnation presentation in Boulder, Colorado. A member of the audience was a friend of Wayne Peterson, the retired US Diplomat and former Director of the Fulbright Scholarship Program, whose reincarnation cases were presented earlier in this book. This person told me that I should investigate a young artist named Alexandra Nechita, as her work is remarkably similar that of Picasso and it has been speculated that she may be the reincarnation of Picasso. I was advised that Alexandra's work was being displayed in Denver, at that time, at Gallery M.

The next day, I took a drive to see Alexandra's work and found myself dumbfounded. Though I had observed how linguistic writing patterns can remain the same across incarnations, such as in the case of Jeff Keene, and in the case of Halle Berry, I witnessed how Berry is demonstrating the acting skill of her heroine and past life persona, Dorothy Dandridge, this was the first time I had the opportunity to see how talent and artistic style could be recapitulated by a painter in a dramatic way. (Keep in mind that I had not yet met with Peter Teekamp and Michelle Moshay). Though I am no expert in art, Alexandra's work was so much like Picasso's it was simply striking.

I asked the director of Gallery M whether there were any photos of Alexandra available, perhaps on a brochure or business card, and whether I could get contact information for Alexandra. The gallery director told me that no photos of Alexandra were on hand and that the artist was a private person and personal contact information could not be given out. In my next session with Kevin Ryerson, though, I asked Ahtun Re whether

Alexandra was indeed the reincarnation of Picasso, which he affirmed.

The meeting in Portland with Peter Teekamp, Michelle Moshay, Kevin Ryerson and I, which was described earlier in this chapter, took place several months later. Peter knew of Alexandra and he stated that he was blown way by her talent. Peter, who had seen her on a television talk show, thought Alexandra could well be Picasso. I asked Peter if Alexandra looked like Picasso and he replied, regarding a resemblance, "I don't see it," which I found inconsistent.

The case of Pablo Picasso/Alexandra Nechita lay dormant for almost two years. Things changed during a visit to Vancouver, British Columbia, in January 2006. There, neurosurgeon Peter Hudoba, MD had sponsored a reincarnation presentation where I would introduce Peter Teekamp to the world as the reincarnation of Gauguin. Dr. Hudoba, our host, had won several Gold Medals in Medicine when he lived in the Soviet Union. He then immigrated to Canada where he served as the Director of Residency Training in Neurosurgery at the University of Saskatewan. It is gratifying, given the subject matter, that I have two academic neurosurgeons, Dr. Hudoba and Norm Shealy, strongly supporting my reincarnation research.

Peter Teekamp, Michelle Moshay and I were in my hotel room preparing for our presentation. The topic of Alexandra Nechita came up and I decided to try again to find an image of her. One the Internet, I found that Alexandra now had a web site with images of herself. I quickly compared her facial features with Picasso's and determined that it was a match. Though Alexandra is a beautiful young woman with fine features and Picasso was a rather rugged looking man, the bone structure, the overall architecture of the face and head, I found to be the same. Though I have grown to trust Ahtun Re's ability to assess whether past life matches are accurate, assessing facial architecture was a crucial point of data that had been missing in the Picasso/Nechita case. So, in Vancouver, in the presence of the reincarnated Gauguin and his wife Mette, I came to the conclusion that Picasso was truly reborn.

Let us briefly review the histories of Pablo Picasso and Alexander Nechita. Picasso was born in Malaga, Spain, on October 25, 1881. Picasso demonstrated artistic gifts early in his boyhood and at the age of 15; he was enrolled in Barcelona's School of the Fine Arts. His painting, *Science and Charity*, won a gold medal at an exhibit in Malaga when he was 16 and by this time, Picasso had his own studio in Barcelona.

In 1900, Picasso made the trek to Paris, where he admired the work of modern artists such as Edgar Degas and Henri Toulouse-Lautrec. Picasso moved to Paris in 1904 and established friendships with writers, such as Gertrude Stein and Max Jacob. Picasso also witnessed the emerging popularity of Paul Gauguin while he was in Paris and Picasso was influenced by his work.

With Georges Braque, Picasso pioneered the "Cubist" style of painting, in which landscape images were composed of what appeared to be small cubes. Picasso did sculpture in innovative ways, using a variety of common objects to create abstract constructions. Picasso also became involved in set design, working for the Ballets Russes in Rome. Picasso's illustrious career culminated in an exhibition at the Louvre, in Paris, which occurred in honor of his 90th birthday, in 1971.

With this event, Picasso was the first living artist to have works displayed at the Louvre. Picasso died in France on April 8, 1973.

Eight years after Picasso died, on August 27, 1985, Alexandra Nechita was born in Romania. Alexandra's father, Niko, unfortunately was not present for his daughter's birth. Niko had left Communist Romania to seek a better future for his family in the United States, when his wife, Viorica, was six months pregnant with Alexandra. Niki would not see his wife and new daughter until 1987, when they were reunited in Los Angeles.

Like Picasso, Alexandra demonstrated artistic talent as a very young child. In fact, Alexandra began to draw as soon as her developing nervous system would allow her to. Alexandra became obsessed with her coloring books, which was a concern for her parents, as she didn't seem interested in the usual things that little girls do, such as playing and skipping rope. Her first pen and ink drawings were done at age two.

A truly startling observation was made by her parents when Alexandra was four years old. Alexandra was drawing abstract figures with two faces and four eyes, as seen in the art of Picasso. Alexandra rapidly built up a collection of original works. At eight years of age, Alexandra's first art exhibit was held at a Los Angeles public library on April 1, 1994. In a symbolic synchronistic event, on the same day that she had her first exhibit, she also saw the art of Picasso for the first time, at the Los Angeles County Art Museum. Alexandra loved the freedom of expression that she saw in Picasso's art, unencumbered by rules.

Alexandra's career advanced rapidly from that point on. As cited on her web site, "She attracted the attention of art critics and the media who began telling the world about this rarest of child prodigies - an artist who had mastered drawing and color, an artist who had created a visual language of her own, in a unique, lyrical, figurative, abstract cubist manner, an artist who had only recently turned nine years old." In fact, the press had dubbed her, "The Petite Picasso."

In 1999, at the age of fourteen, Alexandra was selected to lead a Global Arts Initiative, involving more than one hundred countries, by the World Federation of United Nations. In her still nascent voyage, Alexandra has been a guest on numerous national television shows in the United States, including CBS Sunday Morning, NBC's Today, The Rosie O'Donnell Show, NBC Nightly News with Tom Brokaw and The Oprah Winfrey Show.

If the reincarnation cases of Gauguin and Picasso are accepted, reflect on how these souls have demonstrated such characteristic patterns in their development across two lifetimes. Picasso and Alexandra both drove into art almost in infancy and demonstrated genius already in their teenage years, becoming world renowned artists early in their lives.

On the other hand, Paul Gauguin and Peter Teekamp, as young men, both became carefree world travelers. They both then embarked on business careers as a way to support themselves. Gauguin and Teekamp did pencil sketches, then started painting in adulthood as a hobby. Both only decided to pursue art as a full time profession in maturity. Gauguin died poor and unrecognized and Peter, though an accomplished artist, is at this time relatively unknown. Hopefully, patterns can be consciously changed. One thing that I can tell you for sure, Peter, having observed that a recent Gauguin sold for 39 million dollars, is going to work on the sequence issue in his next lifetime.

Let us also reflect on how these two cases illustrate that we do indeed build upon accomplishments of past lifetimes. The Gauguin/Teekamp sketches, presented at the end of this chapter, of the horse head, women in circles, men in berets and the Christ, drawn from above, demonstrate that Peter Teekamp unconsciously replicated stages in Gauguin's artist development, but at an earlier age. Similarly, Alexandra replicated Picasso's development by drawing abstract figures with two faces and four eyes at the age of four. Picasso became a pioneer of the Cubist style of painting in 1907, when he was 26 years old. The media noted that Alexandra Nechita painted in an "abstract cubist manner," at the age of nine.

In closing, in my mind, it is time for humanity to recognize and celebrate the reincarnation of two of the art world's greatest heroes, Paul Gauguin and Pablo Picasso, in the personas of Peter Teekamp www.peterteekamp.com and Alexandra Nechita. www.nechita.info. Let us recognize through these cases that life on earth is for expression and personal evolution. With this knowledge, let us create a world that we want to return to, where we all, including these two masters of art, can grow and manifest, unfettered by needless war, conflict and strife. Let us celebrate the gift of life.

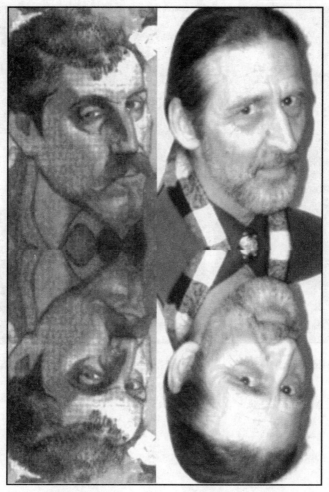

Paul Gauguin   **Peter Teekamp**

**Though not portrayed well in this image, Peter
Teekamp has the same "Inca nose" as Gauguin.**

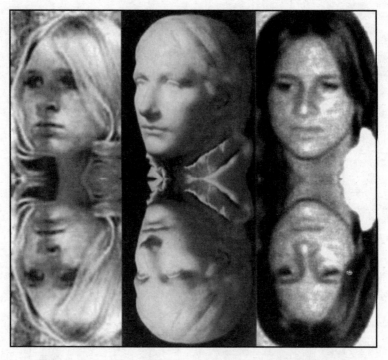

Michelle Moshay   Mette Gauguin   Michelle Moshay

Courtesy of
Michelle Moshay

| Gauguin
Age 43 | Teekamp
Age 16 | Gauguin
Age 41 | Teekamp
Age 22 |

| Gauguin
Age 46 | Teekamp
Age 22 | Gauguin
Age 40 | Teekamp
Age 26 |

Peter Teekamp first saw these Gauguin drawings at the age of 53. These sketch comparisons demonstrate that the artistic development of Gauguin was replicated by Teekamp, but at an earlier age. These sketch comparisons demonstrate that we do indeed build upon accomplishments of prior incarnations.

Gauguin   Teekamp

Pablo Picasso   **Alexandra Nechita**

At the age of four, Alexandra started drawing Picasso like figures
with two faces and four eyes. As a child, she became an accomplished
cubist painter and the media caller her a "Petite Picasso." Alexandra
had her first art show at age eight and went to see a Picasso exhibit
for the first time on the same day.

"The Wine Taster," by Alexandra Nechita,
who has been identified as the reincarnation of
Pablo Picasso.

9

The Three Lives of Penney Peirce and the Phenomenon of Split Incarnation

PENNE PEIRCE AS THE REINCARNATION OF CHARLES PARKHURST

In 1999, I joined an e-mail discussion group called Inpresence, which is made up of published authors whose works focus on the development of intuition and related topics. At one point, I sent an e-mail the describing the reincarnation research that I was doing and I asked if anyone in the Inpresence group knew of other cases that I could study. One person who responded was Penney Peirce, who related that she had a possible a past-life story.

Peirce is a professional intuitive, counselor, perceptual skills trainer and lecturer who works throughout the United States, Europe and Japan. She is the author of *The Intuitive Way: A Guide to Living from Inner Wisdom, The Present Moment: A Daybook of Clarity and Intuition,* and *Dreams for Dummies.* I met with Peirce in her Novato, California home, north of San Francisco, to learn more about her case. Let me share with you her story.

Peirce moved all over the country growing up, with much time spent in the Midwest and some on the East Coast. She moved from New York City to California in the early 1970s. Peirce worked as a corporate art director and graphic designer, but pursued meditation and clairvoyance development in her spare time, in California's then-burgeoning self-help movement.

During that period, a medium, who I will call Bobby Jo, regularly visited the San Francisco Bay area. In her work as a medium, Bobby Jo let non-physical spiritual beings speak through her to provide clients with information about past lives. Bobby Jo, who remained in a meditative state during this process, would have no memory of the information conveyed. Past-life information was reportedly accessed from the Akashic Records, a set of memory banks or a library of the planet's history, found in the spirit realm. Peirce describes Bobby Jo as a dramatic character, with by a jovial nature and a naïve faith. Bobby Jo knew nothing about Peirce when they met, nor did Peirce reveal information about herself at the time of their private session.

Given this background, Peirce was shocked when in her reading Bobby Jo started to rattle off facts regarding a past lifetime as if she were reading out of an encyclopedia. Bobby Jo related that in a past era, Peirce's name was Charles H. Parkhurst, that he had been born on April 17, 1842, in Framingham, Massachusetts, had lived on a farm and then become a prominent minister. Parkhurst enjoyed mountain climbing and used the pulpit to fight crime.

Bobby Jo then reported that Parkhurst had written many books, among them: *The Sunny Side of Christianity; A Little Lower than the Angels; Analysis of the Latin Verb Illustrated by the Sanskrit; What Would the World Be Without Religion?; The Blind Man's Creed and Other Sermons; The Pattern in the Mount; The Pulpit and the Pew; Talks to Young Men; Talks to Young Women;* and *My Forty Years in New York.* Bobby Jo told Peirce that Parkhurst had died on September 8, 1933, at the age of 91, and Bobby Jo then exclaimed in a drawl, "And honey, you died sleepwalking off a roof!"

Given this degree of specific information, after the session was over, Peirce sped off to the nearest library to see if she could verify the past-life detailed by Bobby Jo. In her investigation, Peirce struck gold. She found that there was a record of Charles Parkhurst and that Bobby Jo's description of him was accurate in every detail, including the long list of books Parkhurst had written. She realized that there were many similar personality attributes between Parkhurst and herself, and that there was even a physical resemblance. In assessing this proposed past-life match, Peirce reflected that there was no way that Bobby Jo could have memorized all that data on Parkhurst. Further, in Parkhurst, Bobby Jo had identified an individual with character features that matched closely with Peirce's personality, even though Bobby Jo knew next to nothing about her. Eventually, as Peirce studied the

life of Parkhurst, she came to the conclusion that the
past-life match was accurate.

Let us review some of the similarities between
Charles Parkhurst and Penney Peirce. First of all,
Parkhurst and Peirce share the distinction of being
published authors. Peirce, as a writer, demonstrated
talent at an early age, winning a National Scholastic
Magazine award for a short story. Peirce has had three
books published and in addition, has contributed to a
number of other titles, such as *The Celestine Prophecy
and Tenth Insight Experiential Guides* by Carol Adrienne
and James Redfield; *The Purpose of Your Life* by Carol
Adrienne; *Intuiting the Future* by William Kautz; and
Channeling: The Intuitive Connection, also by Kautz. In
addition to his scholarly works, Parkhurst also wrote
for young people. Similarly, Peirce has been writing
children's books since college and recently has been
incorporating spiritual themes into these stories.

Parkhurst and Peirce have shared an interest in
spirituality and providing service through the ministry.
Parkhurst earned his undergraduate and graduate
degrees from Amherst College, then studied theology
in Halle, Leipzig, and Bonn. He returned to teach at
Williston Seminary, in Massachusetts, and went on to
become a Congregational Minister in Lenox,
Massachusetts, where he spent six years. He then
became the pastor at Madison Square Presbyterian
Church in New York City and earned a Ph.D. and a
doctorate in divinity (DD) from New York University
and Columbia. Penney Peirce also has had a lifelong
affinity for spiritual studies. Ever since she can
remember, Peirce says that "Why" was the word that
motivated her behavior, and she voraciously read

books on world religions, psychic phenomena, and philosophy. Peirce was in search of the core truths contained in all religions and became a licensed minister as a result of this interest. She has even served as a substitute minister at a Unity Church.

Like Parkhust, Peirce has had a natural affinity for ancient languages. Parkhurst taught Greek and Latin and wrote a book called *Analysis of the Latin Verb Illustrated by the Sanskrit*. Peirce took advanced Latin in high school and scored highly in a state Latin competition. She has also had a fascination with Sanskrit and Egyptian hieroglyphs. Peirce relates that she once had a series of dreams that featured ancient Greek words, words that she had no knowledge of in her waking consciousness.

Charles Parkhurst used his pulpit to right social and spiritual wrongs. Parkhurst lived in New York City at a time when political corruption was a major issue. Tammany Hall, the political regime that held power in the late 1800s, was in collusion with crime bosses. Tammany Hall police officials routinely took bribes, while the general populace stuck their heads in the sand and said nothing. Parkhurst, who served as President of the Society for the Prevention of Crime, preached perhaps one of the most famous sermons in American history in which he denounced the corruption.

Parkhurst described New York City as "hell with the lid off" and challenged the public to do something about it. A roving reporter happened to be in the audience and the story made the news, arousing much public excitement and a vehement backlash from officials. Parkhurst was attacked and challenged to prove his accusations. He launched his own investigation and soon appeared before the grand jury with facts in hand. As a result, there ensued the Lexow Investigation and the election of a reform government, the Strong Administration. The appointment of Teddy Roosevelt as the new Police Commissioner followed.

Like Parkhurst, Peirce also has the inclination to act as a whistle-blower and reformer. In her college newspaper, Penney published articles protesting departmental and curriculum changes that she thought were to the detriment of students. When she worked for a large corporation, she launched a letter-writing campaign to warn of unethical practices she observed taking place in her department.

Charles Parkhurst and Penney Peirce both grew up on farms and have shared a love for agriculture. Parkhurst, in his autobiography, wrote: "Agriculture is the physical basis of all civilization. It stands to civilization as the body stands to the soul."[1] Parkhurst went on to say that, "working the soil is the great original art."[2] Peirce began keeping a journal at age seven and much of her inspiration stemmed from nature and the farm. Further, the National Scholastic Magazine award she won was for a short story about the wheat fields of Kansas. Peirce has also loved "working the soil" and has planted a vegetable garden every year since she was twenty.

Parkhurst and Peirce also have shared a love of climbing. Parkhurst was an avid mountaineer, who vacationed annually in the Alps, climbing the Matterhorn, Weisshorn, and other great peaks. Peirce demonstrated an early affinity for climbing also. At the age of three, she climbed a cedar tree adjacent to her home and peered into the family's second story bathroom, where her mother was applying makeup. When Penney's mother looked outside and witnessed her three-year old daughter waving to her from a tree, she almost had a stroke!

In a tragic, though amusing, incident, Parkhurst's demise was associated with his love of heights. At the age of 91, Parkhurst had an episode of sleepwalking during which he strode off the roof of his porch, falling to his death. In what appears to be a residual effect of this traumatic event, Penney Peirce relates that for years she experienced recurring nightmares of driving off cliffs, falling in elevators, and falling out of trees. At the end of every dream, when she realized that she would die, Peirce would wake agitatedly.

When Peirce had her session with Bobby Jo and learned that Parkhurst had died by falling off a roof, her nightmares abated. She had one last dream in which she fell out of a tree in "super slow motion," consciously reviewing the stages one goes through in dying by falling. After that dream, the nightmares stopped entirely.

Peirce believes she had these nocturnal images of falling because Parkhurst was asleep and confused when he died, and that the experience had never been processed in a conscious manner. Peirce also feels that Parkhurst's death by sleepwalking out a window and off a roof might be related to her own subliminal desire to leap off high places and fly like a bird. Perhaps Parkhurst had the same urge and found a way to let himself fly. Peirce notes that to this day she still has an attraction, rather than an aversion, to elevated locations. Fortunately, in this lifetime Peirce lives in a one-story, ranch-style house.

PENNY PEIRCE AS THE REINCARNATION OF ALICE CARY

In her session with the medium, Peirce was told about an even earlier incarnation. Bobby Jo conveyed that Penney's name, in that lifetime, was Alice Cary, that she was born on a farm near Cincinnati, Ohio, on April 26, 1820, and that she died on February 12, 1871. As in the Parkhurst case, Bobby Jo rattled off a series of books that Alice Cary had written, which included the following titles: *Poems of Alice and Phoebe Cary; Clovernook: Recollections of Our Neighborhood in the West; Hagar: A Story for Today; Lyra and Other Poems; Clovernook Children; Married, Not Mated; Adopted Daughter, and Other Tales; The Josephine Gallery; Pictures of Country Life; Ballads, Lyrics and Hymns; The Bishop's Son, A Lover's Diary; The Born Thrall; Snow-Berries: A Book for Young Folks;* and *Ballads for Little Folks.* Once again, Bobby Jo appeared to have access to an incredible amount of detailed information on an extemporary basis. Bobby Jo also told Peirce that Alice Cary had been inseparable from her younger sister, Phoebe, in that lifetime. Bobby Jo noted that Phoebe was Peirce's younger sister, Paula, today.

Parallels between Penney Peirce, Alice Cary, and Charles Parkhurst are apparent from this list of book titles alone. Obviously, all three are accomplished writers and all three have written children's books. Like Alice Cary, Peirce is a prolific poet as well as a writer of nonfiction. In an interesting synchronicity,

Alice Cary wrote under the pen name "Patty Lee," which corresponds to Peirce's first and middle names, "Penney Lee."

There are also geographical correspondences between the three lives. Past-life regression therapists have noted that souls often like to retrace their steps, from one lifetime to another. It is almost as if the soul is nostalgic for familiar places and settings of past lives. The soul then appears to engineer a life path that will take it to these familiar haunts. As an example, Peirce went to college at the University of Cincinnati, only a few miles from where Alice was born. Here, like Cary, Peirce began writing poetry in earnest. Also in college, Peirce had a boyfriend who wrote poems to and drew portraits of a fictitious woman. Her boyfriend referred to this woman as his muse and he called her "Alice." Interestingly, Alice Cary had been jilted by a boyfriend when living in Ohio, which prompted her to suddenly move to New York City. Peirce wonders whether her college boyfriend might have been the same man who jilted Cary.

After Cary moved to New York, her sister Phoebe soon followed. The women had moved to the city with the intention of making their living from literature— a very adventurous thing to do. Together, they wrote and published many books of poetry and fiction. In New York, Alice and Phoebe Cary were fondly known as "The Sisters of the West," as Ohio was still considered the western edge of adolescent America at that time.

The Cary sisters became beloved by the intelligentsia and other types as they hosted a popular literary salon in their home for over fifteen years.

Attendees included thinkers, philosophers, early feminists, writers and prominent personalities of the time, such as Horace Greeley, Edgar Allen Poe, John Greenleaf Whittier, and PT Barnum.

In what appears to be a parallel path, Peirce also left Ohio abruptly, before graduating from college, and moved to New York City. In New York, Peirce, like Alice Cary, soon became involved with a group of feminist writers and other authors. In another geographic correspondence, Peirce's job was situated near Gramercy Park, only blocks from where Alice and Phoebe Cary had lived. In New York, the life of Charles Parkhurst also becomes interwined with theirs.

Peirce's apartment on West 80th Street was only blocks from where Charles Parkhurst resided on West 74th. She attended night school at NYU and Columbia, which Parkhurst also attended. In time, Peirce moved to Park Slope, Brooklyn, close to where Alice and Phoebe are buried in Greenwood Cemetery. In another odd parallel, Parkhurst, late in life, traveled from New York to Los Angeles to marry a second time. Similarly, Peirce left New York City for Los Angeles to complete her design degree at the California Institute of the Arts. She also notes that in the year after her reading with Bobby Jo, her parents moved near Framingham, the birthplace and childhood home of Charles Parkhurst. In visits to her parents, Penney has been able to survey Parkhurst's old stomping grounds.

Like Penney Peirce and Charles Parkhurst, Alice Cary had an early quest for knowledge, even reading at night by the light of burning lard when candles were not available to her. Cary loved nature and wrote prolifically about scenes from rural life. Peirce has a love for nature, as did Cary and Parkhurst, and she lives in a setting of rolling farmland. As mentioned previously, Penney began keeping a journal at age seven and much of her inspiration stemmed from nature, animals, and the farm. Like Alice Cary, Penney published articles and poems in her teens. The National Scholastic Magazine award she won, we recall, was for a short story about Kansas wheat fields.

In an interesting correspondence, John Greenleaf Whittier wrote a poem for Alice called *The Singer*, which ends with a reference to wheat. Whittier wrote of Alice: "Her modest lips were sweet with song/A memory haunted all her words/Of clover-fields and singing birds/Her dark, dilating eyes expressed/The broad horizons of the west/Her speech dropped prairie flowers; the gold/Of harvest wheat about her rolled."[3]

In addition to her literary pursuits, Alice Cary was a social activist, like Parkhurst and Peirce. Alice was a firm believer in the abolition of slavery and a proponent of women's rights. She became the first president of first women's club in America, the Sorority of Sisters (Sorosis), and was friends with Jane Croly, Elizabeth Cady Stanton, and Susan B. Anthony. In a similar way, Penney became involved with the feminist movement in New York and California, and became the art director for a feminist magazine. Alice Cary hated human repression or coercion in any form. Penney Peirce started a nonprofit organization in college to study the harmful brainwashing affects of the mass media and advertising on the general public.

Spiritually, Alice was attached to the Universalist Church and accepted its doctrines, including the belief in reincarnation and that spirits of the deceased could communicate with the living. She wrote: "Laugh, you who never had/Your dead come back; but do not take from me/...my foolish dream:/That these our mortal eyes,/Which outwardly reflect the earth and skies,/ Do introvert upon eternity."[4] Cary's biographer notes that Alice also had an interest in prophecy. Alice's sister and friends related that she would "tell us each our fortune anew, casting our horoscope afresh in her teacup each morning." Similarly, Peirce pursued parapsychology and clairvoyance development very early in her career.

Peirce has noticed many parallels between her own writings and those of Alice Cary and Charles Parkhurst. As an example, all three focused on the need to demonstrate spiritual values in everyday life, in intention and through small actions, and that the practice, the process, and the experience itself is more important than just talking about lofty goals. Peirce has selected the following quotes from their books to illustrate this point.

> Cary: "True worth is in being, not seeming—in doing, each day that goes by, some little good."[5]
> Parkhurst: "Character is the impulse reined down into steady continuance."[6]
> Peirce: "The process, not necessarily the answers, is the sacred thing."[7]

In another example, all three write about truth. Parkhurst wrote: "Truth, of course, is from everlasting and has its existence in the being of God, while an idea is only an attempt at truth and comes and goes with the mind that develops it."[8] Peirce wrote in her journal: "Information is of the mind. Knowledge is truth, the result of the direct experience of being or Soul. Information is facts, the mere *description* of knowledge."[9] Alice wrote: "For sometimes, keen, and cold, and pitiless truth,/In spite of us, will press to open light/The naked angularities of things,/And from the steep ideal the soul drop/In wild and sorrowful beauty, like a star/From the blue heights of heaven into the sea."[10]

And, about gratitude, Parkhurst wrote: "We have enough to make us all happy and thankful if we will be quiet long enough to take an affectionate inventory of our commonplace mercies, and let our hearts feel of them and mix themselves with them till we become saturated with their comfort and awaken into a loving sense of the patient goodness of their Giver."[11] Peirce wrote: "Slow down enough to describe in simple terms the things you feel, as though you're taking inventory. By noticing things, you connect with your world. The 'feminine mind' brings you into a sense of beneficence and providence, and as you experience this fully, you may weep, or overflow with praises, or beam with feelings of ecstasy."[12] Alice Cary wrote, When I think of the gifts that have honored Love's shrine—/Heart, hope, soul, and body, all the mortal can give—/For the sake of a passion superbly divine,/I am glad, nay, and more, I am proud that I live!"[13]

Peirce notes that she seems to be an interesting link between the masculine, more intellectual, minister, Charles Parkhurst, and the emotional, feminine poet, Alice Cary. In her writings, Peirce combines elements of both. It is interesting to observe that in Penney's case, though the styles of rhetoric may vary with changes in gender and era, core ideas stay the same. Another interesting parallel in these cases is the possible carryover from previous lives of physical infirmity and injury. Ian Stevenson, M.D., in his research of children who spontaneously remember past lives, observed that when an individual perishes from a traumatic injury, such as a knife or bullet wound, in the subsequent lifetime, a birthmark is found at the location of the traumatic wound. Peirce poses the hypothesis that a similar carryover may occur with chronic illnesses. Alice Cary died of tuberculosis, which she courageously suffered for many years. Penney Peirce was born with severe lung problems, which manifested as chronic bronchitis and pneumonia for about the first 15 years of her life. Peirce also notes that when Charles Parkhurst died of injuries sustained in his fall, one of his injuries was a broken left leg. Peirce notes that she has received many injuries to her left leg, including a cracked ankle. The question of whether residuals from illnesses and injuries from one lifetime can be carried through in another is a subject for further study.

The case of Alice Cary/Penney Peirce features a karmic relationship that seems to have persisted from one lifetime to another. Recall that Bobby Jo told Peirce that Alice Cary had a sister named Phoebe and that in this lifetime, Phoebe is Paula, Penny's contemporary sister. It appears that Bobby Jo's statement is valid, as Paula has facial features that are consistent with those of Phoebe Cary. There are also similarities in personality traits. Phoebe was considered to be one of the wittiest women in America, known for her ability to see the ludicrous in the glamorous, and for her great ability for parody. Peirce has observed that these traits are consistent with Paula, who has earned a Ph.D. and who is described as witty, like Phoebe. Peirce once wrote that Paula is characterized by a "dry wit and cheerful, diplomatic disposition." In a more mundane similarity, Pheobe was known to have an aversion to housework. In this lifetime, Paula has the same aversion. Paula sets money aside, so that she can utilize a maid service, rather than do housework herself.

Another significant parallel is observed in the relationships between the sisters, Alice and Phoebe and Penney and Paula. Both sets of sisters are approximately the same number of years apart in age, and both have had incredibly close relationships with each other. Regarding Alice and Phoebe Cary, a biographer wrote: "The connection between the sisters, who had always treated one another with the utmost consideration and delicacy, was one of the most charming things about their unique dwelling."[14] The emotional bond between the sisters was so great, in fact, that they practically died together. After Alice succumbed to tuberculosis, Phoebe was so drained with grief that she passed away six months later. This close connection between the sisters persists in contemporary times. Peirce has noted, "Throughout my life, my younger sister Paula has been my best friend."

The bond between the sisters was rekindled early, as Penney recalls that when Paula was born, she had no feelings of jealousy or sibling rivalry; rather, Penney wanted to be close to her little sister. Later in life, Penney seems to have unconsciously intuited the past-life identity of her sister. Penney relates that as a young woman, she fantasized about a list of names that she would give to her children someday. Interestingly, her favorite name was Phoebe, which she learned meant "shining and bright."

THE PHENOMENON OF SPLIT INCARNATION

The case of Alice Cary/Charles Parkhurst/Penney Peirce, if it is accepted as valid, demonstrates an interesting phenomenon, that a soul can animate two different bodies or personalities at the same time. Alice Cary, the earliest incarnation in this series of lives, was born in 1820 and died in 1871. Charles Parkhurst was born in 1842, at a time when Alice Cary was 22 years old. Alice Cary died in 1871 at the age of 51, at time when Parkhurst was 29 years old. Parkhurst died 52 years after the death of Alice Cary, in 1933. Penney Peirce was born 16 years after Parkhurst's death, in 1949, 50 miles from the location where Parkhurst died. In reviewing this chronology, we observe that there is an overlap of 29 years between Parkhurst's birth in 1842 and Cary's death in 1871. In this period of 29 years, it appears that the same soul was animating two bodies.

It is of interest to wonder if Alice Cary and Charles Parkhurst ever crossed paths. Though there is no evidence to support that Cary and Parkhurst ever met, it appears that they did come in close proximity to each other. In 1850, Alice, at 30 years of age, journeyed from Ohio to visit John Greenleaf Whittier at his Massachusetts home, not far from where Parkhurst was living on his family's farm in Framingham, as an 8-year-old boy. Alice subsequently moved to New York later that same year.

The two people had another episode of geographic proximity 20 years later, in the summer of 1870 when Alice Cary made her last foray out of New York to visit friends in Northampton, Massachusetts. Parkhurst was living nearby at the time and only months later, in November, Charles Parkhurst married his first wife in Northampton. Parkhurst moved to New York, in 1880, nine years after Cary died. Though it appears that the two never met, it is likely that Parkhurst knew of Cary. When Parkhurst was a young man, Cary was in her prime as an author, contributing to many popular magazines of the time. It is possible that Parkhurst read articles written by his alter ego, Alice Cary.

In sum, the case of Alice Cary/Charles Parkhurst/ Penney Peirce demonstrates how facial architecture, personality traits, and even geographical locations can remain consistent over three lifetimes. In addition, the relationship between Alice and Phoebe in one era, and that of Penney and Paula in another, shows how karmic and emotional bonds are maintained from one incarnation to another. The 29-year period when Alice Cary and Charles Parkhurst were both incarnated simultaneously appears to demonstrate that a soul can animate two bodies at the same time. This phenomenon might help explain why there are so many more people on the planet at this time in comparison to ages past.

Charles Parkhurst

Courtesy of the Library of Congress

Penney Pierce

Courtesy of Penney Pierce

Alice Cary   **Penney Pierce**

The lifetime of Charles Parkhurst and Alice Cary overlapped by 29 years, demonstrating that a soul can animate two bodies at one time, a phenomenon termed split incarnation.

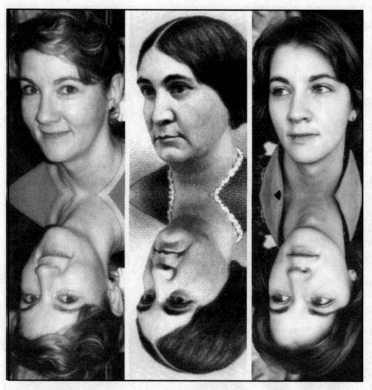

Paula Pierce   **Phoebe Cary**   **Paula Pierce**

**The sisters Alice and Phoebe Cary reincarnated as sisters
Penney and Paula Pierce**

Born Again

SECTION TWO

Cases Solved though Kevin Ryerson and Ahtun Re

10

Introducing Kevin Ryerson, Tom MacPherson and Ahtun Re

The way in which I became involved in reincarnation research is that in 1984, on a lark, I went to a medium, much like the one that Penney Peirce went to see, as discussed in the preceding chapter. It was a time when I was in my medical training in Chicago, Illinois. A friend called me and suggested that I have a session with a medium who was working out of a local metaphysical bookstore. Being a skeptic by nature, I had never even considered going to a psychic before. It had been a dreary winter, though, with little to do but study, and I reasoned that a session with a medium might break the monotony.

During the session, the medium went into a meditative state and in doing so, allowed spirit guides to talk through him. These guides told me about family issues with surprising accuracy. The guides then told me about two past lives, one of which was during the

American Revolution. In short, they told me that I was John Adams, an American Revolutionary who eventually became the first Vice President, under Washington, then the second President of the United States. I had heard that psychics often tell people that they were someone famous in a past lifetime. At the time, I did not find is plausible that I was Adams, so in 1984, I dismissed the information and did not pursue the Adams connection for about 12 years.

At the end of 1995, I was fully engaged in my medical career and was on a business trip in Hawaii. I was working as a medical director of an oil company called Unocal 76, whose slogan happened to be, "The Spirit of 1776," a reference to the spirit of the American Revolution. Out of the blue, out of nowhere, I received a command from my soul like I had never experienced before. It was as if a booming, yet silent voice, entered my mind and commanded, "Study the lifetime of Adams." The message conveyed by this voice was firm and undeniable, and powerful enough to make me go to a bookstore in Honolulu that evening, where I purchased books on the American Revolution and John Adams.

In the session in 1984, the spirit guides told me that if I researched John Adams, I would see myself in physical attributes, personality and habits. As I read about Adams over the course of 1996, that is exactly what I found. I had the same personality, the same strengths, same weaknesses and in certain portraits, such as the one done for the Paris peace conference after the Revolutionary War, I had the very same face as Adams. Over time, I identified 60 people who where affiliated with Adams, who seemed to be reincarnated in around me in my life. For example, my brother George seemed to be Peter Adams, the brother of John Adams, based on similarities in appearance and personality.

Over a period two years, I slowly started to believe that I might indeed be the reincarnation of John Adams. If this was true, I reasoned that the information might be valuable in understanding how reincarnation works, but I didn't know what to do with the information. I certainly wasn't ready to go public. After all, I was a physician making a good salary. I didn't want to lose my job by running around saying that I was John Adams, if I was not. I needed some type of validation or confirmation.

Not knowing what else to do, I started going to psychics in the community, who had good reputations, to see what they would say. First, I visited Michael Tamura, who directed the Berkeley Psychic Center for almost 20 years. In this position, he trained other clairvoyants, so I though he might be a reliable resource. In my session with Michael he stated, "Yes you were John Adams and you are here to bring the Founding Fathers back." That was nice, but I still wasn't convinced. I went to several other psychics and they all told me the same thing, that I was reincarnation of John Adams. In my continuing tour, I eventually was referred to Kevin Ryerson, the trance medium who has worked with Shirley MacLaine for 30 years or so and who is featured in three of her books.

I found that Kevin is a trance channel, which means that when he works, he goes into a meditative state or trance and allows spirit beings to speak through him.

The spirit being that I began to work with through Kevin is named Ahtun Re, who identifies himself as an Egyptian of Nubian origin. Ahtun Re explained that he had evolved through a series of human lifetimes and then ascended, like Buddha, Jesus, Mohammed and other spiritual masters. Ahtun Re's last incarnation, he told me, was in Egypt, during the time of Pharaoh Akhenaton (1379-1362 BC), known as the "Father of Monotheism." Ahtun Re served as a High Priest and advisor to Akhenaton and as such, Ahtun Re's last incarnation occurred approximately 3350 years ago.

Speaking to an Egyptian spirit guide that has been dead for over 3000 years was a novel experience for me. I was open minded but skeptical and in the beginning, I did not assume that Ahtun Re was accurate. Like any reasonable person, and especially since my background is in science, I needed evidence to be convinced that Ahtun Re produced valid information.

First of all, Ahtun Re also confirmed that I am the reincarnation of John Adams. I then reviewed the list of almost 60 past life matches that I had hypothesized regarding the group that was incarnate around John Adams, who I thought I had identified in contemporary times. As we went through each match, Ahtun Re told me if I was right or wrong. In total, he validated about 85 percent of the matches that I had hypothesized and he indicated that 15 percent or so were inaccurate. Still, I wasn't sure whether there was any reason to place trust in Ahtun Re. How did I know that his determinations were valid?

A breakthrough occurred when I started to ask about matches in which I had no hypothesized matches and I asked Ahtun Re to tell me who a person was in a past lifetime, or who a person from history was in contemporary times. What I found was that Ahtun Re could make past life identifications, which when I researched, appeared to be valid and accurate. The matches he made, when investigated, demonstrated similar facial features, personality traits, talents and appropriate karmic groupings.

Further, at times the matches involved individuals in history that were so obscure, so hard to get information on, that there was no way that Ahtun Re (or Kevin Ryerson for that matter), could have made the matches without accessing some spiritual source of accurate data. Some might call this source of information the Akashic Record, some may call it Universal Mind. The cases which clearly demonstrate Ahtun Re's ability to make accurate past life matches include those of the 2000 American Green Party Candidate for President, Ralph Nader, the astronomer Carl Sagan and Neale Donald Walsch, author of the *Conversations with God* book series. These cases will be presented in subsequent chapters.

Before I proceed with presenting cases solved through Ahtun Re, I would like to share an anecdote which demonstrates that the spirit guides that Kevin channels can monitor events on earth. In my book, *Return of the Revolutionaries*, Shirley MacLaine is identified as a reincarnated American Revolutionary and signer of the Declaration of Independence, a match that Ahtun Re confirmed. Ms. MacLaine was gracious enough to agree to be in my book, though she herself had not had an opportunity to have a session with Kevin prior to my book's publication, to have this past lifetime confirmed directly.

A few months after publication of *Return of the Revolutionaries*, Ms MacLaine was conducting a series of workshops at the Academy of Art College, in San Francisco, in October 2003. As I was living in San Francisco, it was an opportunity for me to meet Ms. MacLaine for the first time. In the interim months, I understood from Kevin that Shirley did have session with him and Ahtun Re.

I myself happened to have a session with Kevin Ryerson scheduled on the day before Shirley's event. In the session, I asked Ahtun Re whether I should bring a gift to Shirley. Ahtun Re, speaking through Kevin in his deep bass voice, told me to have a T Shirt manufactured that had an image of Shirley's revolutionary persona on the front, with a caption underneath that states: "In my next lifetime, I want to be Shirley MacLaine" On the back of the T Shirt, Ahtun Re told me that I should emboss the following line, "One Hundred Lifetimes and All I Get Is this Crummy T Shirt." Ahtun Re not only can make accurate past life matches, he also has a sense of humor.

Well, almost miraculously, I was able to get the T Shirt manufactured within a day and I had it with me when I went to see Shirley speak. After a wonderful morning session, I introduced myself to Shirley at the lunch break. I was not prepared for what happened next. At the start of the afternoon session, Shirley invited me to join her on stage.

For almost two hours, a three way conversation ensued between Shirley, her audience of two to three hundred people and me, regarding reincarnation, my book and her reincarnation case. Though I was having the time of my life, I was nervous about being on stage with one of the most famous celebrities on the planet. My anxiety was channeled to my right hand, which was holding the microphone. My hand grasped the microphone with greater and greater force until it started to cramp. At that point, perhaps forty minutes into our discussion, I passed the microphone to my left hand. After a few minutes, my left hand started to cramp and I had to pass the microphone back to my right hand. This passing of the microphone baton continued thoughout the duration of my stage appearance with Shirley.

What is remarkable about this incident with Shirley is that Kevin Ryerson's spirit guides were watching the proceedings from the other side. Several months after Shirley's Acadamy of Art College engagement, Kevin Ryerson came into San Francisco to do a lecture and a public demonstration of channeling. In the session, another spirit guide channeled through Kevin, Tom MacPherson, came through. MacPherson often came through in sessions for Shirley MacLaine, as Tom was last incarnate as an actor in Shakespeare's troupe, so he and Shirley have a common interest in drama. Tom, through Kevin, addressed the audience in his Irish accent and he called out for me. Tom inquired, "So, Laddy, did you have a nice time with the redhead?"

The redhead that Tom was referring to, of course, was Shirley MacLaine. I responded that I had a wonderful time on stage with Shirley. Tom then noted:

"You were a wee bit nervous, though, passing the microphone to and fro from one hand to another."

I was shocked when Tom made that statement, as

I had not told Kevin of the microphone incident. Later upon questioning, Kevin confirmed that he had no knowledge of my problem with the microphone when I was on stage with Shirley. This made me realize that Kevin's guides could monitor events on earth, regardless of where Kevin himself was physically located.

Over the years that I have worked with Kevin since we first met in October 2001, we have become good friends. In addition, since I have had over 70 sessions with Kevin, I also feel that Ahtun Re is a friend of mine. In the sessions, Ahtun Re is as warm and human as anyone else that you might speak to over the telephone. The only difference is that with Ahtun Re, the telephone is Kevin Ryerson. MacPherson has also come through a handful of times, but it has been Ahtun Re who has been the dominant spirit guide that I have worked with. With this introduction, let us review cases solved through Ahtun Re.

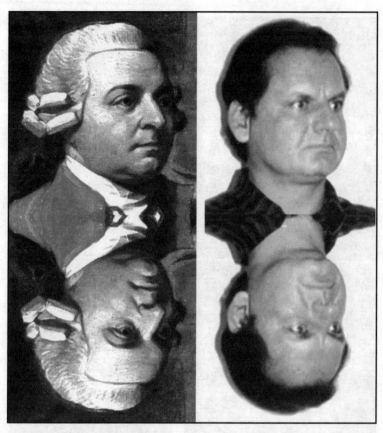

John Adams

Detail of unfinished painting
"Treaty of Paris" by Benjamin West,
Courtesy of Winterthur Museum

Walter Semkiw

Courtesy of Walter Semkiw

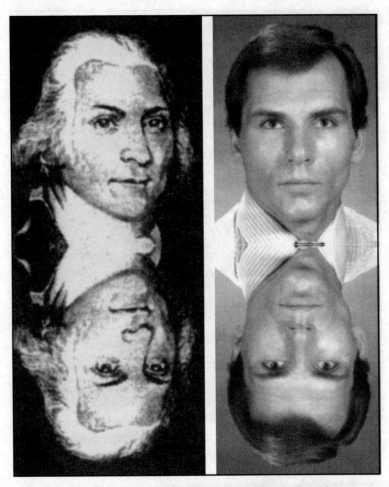

Peter Adams   **George Semkiw**

Peter was the brother of John Adams and George is the brother of Walter Semkiw. This case demonstrates how souls reincarnate in groups and that family members can return as family again.

11

The Reincarnation cases of
Ralph Nader, Carl Sagan and
Neale Donald Walsch

As described in the previous chapter, when my working relation was established with Kevin Ryerson and Ahtun Re at the end of 2001, I decided to see if Ahtun Re could make past life matches where I myself had no hypotheses. For example, I had the feeling that Ralph Nader, who ran for US President in 2000, was part of the Revolutionary group, I had no clue, though, as to who he may have been. In a session with Kevin, I asked Ahtun Re if Nader was incarnate during the period of the American Revolution and if so, who he was. Ahtun Re confirmed that Nader was alive in the 18th century and that his name was Thomson or Thomason. Ahtun Re told me that he was a major player in the Continental Congress and Ahtun Re stated that I would find that Thomson had the same chiseled facial features as Ralph Nader.

Initially, I was frustrated in locating information on someone named Thomson in the books and other resources that I had collected on the American Revolution. Time was an issue, as I had signed a contract for *Revolutionaries* on October 30, 2001, which as mentioned, was John Adams' birthday, and my publisher's deadline for the book's submission was fast approaching.

I decided to give Nader's case one last chance try by visiting the San Francisco Public Library. I went to the section on American history dealing with the Continental Congress and the Constitutional Convention, which featured three full bookcases of material. I systematically went through the index of each, hoping to find mention of a Thomson, or Thomason. After going through a hundred books or so without success, my hopes began to dim. Suddenly, in a large text, which most likely hadn't been opened in years, I saw the name of Charles Thomson in the index, with a portrait also identified by a page number. Could this be what I was looking for? As I turned to the page with the portrait, I saw Ralph Nader's face, with his distinctive eyebrows and the sharp vertical line on one side, symmetrically reflected in the face of Charles Thomson.

In a subsequent session with Kevin Ryerson, Ahtun Re confirmed that Ralph Nader was Charles Thomson in the Revolutionary Era. In addition to having matching facial architecture, I found that the personality traits of Thomson and Nader were uncannily similar. Both were consumer advocates, both fought for the underdog and both were considered too radical to be elected to office themselves. In *Return of the Revolutionaries,* I have dedicated an entire chapter on the Thomson/Nader match, in which I compare quotes from Thomson's and Nader's writings, showing how their values and thoughts are essentially the same. This case had profound significance for me, for it demonstrated that Ahtun Re had the capability of establishing past-life identities accurately.

CARL SAGAN AS THE REINCARNATION OF DAVID RITTENHOUSE

Charles Thomson was an American Revolutionary in Philadelphia. Thomas Paine lived in Philadelphia when he wrote his pamphlet, *Common Sense. Common Sense,* with its straightforward arguments as to why independence from Britain was desirable, became a huge best seller that helped influence people's emotions and positions, and helped launch the Revolutionary War. In reading about the history of *Common Sense,* I learned that a Philadelphia resident named David Rittenhouse served as an editor. That is all I knew about this man, when I asked about Rittenhouse in a session with Kevin Ryerson. Specifically, I asked Ahtun Re if Rittenhouse had reincarnated in contemporary times. When Ahtun Re told me that David Rittenhouse had reincarnated as Carl Sagan, I was certain that he was wrong. By now, I had observed that souls tend to express themselves in similar ways, from lifetime to lifetime, and that they tended to demonstrate similar talents. It made no sense to me that Rittenhouse, who I perceived to be a little known Philadelphia revolutionary, would

reincarnate as a world famous astronomer. I
determined that Ahtun Re was wrong and I became
discouraged about his being a reliable resource in
making reincarnation matches. But I was the one who
was wrong.

When I researched David Rittenhouse more
thoroughly, I found that he was an instrument maker
who built the first telescope in America. I also found
that he was a mathematician who, based on his
telescope observations, built an orrery—a precursor
to the planetarium, which portrayed the solar system
with great accuracy. I then found a portrait of
Rittenhouse and found that he had the same face as
Carl Sagan. This all occurred early in my work with
Kevin Ryerson and when I realized that Ahtun Re had
made this match, which to me now seemed to be
uncannily accurate, I realized that something very big
was happening, that I had a resource that could
accurately identify souls in past and contemporary
incarnations.

NEALE DONALD WALSCH AS THE REINCARNATION OF REVEREND WILLIAM WALTER

In my reincarnation research, even before I met
Kevin Ryerson, I had established that the author
Marianne Williamson and physicist John Hagelin were
part of the Revolutionary Group in Boston. Hagelin
had run for President under the Maharishi Mahesh
Yogi's Natural Law Party. Ahtun Re later confirmed
these matches, as they were part of the 60 pairings
that I had reviewed with him during our first few

sessions. They were Boston revolutionaries that were close to John Adams. In fact, Marianne Williamson was confirmed to be Abigail Adams, the wife of John Adams. Synchronistic events would lead us to meet for the first time on Valentine's Day, in 2001, when Marianne agreed to be included in *Return of the Revolutionaries* as the reincarnation of Abigail. John Hagelin was confirmed to be the reincarnation of James Otis, a Boston lawyer, considered a genius, who helped spark the revolutionary movement by taking the British to court regarding the Writs of Assistance, an illegal search and seizure law.

In contemporary times, Neale Donald Walsch, author of the best selling *Conversations with God* series, has been close to both Williamson and Hagelin. Walsh and Williamson both supported Hagelin's presidential bid in 2000 and Williamson and Walsch together found the Global Renaissance Alliance. As such, I wondered if Neale was in Boston during the American Revolution too. In a session with Kevin Ryerson, Ahtun Re told me that Walsch was indeed a minister in Boston who was good friends with John and Abigail Adams, and that he was also an associate of John Hagelin in those times. I asked Ahtun Re what Neale's name was in that era. Ahtun Re told me that Neale was known as Reverend Walter and that he was a Freemason, who also supported Anglican causes.

Reverend Walter is in no history book, but I was able to find him through the New England Genealogical and Historical Society (NEGHS). A biography from Harvard College was available that confirmed that he was a Freemason. A subsequent search of the diaries of John Adams revealed only one minister known to the Adamses by the name of Walter. That minister was William Walter, born on October 7, 1737. Walter received his license as a minister in England, by the Bishop of London. Reverend Walter then returned to Boston and was inducted into the ministry in July 1764, at Trinity Church. On April 4, 1768, Walter was chosen to be Rector of Trinity.

The entry from John Adams's diary regarding Reverend William Walter, made on May 24, 1773, is provided below. This entry mentions two other men, Colonel and Major Otis, who were father and son. The son, Major Otis, refers to James Otis, who in contemporary times has been identified as John Hagelin. Let us now turn to the notes of John Adams. I have placed the contemporary identities of the players involved in brackets, for clarity. John Adams wrote:

> *Spent this Evening at Wheelwrights, with Parson Williams of Sandwich. . . . Williams took up the whole Evening with Stories about Col. Otis and his Son the Major [John Hagelin]. The Major [John Hagelin] employed . . . Parson Walter [Neale Donald Walsch] to represent him to the Governor as a Friend to Government, in order to get the Commission of Lieutenant Colonel.*
>
> *The Major [John Hagelin] has Liberty written over his Manufactory House. . . . Col Otis reads to large Circles of the common People, Allens Oration on the beauties of Liberty and recommends it as an excellent Production.*[1]

Note that Major James Otis/John Hagelin asked Parson Walter/Neale Donald Walsch for assistance in obtaining a higher military rank within the Royal British government. Keep in mind that this event took place prior to the American Revolution and that many patriot leaders served in leadership roles within the British system before independence was declared. Clergy and ministers were leaders of the community and as such, Reverend William Walter/Neale Donald Walsch was in a position to assist James Otis/John Hagelin in procuring greater influence within the government.

Note too that this situation is parallel to contemporary circumstances involving Hagelin and Walsch. As part of his 2000 presidential campaign, Hagelin tapped Walsch for fundraising help, just as Otis tapped Reverend Walter in his campaign to procure the rank of lieutenant colonel. So here we have established, if the proposed past-life identities are valid, a Revolutionary karmic connection between John Hagelin and Neale Donald Walsch.

Reverend Walter tried to maintain a neutral stance between the Loyalists and Revolutionaries within his congregation. As such, Reverend Walter remained in the good graces of Patriots and Loyalists alike until an unfortunate incident occurred. In February 1776, just as Paine's *Common Sense* was making a splash, Reverend Walter was accused of trying to spread smallpox within the Patriot army. A vaccine for smallpox had recently been invented, but there was great controversy as to whether the vaccine did more harm than good. People who were inoculated could spread the disease to others for a period of time, so the vaccinated had to go into temporary quarantine.

The incident in question involves a small boy who

accused Reverend Walter of forcing inoculation on him. The boy claimed that Reverend Walter then instructed him to go to a Patriot army base where the boy came down with the pox. This placed the Patriot army in danger of contracting the disease. Though it is difficult to imagine that this account was accurate, certain Bostonians apparently accepted the story and accused Walter of trying to spread smallpox within the Patriot armed forces. They branded him a Loyalist and traitor. As a result, Reverend Walter's house was ransacked and he was forced to take refuge in England in 1776.

In the spring of 1777, Walter returned to New York while the Revolutionary War was on, and was appointed as a chaplain to Britain's Third Battalion. In this capacity, Reverend Walter tended to Patriot prisoners of war. A biographer wrote that Walter's "kindness to the American prisoners was famous."[2] This service to the Patriot prisoners is consistent with Ahtun Re's statement that Walsch gave shelter or assistance to revolutionaries. It is also interesting that Reverend Walter attended to a prison population, as Neale Donald Walsch has created a special program to provide books to contemporary prison inmates. As such, William Walter and Neale Donald Walsch both have a common history of serving prison populations.

In December of 1783, Reverend Walter returned to England and in July 1784 he called upon Abigail Adams to welcome her to London. Abigail had just arrived to join her husband John, who was serving as the American minister to England. This visit acknowledges a karmic connection between William Walter/Neale Donald Walsch and Abigail Adams/ Marianne Williamson in the Revolutionary era. As noted previously, in contemporary times, Marianne Williamson has founded the Global Renaissance Alliance with Walsch cited as a co-founder.

In July and August 1787, Reverend Walter was back in Boston and was invited to preach in the Anglican church, which derived from the Church of England. Prior to his exile in England, Walter was known to support the establishment of an Anglican bishop in America, which caused consternation among independent-minded Americans. This association with Anglican churches and the calling for an Anglican bishop are consistent with Ahtun Re's statement that Walsch, in his Revolutionary lifetime, supported Anglican causes. It is also documented that Reverend Walter was a Freemason and spoke at Masonic events. An observer wrote: "Dr. Walter was an ardent Mason because he saw the function of that organization to be to further love of mankind."[3] This statement is consistent with Ahtun Re's other proclamation, that Walsch, in the Revolutionary era, was a Freemason.

As the years went on after his return from England, the people of Boston reaccepted Reverend Walter and, eventually, he was made Rector of Christ Church in Boston. Reverend Walter also frequently preached at Christ Church in Cambridge. He died on December 5, 1800, and was buried with Masonic honors in a family tomb under Christ Church. A memorial window was erected in Trinity Church in honor of William Walter. Reverend Walter was survived by seven children.

In addition to historical details that match Ahtun Re's description of Walsch in the Revolutionary era and the existence of karmic ties to Abigail Adams/ Marianne Williamson and James Otis/John Hagelin, common personality and character traits can be noted between Reverend Walter and Walsch.

For example, I have been told that Walsch is congenial in public and that he likes to dress well. Walsch himself has publicly joked about his vanity. At fundraising events held for John Hagelin, Walsch has told the story that when he was growing up one of his greatest concerns was his "hair" and how it was styled. This is consistent with how the ladies of Boston remembered Reverend Walter. One of these ladies remarked:

> Dr. Walter was a remarkably handsome man, tall and well proportioned. When in the street, he wore a long blue cloth cloak over his cassock and gown; a full-bottomed wig, dressed and powdered; a three-cornered hat; knee breeches of fine black cloth, with black silk hose; and square quartered shoes, with silver buckles.[4]

Walsch, I understand, is also fond of fine footwear. Walsch is also a former actor and radio personality. These roles are consistent with statements made regarding Reverend Walter: "His whole attention is given to dress, balls, assemblies, and plays;"[5] "his voice was clear, musical and well modulated."[6]

Walsch demonstrates great love and emotion towards his wife, Nancy. This is evident in words he uses to describe her in the foreword of his books. For example, in *Conversations with God, Book 3,* Walsch writes:

> Next, I would like to acknowledge and thank my wonderful life partner, Nancy, to whom this book is

dedicated. When I think of Nancy, my words of gratitude seem feeble next to her deeds, and I feel struck with not being able to find a way to express how really extraordinary she is. This much I know. My work would have not been possible without her.

This affectionate relationship is consistent with that of Reverend Walter's relationship with his wife, Lydia Lynde, who he married on Sept 30, 1766. What stuck me in reading about Reverend Walter was his reaction when he lost his beloved wife in 1789. It is documented that Walter could barely finish the sermon at her funeral. As an observer noted, the "funeral sermon which he preached for her was rendered almost illegible by his tears."[7] Reverend Walter's depth of emotion for his wife appears to reflect Walsch's deep love for Nancy.

Another common feature between Reverend Walter and Walsch is that both have produced spiritual and metaphysical works that have enjoyed great popularity. Walsch, of course, has written the *Conversations with God* series, which has sold in the millions. Reverend Walter, in like fashion, produced sermons of great popularity that had a metaphysical quality. The following quotes regarding Reverend Walter illustrate these points. "The popularity of the young man's preaching was amazing."[8] Of a sermon made by Walter, a listener wrote, "metaphysical but well picked and adapted to the present season."[9]

What is most striking is that Reverend Walter in the 18th century gave sermons that involved references to extraterrestrial beings. This subject matter is consistent with material in *Conversations with God, Book*

3 where Walsch writes about "highly evolved beings" who are extraterrestrials (ETs) from other planets. Walsh writes that these highly evolved beings are benevolent and more advanced than humans on the evolutionary scale. Let us now reflect on the words of Reverend William Walter, written in the 18th century, as he describes God creating the universe, with planets populated with life forms, and endowed with varying degrees of intelligence.

> *He speaks, and behold! those Suns which appear so magnificent in the great Concave, instantly exist; Suns which the Eye of an Herschel or a Newton . . . is unable to number: He commands, and behold! those Suns are surrounded with Planets, and their concomitant Satellites, prepared with all the Accommodations for embodied Spirits. It is not improbable that the Inhabitants of those countless Worlds which roll incessantly around their central fires, forming Systems beyond Systems, are en dowed with different Degrees of Intellect, and different Modes of attaining that Happiness for which they were made.*[10]

So Reverend William Walter speaks of beings living on other planets, each with their own ways of attaining happiness. This is consistent with Walsch's message about intelligent ETs evolving in their own manner.

In sum, the information that Ahtun Re provided regarding the past-life identity of Neale Donald Walsch appears to be fulfilled in the persona of Reverend William Walter. In addition, appropriate karmic connections exist between William Walter and James Otis/John Hagelin and Abigail Adams/Marianne Williamson. Personality traits and intellectual interests appear to be consistent too. As mentioned, facial architecture also matches, particularly in the area of the eyes and forehead. For all these reasons, it appears that Neale Donald Walsch was indeed Reverend William Walter in a past lifetime. Ahtun Re also identified Nancy, Neale's wife, as Lydia Lynde, Reverend Walter's great love. So we see, the romance continues.

In closing, the three cases of Charles Thomson/ Ralph Nader, David Rittenhouse/Carl Sagan and Reverend William Walter, served to demonstrate to me that Ahtun Re could make accurate past life matches. All three cases were very compelling to me, but the Walter/Walsch case was the most profound, as Ahtun Re gave very specific information about an individual, Reverend William Walter, who was in no history book, but through extensive research, everything that Ahtun Re said about the case was confirmed. Further, when I sent the reincarnation case information to Neale Donald Walsch and I stated that I thought that in a past lifetime, he was Reverend William Walter, that his friend Marianne Williamson was Abigail Adams and that John Hagelin was the Boston Revolutionary James Otis, Neale Donald Walsch telephoned me and stated, "I think there is something to this." Neale then agreed to be included in *Return of the Revolutionaries* as the reincarnation of Reverend William Walter. Coming from a man who has *Conversations with God*, I found his cooperation to be a validating experience.

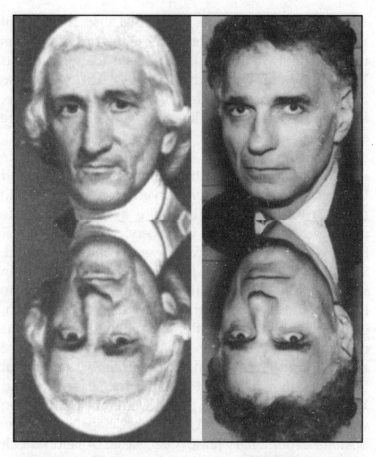

Charles Thomson　　　　　　**Ralph Nader**

From the Collection of Mrs. Paul Bartlett　　　Photo by Beverly An

When Dr. Semkiw asked Ahtun Re, the spirit guide channeled through Kevin Kyerson, the trance medium who has been featured in three of Shirley MacLaine's books, who Ralph Nader may have been in the era of the American Revolution, Ahtun Re said Nader was a leader of the Continental Congress named Thomson. Research revealed that Charles Thomson was the secretary of the Congress and that his facial features and personality traits matched precisely with those of Nader. This case made Dr. Semkiw take Ahtun Re seriously.

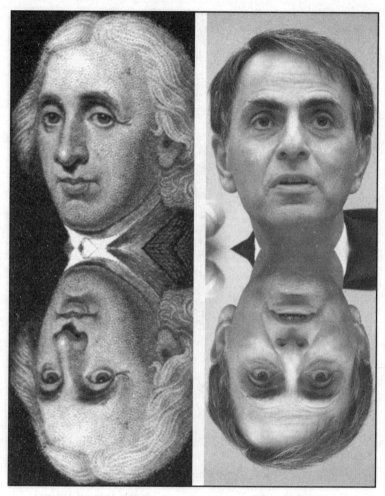

David Rittenhouse

Carl Sagan

Courtesy of Edward Savage, David
Rittenhouse, L.L.D., F.R.S., Yale University
Art Gallery, Mabel

Detail © Bettman/CORBIS

David Rittenhouse, who was an American Revolutionary, built the
first telescope in America, as well as an early planetarium, which
accurately depicted our solar system. He reincarnated as astronomer
Carl Sagan.

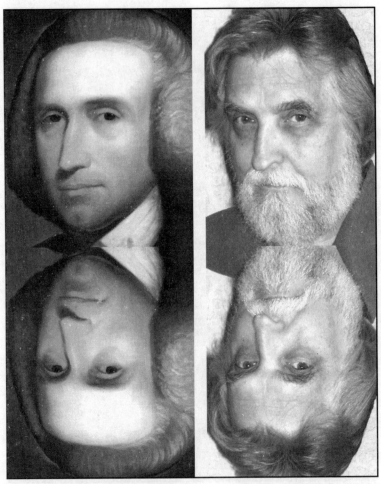

Reverend William Walter

Detail, Virginia Historical Society,
Richmond, Virginia

Neale Donald Walsch

Photo by Walter Semkiw

Mr. Walsch, author of "Conversations with God," agreed to be featured as the reincarnation of Rev. Walter in "Return of the Revolutionaries." This case dramaticaly demonstrates Ahtun Re's ability to make accurate past life matches.

12

The Reincarnation Cases of George W. Bush, Bill Clinton and Al Gore; With the Phenomena of Xenoglossy

I will present only a few cases from the American Revolution that may be of interest. A much more extensive discussion of such cases may be found in *Return of the Revolutionaries*. As George W. Bush is the current President of the United States, his case will be provided in detail. Though the cases of George W. Bush, Bill Clinton and Al Gore were all confirmed by Kevin Ryerson' guide, Ahtun Re, they were initially derived though intuitive guidance. At this point, I would like to present an example of how useful intuitive guidance can be. In this example, a case of xenoglossy, where an individual can speak a language that has not been learned, was discovered though intuitive, spiritual guidance.

This story involves my good friend, Igor Shochetman, who is a Russian pianist I know in San Francisco. Early on in my research regarding my own past lifetime as John Adams, I came to the hypothesis that Igor was a member of the French court that John Adams knew, based on similarities in physical appearance, personality traits and interests. Later on, Ahtun Re confirmed the match of Igor and the Frenchman. I kept this match quiet, though, and did not tell Igor of my hypothesis because Igor was an atheist. In the past, whenever I would tell Igor about my reincarnation theories, I could tell that he was just humoring me and didn't believe one word. As such, I learned not to discuss reincarnation with him.

One evening, I was sitting in Igor's kitchen along with him and Holly, Igor's girlfriend. Holly and Igor had been together for about six months. Igor spoke of Holly frequently, but I didn't see her very often, as she lived in a different city, Seattle, where she was getting a masters degree in mathematics. As I was sitting in Igor's kitchen, suddenly, out of nowhere, I received a strong intuitive, telepathic message. An inner voice proclaimed, "Tell them now, tell them now." This surprised me, as I was not accustomed to hearing such strong verbal messages very often. Indeed, the message seemed to come from outside of me.

I knew immediately that the voice was referring to the past life information regarding Igor, but I was resistant to revealing Igor's past life identity. I even tried to argue with this inner voice or spirit guide, whatever it was, and I silently thought to myself, hoping to get a response from the voice, "Why should I tell them about Igor's French past lifetime? First of all, Igor will never believe it. Secondly, I could have told him a year ago, why should I tell him now?"

There was no response to these questions that I posed internally, in my mind. Despite my initial reluctance, I reflected that this occurrence, with the telepathic message, was strange and powerful enough that I should not ignore it. Accordingly, I said out loud to Igor and Holly, "Igor, remember the reincarnation research that I have been doing in relation to John Adams? Well, I believe that in the era of the American Revolution, you were a Frenchman that John Adams knew and worked with, when Adams was in Paris as a foreign minister." At this point, I expected Igor to laugh this information off, but instead, what happened next really floored me. Holly, Igor's girlfriend exclaimed, "That is really strange, because Igor speaks French in his sleep."

Igor then admitted that this is true; that he has been told multiple times that he talks in French in his sleep, though in his waking consciousness, he cannot speak French. Igor is Russian and he has never learned French. In reincarnation research, the phenomenon of being able to speak a language that has not been learned is called "xenoglossy." Xenoglossy is a very rare phenomenon that is thought to represent knowledge from a past lifetime being transmitted into a contemporary incarnation. Recall the sketches that demonstrated how Peter Teekamp replicated the artistic development of Gauguin at a younger age. One can imagine xenoglossy as a similar phenomenon, where knowledge of a language is unconsciously accessed from a past lifetime. In the case of Igor, he demonstrates a variant of xenoglossy, in which he is able to speak French, a language he has not learned, but he can do so only in his sleep.

Given the rare nature of xenoglossy, the incident in Igor's kitchen helped validate that I was on the right track in my hypothesis that Igor was the Frenchman that John Adams knew. I also realized that the intuition, or telepathic message, that prompted me to discuss this French past life information in the presence of Holly was timed so that she would reveal Igor's nocturnal conversations in French, for I do not believe that Igor himself would have volunteered this information to me, given the skepticism he had previously demonstrated regarding these types of matters.

In a similar manner, the reincarnation cases involving Bush, Clinton and Gore were derived through intuitive guidance. Back in 2000 or so, before I met Kevin Ryerson, I was pondering the match that I had made for John Hagelin as the American Revolutionary, James Otis. Hagelin, a devotee of Maharishi Mahesh Yogi, was running for President of the US as candidate under the Natural Law Party, an organization supported by Maharishi Mahesh Yogi. I thought to myself, if James Otis is reincarnated and running for president, perhaps other American Revolutionaries are reincarnated and active in politics too.

As I reflected on this possibility, an unexpected directive popped into my mind regarding Bill Clinton, "Look in the Randolph family." I realized that the intuitive voice was referring to the Randolph's of Virginia, ancestors of Thomas Jefferson. I quickly did a search with the encyclopedia in my computer and

Peyton Randolph, who matched Bill Clinton in appearance and personality. Peyton even had the ball at the tip of his nose that is so characteristic of Clinton.

When I thought about George W. Bush and Al Gore, I received the very specific intuitive guidance to go look in a green book that I had on my shelf regarding George Washington and his generals. As I skimmed through the book, I quickly found that Bush bore a strong resemblance to Daniel Morgan, who commanded the Continental Rangers, the Patriot army's equivalent of a Special Forces unit. Al Gore bore a strong resemblance to General Horatio Gates. Later on, when I started working with Kevin Ryerson, Ahtun Re confirmed these reincarnation matches for Clinton, Bush and Gore. Let us now review the reincarnation cases of Daniel Morgan/George W. Bush and Horatio Gates/Al Gore, which are closely intertwined. The close past life relationship of Gates and Morgan is interesting, given that Bush and Gore ran against each other in hotly contested presidential race of 2000.

Let us first address the case of Gates/Gore. In addition to having nearly identical facial architecture, Horatio Gates and Albert Gore share similar personality traits. In particular, the two men share reputations as organizers and technocrats. Horatio Gates was a master at getting an army into fighting shape. He was a professional soldier, described by one historian as having "rare abilities as a military organizer."[1] Gates, upon numerous occasions, was able to convert undisciplined and demoralized troops into fighting units that even the British admired. This is significant, as the British considered the American forces as amateurs, which in many ways, they were. The Continental Congress also recognized the administrative abilities of Horatio Gates and eventually, Gates was made the President of the Board of War, which technically made Gates superior in rank to George Washington.

Though Gates was a military disciplinarian, he cared a great deal about the common soldier. Perhaps this arose from a battle during the French and Indian War, in which Gates was wounded by a musket ball; an infantryman dragged him from the field, saving his life. General Gates always tried to make sure that his troops were fed and sheltered. He made it a point to camp with his men, and in this way Gates won the affection and admiration of his troops. Samuel Adams described Gates' relationship with his men in the following way: "He has the Art of gaining the Love of his Soldiers principally because he is always present with them in Fatigue and Danger."[2]

Al Gore has been described as having similar abilities as an organizer and administrator. While Horatio Gates was a master of military organization, Gore is a master of the intricacies of government. Some have called Gore a technocrat in this regard. There are other similarities in the lives of Horatio Gates and Al Gore. In the period between the French and Indian War (1754–1763) and the Revolutionary War (1775–1782), Gates went through a period of "guzzling and gaming,"[3] as one historian has noted. Al Gore has had his own history of partying days, and Gore went through a similar "gaming" stage when he was a student at Harvard. Gates later experienced a religious conversion, a profound personal spiritual experience.

Gore has also had religious or mystical experiences, similar to the spiritual conversion of Horatio Gates; following these spiritual experiences, Gore adopted the habit of asking, "What would Jesus do?" when pondering difficult issues.

Let us now return to the battle of Saratoga. Horatio Gates/Albert Gore was in command of a demoralized and disorganized Northern army, which he transformed into an effective fighting unit. It was Gates' superior understanding of military strategy, terrain, and the mind of his enemy, which led to victory at Saratoga and the surrender of a large segment of the British forces. In fact, one fifth of the British troops on American soil (5,700 men) laid down their arms on that day. This was the first victory for the American Continental Army, and this achievement gave the colonists hope that they could succeed in their war against the British who possessed the most powerful army in the world.

More importantly, it was the victory at Saratoga that convinced France to join America in the struggle against Britain, committing military and financial aid to the American cause. John Adams, serving as an ambassador in Paris at the time, made the following statement regarding the international importance of the military event that shook the world: "General Gates was the ablest negotiator you ever had in Europe."[4] The negotiating chip Gates produced was Saratoga. (It was while Adams was in Paris, by the way, that he came to know the Frenchman who has reincarnated as Igor, our friend who speaks French in his sleep.)

Years later, at the siege of Yorktown, victory for the Americans came only with the assistance of the

French Navy and Army. Without the support of Louis XVI, the victory at Yorktown, which effectively ended the Revolutionary War, could never have been achieved. The importance of Saratoga, both as America's first strategic military victory and as the inducement for France to become America's ally, cannot be overemphasized. Due to his role in this critical campaign, some historians feel that Horatio Gates should be considered one of the Founding Fathers of America.

Though Horatio Gates/Albert Gore was the commanding general at Saratoga, he could not have won the battle without the help of Daniel Morgan, who held the rank of colonel at the time. At Saratoga, Colonel Morgan led a corps of elite sharpshooters or riflemen, called the Continental Rangers. As mentioned, Daniel Morgan has been confirmed by Ahtun Re to be reincarnated in our contemporary times as President George W. Bush. Let us briefly review a history of Morgan's contribution to the American Revolution.

Daniel Morgan was noted to have awkward speech and coarse manners when he made his debut on the Virginia frontier at age seventeen. George W. Bush, it is interesting to note, has also been observed to have difficulty with speech, and it was even speculated, during the presidential campaign of 2000, that he might have dyslexia. During the French and Indian War, Morgan served with the Virginia Rangers and he developed skill with the Kentucky rifle. During the Revolutionary War, on the basis of Morgan's courage, determination, and leadership skills, George Washington selected him as commander of the country's first special-forces unit. Five hundred members of the Continental Army, selected for marksmanship and fighting skills, were assembled. They were officially known as the Rangers, but many referred to the unit as Morgan's Riflemen. The Rangers were one of the premier units of the Army and participated in many important battles of the Revolution. In campaigns, Morgan himself demonstrated remarkable bravery, physical stamina and strength. Eventually, Morgan was made a brigadier general.

It has been mentioned that often time's symbols from a past lifetime can be found in contemporary incarnations. It is interesting to observe that George W. Bush has been affiliated with the Texas Rangers, the baseball team he once partially owned, which seems to reflect Daniel Morgan service with the Virginia and Continental Rangers.

Morgan, like Horatio Gates, first saw military action in the French and Indian War. Morgan was also wounded in this war, as was Horatio Gates/Albert Gore. During the conflict, Morgan's personality traits were observed and recorded. Morgan was a rowdy sort. One historian notes that during the war, Morgan and his pals "exasperated" officers with their "drinking, brawling, and lusty flirtations with Indian women." These characteristics were also noted after his period of enlistment was over. The same historian wrote:

> The years following "the French War" were carefree and roistering ones for Daniel Morgan. He was constantly in trouble with the law either for brawling

in taverns or for not paying his liquor bills and card debts. But by 1763, when Morgan formed a common-law union with sixteen-year-old Abigail Curry, his conduct underwent a marked change. He settled down, purchased a farm . . . and began enjoying a more prosperous and peaceful existence. His changed way of life soon gained him the respect of the more important members of his rural community.[5]

It is interesting that George W. Bush takes a certain pride in his partying days at Yale. Later on, Bush got into trouble with the law and was arrested for driving while under the influence of alcohol. We can image that Daniel Morgan in the 20th century would likely have earned a DUI, too. Like Morgan, Bush then became more serious and sober, earning the respect of Texas voters. Just as Morgan was a denizen of a rural community, George W. Bush is famous for his love of the land and his ranch in the small town of Crawford, Texas.

Under the command of Horatio Gates, Daniel Morgan played an important role in the battle of Saratoga. Accordingly, Horatio Gates/Albert Gore hugged Daniel Morgan/George W. Bush following the victory at Saratoga and said, "Morgan, you have done wonders."[6] In his report to Congress regarding the battle, an appreciative General Gates wrote, "too much praise cannot be given to the Corps commanded by Col. Morgan."[9] So important was this victory to Morgan that, in retirement, Morgan would call his home "Saratoga."

Morgan and his men shared winter quarters with George Washington at Valley Forge. Later, Morgan signed on once again with Horatio Gates, who was made commander of the Southern army. Unfortunately, Gates was not as successful in the South as he was at Saratoga. Later on, Morgan was given an independent command in the South. In was in this theater that Morgan, now a brigadier general, had his greatest military moment. The battle occurred at a place called Cowpens in the Carolinas. Crack British units were chasing Morgan, his riflemen, and American Regulars when nightfall descended and troops had to settle until daybreak. Morgan devised a battle plan in which his riflemen and militia formed a skirmish line below the crest of a hill. In the morning, as the British advanced, Morgan's sharpshooters let out two sets of volleys and then retreated. The British took the retreat as a signal to charge forward, only to be met at the top of the hill by American regulars. The American victory at Cowpens is roughly replicated in the last battle of the movie *The Patriot*. Cowpens has been called "one of the tactical masterpieces of the war."

In another reflection of George W. Bush's proposed past-life as Daniel Morgan, I would like to cite a painting that was hung on George W. Bush's wall when he was governor of Texas. The painting is also found on the back cover of Bush's autobiography, which is called *A Charge to Keep*. In this painting, a group of mountain men are charging up a hill. The scene features an unnamed horseman who sports a determined look in his eye, similar to the gaze we see in portraits of Daniel Morgan. The hills in the painting, indeed, are reminiscent of the mountains of Virginia. I submit that if there is one painting that Daniel Morgan could pick to place on his wall, it would be

George W. Bush's favorite, of determined mountain men, making a "charge to keep."

Daniel Morgan can also be seen in Bush's military management of the war in Afghanistan. When the war was starting out, after the destruction of the World Trade Center, Bush made a statement regarding the perpetrators: "We are going to smoke them out of their holes and get them." This way of speech reflects the personality of the mountain man, the Virginia Ranger, Daniel Morgan. Further, after a tentative start in this presidency, George W. Bush took charge after the World Trade Center disaster and indeed, in conducting war, George W. Bush demonstrated that he clearly was in his element.

Bush's natural ease in this role, I believe, reflects his past experience as one of the bravest and most effective warriors of the American Revolution. Let this statement, though, not encourage us to pursue war. As proclaimed in the first chapter, one of the primary motivations for writing this book is to eliminate war from this planet. No one group is "evil." The reality is that we, Hindu's, Sikh's, Christians, Jews and Muslims, are only separated by religious beliefs than can change from one lifetime to another. Only once we understand our true nature, as universal humans, who experience all these and other religions in successive lifetimes, only then will acrimony be quelled. Only then, will the delusion of separation be shattered.

The conflagration in the Middle East, surfacing during Bush's presidency, has revealed a past-life karmic connection with a European ally. During the Revolutionary War, the French military leader, the Marquis de Lafayette, rallied to the American cause.

Lafayette fought with American forces and became a close friend of George Washington. Lafayette saw the American Revolution not just as a mission for the United States, but as a cause for all mankind. The cause was to establish democracy in the world.

In contemporary times, America has another ally from Europe, who has even been called a "cheerleader" by the press, in America's war on terrorism. Tony Blair, England's Prime Minister, has spent time at President George W. Bush's Crawford ranch in efforts to join forces with America in a common cause. This parallels Lafayette's role, though the common cause this time is terrorism. Based on the similar role that Blair is playing, as well as consistent facial architecture, I arrived at the hypothesis that Tony Blair is the reincarnation of the Marquis de Lafayette. In a session with Kevin Ryerson, Ahtun Re confirmed this match

In closing, I would like to point out again that personality traits and predispositions stay the same from lifetime to lifetime. Just as Horatio Gates and Al Gore have both demonstrated qualities of organization and mastery of detail, Daniel Morgan and George W. Bush both have the qualities of a "Ranger." I believe that Bush's affinity for firearms is a link to his lifetime as a rifleman.

Horatio Gates and Daniel Morgan, by the way, were both friends of John Adams. John and Samuel Adams were Horatio Gates' strongest supporters in the Continental Congress. It was they who lobbied for his military commands. It is interesting to note that Al Gore was made aware of his past-life connection to Gates in the period of time surrounding the 2000 election. Through a mutual friend, I became acquainted with the famous psychic, Uri Geller, who interviewed me on the Thursday before the November 2000 election day. On Uri Geller's international radio show, I disclosed the past-life connections between Gore, Bush and Clinton and their Revolutionary counterparts. Though I was not aware of it beforehand, it turned out that Uri Geller is a friend of Al Gore. After the interview, Uri Geller contacted the White House to inform Al Gore of my work, and the past-life connections regarding Clinton, Gore, and Bush.

Daniel Morgan, a fierce Federalist, was also an ally of John Adams. Daniel Morgan thought that Jefferson's Republicans were "trying to destroy the constitution." Daniel Morgan/George W. Bush became a member of the US House of Representatives to support Adams in his presidency and to oppose the Jeffersonian Republicans. As a member of the House, Morgan even threatened to call out his Virginia militiamen against the "seditious" Jeffersonians within his own state.

So we see that from lifetime to lifetime, facial architecture, personality traits and karmic connections persist. Further, partners on the battlefield in one lifetime (Gates and Morgan) may become political competitors (Gore and Bush) in a subsequent lifetime. Another karmic connection that I would like to reveal at this time involves the Commander in Chief, George Washington, who Gates and Morgan reported to. Ahtun Re has revealed that Washington, in contemporary times, has reincarnated as Tommy Franks, who commanded US troops in Afghanistan and Iraq. In this case, we observe a role reversal. Whereas Daniel Morgan reported to Washington, in contemporary times, Washington/Franks had his

Commander in Chief in Morgan/Bush. Whereas Washington served as President in Revolutionary times, Bush has become President of the US in contemporary times.

In closing, the cases of Bush, Gore and Clinton were first derived through intuitive guidance and then confirmed through Kevin Ryerson's guide, Ahtun Re. It is important to note that John Adams too was a strong believer in the power of intuition. In addition, Adams, at the end of his life, dedicated himself to the study of metaphysics and even wrote to Jefferson regarding the concept of reincarnation. It seems that I have picked up where John Adams left off.

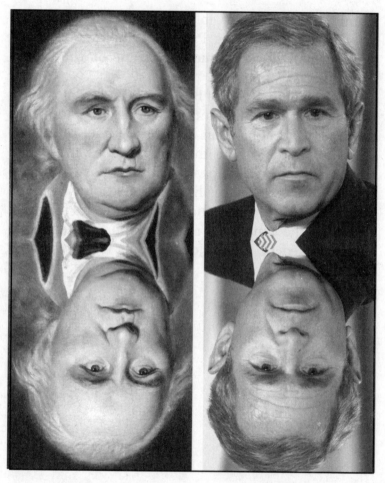

Daniel Morgan   **George W. Bush**

Courtesy of the Library of Congress   Detail of Photo by Robert Trippett, Sipa

During the American Revolution, Daniel Morgan led the Continental Rangers, a special forces unit of the Patriot army. Morgan reported to George Washington, who in contemporary times has been identified as US General Tommy Franks. Morgan was promoted to the rank of General and later was elected to the US Congress.

13

Oprah Winfrey and the American Revolution

Once I had gained confidence that Ahtun Re, Kevin Ryerson's spirit guide, could make accurate past life matches, I was interested in deriving reincarnation cases of celebrities. One of the most famous women in contemporary society is Oprah Winfrey and in a session with Kevin, I asked for a past lifetime for Oprah. I was surprised by his response.

Ahtun Re stated that Oprah was a significant figure in the Constitutional Convention, an Abolitionist, and involved in debates regarding the "three-fifths clause." When I asked Ahtun Re for Oprah's name in the Revolutionary era, he responded with the words, "One moment," as was his fashion when I asked for more specific information. After a pause, during which Ahtun Re presumably checked the Akashic Records, he revealed that Oprah's name was Wilson. In reviewing participants of the Constitutional Convention, a James Wilson matched the description given by Ahtun Re. In a subsequent session, Ahtun Re confirmed this match.

James Wilson was born in Scotland in 1741. After attending several universities without obtaining a degree, he immigrated to Philadelphia in 1765. Wilson then established himself in the Scottish settlement of Carlisle, Pennsylvania. In addition to occupying himself with a very successful law practice, Wilson taught English literature at the College of Philadelphia. He became involved in the Revolutionary movement when he became chairman of the Carlisle Committee of Correspondence. This put him in contact a with fellow Pennsylvania Patriot letter writers Charles Thomson/Ralph Nader. Wilson soon wrote an influential pamphlet on the relationship between the Colonies and Britain and argued that Parliament did not have the right to rule the Colonies. This pamphlet elevated Wilson to a position of leadership and in 1775 led to his election as a delegate to the Continental Congress.

In the Continental Congress, Wilson served on military committees and committees dealing with Indian Affairs. Charles Thomson/Ralph Nader also had expertise in Indian Affairs, so it is likely that James Wilson/Oprah Winfrey and Thomson/Nader conferred on this subject. Though there was some ambivalence in Pennsylvania regarding severing ties with Britain, after conferring with his constituents in Carlisle, James Wilson voted for Independence on July 2, 1776. Wilson signed the Declaration on August 2, 1776.

As the Revolutionary War progressed, many economic hardships were encountered. In 1779, there were food shortages, and rampant inflation made paper currency worthless. In frustration, a mob, whose members perceived Wilson as a wealthy benefactor of the economic turmoil, attacked Wilson and thirty five associates who were trapped in his home, which was dubbed Fort Wilson. Gunshots were fired and several people on both sides of the conflict were killed. The affair was called the Fort Wilson riot and one of the defenders of the fort, along with Wilson, was the past life persona of Shirley MacLaine.

During the Revolution, Shirley MacLaine and James Wilson/Oprah Winfrey were closely involved in financial dealings over many years. As a result, in 1781, Wilson/Winfrey was made a director of the Bank of North America, which was the brain-child of Shirley MacLaine. It is interesting to note, that when Oprah's Chicago-based talk show first originated, Shirley MacLaine was one of her first guests.

James Wilson's greatest service to the United States came later, though, as a delegate in the Constitutional Convention of 1787. Wilson was one of the most influential participants of the Convention, only superseded by James Madison. In fact, in the book *Miracle at Philadelphia*, Catherine Drinker Bowen called Wilson "the unsung hero of the Federal Convention." The historian Lord Bryce referred to Wilson at the convention as one of the "deepest thinkers and most exact reasoners"[1] and stated that "he thought as he chose, independently of other men, a trait that invited stormy episodes."[2] Oprah too, has been known to speak her mind.

In the debates regarding methods of establishing representation within the national legislature, Wilson proposed the "three-fifths clause." Though Wilson was against slavery, a compromise had to be struck on how slaves would be counted in a slave-owning state's population, which would in turn determine the number of representatives from that state to a national congress. Northern states claimed that slaves shouldn't be counted, as they had no voting rights, while southern states demanded that slaves be included in a state's population. A compromise was settled upon that the slave population of a state would be multiplied by three fifths to determine the state's representation. In other words, a slave would count for three fifths of a person.

After the Constitutional Convention finished its work and a new Federal government was formed, George Washington appointed Wilson as one of the original justices of the Supreme Court. Wilson died in 1798.

James Wilson and Oprah Winfrey share a number of personality traits. One striking feature about Oprah is that ever since childhood, she has displayed a natural gift for speech and oration. At age three, she gave a recitation to the congregation of her church. Adults gave Oprah praise, while the other children scorned her, jealous of her gift. At the age of seven in the third grade, she was paid $500 to give a speech to a church group, an amazing accomplishment for someone born into poverty and raised on a pig farm. Biographer George Mair commented on her natural "poise and ability to engage an audience."[3] At the age of seventeen, Oprah participated in a White House conference on youth, as well as a national speaking competition. Oprah continued to speak in churches and developed a lifelong interest in women's rights. Mair has pointed out how "Oprah would stand before the congregation or audience and thunder out the words on behalf of women's equality."[4]

James Wilson was also a great speaker. One historian writes, "Wilson was one of the early congresses greatest orators."[5] Thomas Kindig comments, "James Wilson's power of oration, the passion of his delivery and the logic he employed in debate, were commented on favorably by many members of Congress."[6] This mirrors Oprah's style, as reflected in a comment by Mair on Oprah's speeches on ex-slave women, who Oprah reveres. Mair writes, "Her articulate and passionate speeches about them as a teenager began winning her recognition and prizes."[7]

At the Constitutional Convention, only James Madison had more influence than Wilson and only two others gave more speeches than Wilson. These traits of Wilson are consistent with Oprah, as demonstrated by Mairs's comment that Oprah had the ability to "thunder out words." Bowen, in *Miracle at Philadelphia*, wrote that, "In the records of the Convention, when Wilson rises to speak it is as if an electric charge passes down the page." Bowen further notes that Wilson's was a "clear and powerful voice."

As the Constitutional Convention drew to a conclusion, there was fear that dissenting delegates would not sign the new Constitution. In an effort to promote unity, Benjamin Franklin wrote a speech and invited supporters to his home, over a weekend break, to review the oration. James Wilson attended and was chosen to read Franklin's speech on the following Monday. The speech was successful. After the Constitution was ratified, Philadelphia had a celebration on the Fourth of July, 1788, and seventeen thousand people attended. The crowd settled at the newly named "Union Green," at the foot of Bush hill, near the city's harbor. James Wilson was, once again, selected to make a speech. Ten toasts were made. A trumpet sounded and artillery boomed from the ship *Rising Sun* after each toast.

At the end of the day, Philadelphia was lit by the aurora borealis and Benjamin Rush wrote his famous words, "Tis done, we have become a nation." In these examples, we see that James Wilson was repeatedly chosen to speak at public gatherings, much as Oprah was chosen to speak from an early age. It appears that Oprah's gift for oration is a continuation of James Wilson's talent with words.

Wilson and Oprah can both be characterized as hard workers, driven by ambition and blessed with a fine mind. Like Oprah, Wilson was born in humble circumstances. Historian Stephen Conrad wrote that Wilson "achieved fame and fortune, though industry and intellect."[8] After immigrating to Philadelphia at 23 years of age, Wilson quickly connected himself with leading figures and established a lucrative law practice. As mentioned, Wilson soon wrote a political pamphlet that supported American self-rule and thereafter became a leader in the Continental Congress. Benjamin Franklin liked to refer to Wilson as "my learned colleague" and Benjamin Rush referred to Wilson's mind as "one blaze of light."

This mirrors Oprah's path. Oprah's intelligence was recognized early on when teachers determined that she could skip kindergarten and move directly to the first grade. Oprah also demonstrates Wilson's trait of industry. Mair wrote of the teenage Oprah, "She possessed a driving ambition and a determination to be somebody."[9] Oprah is said to have been inspired by Jesse Jackson's admonition to work hard to achieve. Oprah's television producer made the comment that she never saw anyone work as hard, and said of Oprah, "Her stamina was boggling."[10]

Significantly, James Wilson and Oprah, both have demonstrated a love of books. Despite his heavy schedule as a lawyer and revolutionary, Wilson taught English literature at the College of Philadelphia. Oprah demonstrated an early love of books; during childhood on her grandmother's farm, Oprah's life revolved around reading. Oprah read Bible stories aloud to farm animals she tended. In her adolescence, during periods of trouble and alienation, Oprah would withdraw into books. In later years, as her show became the most watched daytime program, she got America reading again and her book club became a cultural institution.

James Wilson was an early voice against slavery. In his pre-Revolutionary pamphlet, *Considerations on the Nature and Extent of the Legislative Authority of the British Parliament,* Wilson wrote "All men are by nature, equal and free. No one has a right a right to any authority over another without his consent." Though the pamphlet dealt primarily with British rule, this statement reflects Wilson's idealism. In the Continental Congress, Wilson voiced his opposition to slavery at a time when many ignored the issue in order to preserve unity between the colonies.

Human bondage has been an issue for Oprah also. Oprah, in her shows and movies, has explored the detrimental effect slavery has had on the psyche of African Americans. In this context, Oprah has said, "Slavery taught us to hate ourselves." It is important to note, that though being black in America has been a central issue in Oprah's life, she does not fully identify with black issues. Sherry Burns, an Oprah producer, said: "She's the universal woman; she gets past the black thing."[11]

Wilson and Oprah have both been characterized as being wealthy and both associated with the "aristocratic" elements of society. Though Oprah has shown devotion to her black heritage, Mair writes of Oprah, "She identifies with the white power structure, with whom she shares the same socioeconomic class, as does a virtually invisible class of successful, wealthy blacks."[9] Mair notes, "Oprah quickly slipped into the role of the rich woman who could order up limousines, fancy meals, and chartered jets at the snap of her fingers."[12] Oprah makes it a point to maintain close fiscal control of her wealth and operations, rather than delegating the control of money to others.

These traits are consistent with those observed in James Wilson. One historian notes, "Wilson affirmed his newly acquired political stance by closely identifying with aristocratic and wealthy republican groups, multiplying his business interests."[13] Wilson eventually was perceived as one of the wealthiest citizens of Philadelphia. As mentioned previously, when rampant inflation and food shortages occurred in 1779, this image of wealth worked against Wilson and other well-to-do cohorts. In the fall of 1779, Robert Morris and over 30 other aristocrats were chased into James Wilson's home by an armed mob. Shots were fired and there were deaths on both sides. Local troops had to rescue the barricaded group in what became known as the Fort Wilson Riot.

Though Wilson and Oprah both have demonstrated a drive for wealth and achievement, both have also had a tendency to be loose with their money. As a young woman, when Oprah was asked during a beauty contest what she would do with a million dollars, she replied she would be "a spending fool." This prediction has come true on many occasions. Biographer Mair has noted that between 1988 and 1990, Oprah spent $35 million on personal items. In addition, when problems arise with key staff members or in relationships, Oprah's impulse is to spend money lavishly, on gifts, vacations, new dwellings, and other perks, hoping that her generosity will quell the disturbance.

James Wilson was also a big spender, but more in terms of business ventures and land speculation. James Wilson purchased frontier land in Illinois and was made president of the Illinois Wabash Company. Ironically, in this way, Wilson owned the land that later sprouted the city of Chicago, Oprah's adopted home town and base of operations. The title "spending fool" is apropos for Wilson also, as his spending and speculation drove Wilson into bankruptcy. James Wilson/Oprah Wintrey even served time in debtors' prison.

Like James Wilson, Oprah has been involved in the workings of government and has sponsored legislation. Oprah hired former Illinois governor James Thompson to guide passage of the National Child Protection Act, which helps prevent convicted child abusers from taking jobs involving child care. The bill was also known as "Oprah's Act," and Oprah was present when President Clinton signed it into law. Interestingly, Oprah as James Wilson would have known Clinton as Peyton Randolph in Revolutionary times. James Wilson/Oprah Winfrey was elected to the First Continental Congress in 1775. Peyton Randolph/Bill Clinton served as the President of the First Continental Congress until he suddenly and unexpectedly died in October 1775.

In a final similarity, Oprah and Wilson both have demonstrated an inclination for weight gain. James Madison noted that James Wilson was "inclined to stoutness." John Adams had this tendency also, as have I in certain years. It appears that the characteristic of a good appetite is a personality trait that can be carried through from lifetime to lifetime. Oprah seems to have learned to control this tendency, as she has looked quite beautiful in recent years. It seems that James Wilson has gone on a diet.

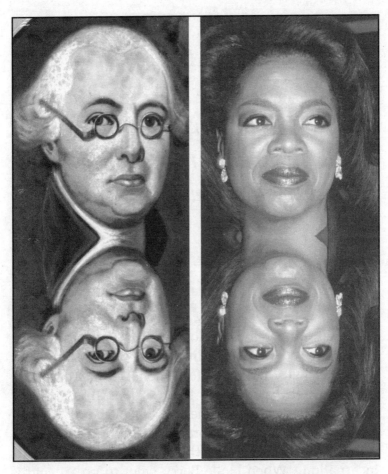

James Wilson

Oprah Winfrey

by Philip Fishbourne Wharton, after James
Baron Longarce's engraving from a
painting by Jean Pierre Henri Elouis, 1873,
Independence National Historical Park

Detail © Ariel Ramerez/CORBIS

James Wilson was considered one of the greatest orators of the American Revolution. Oprah showed a talent for public speaking early in her youth. In Philadelphia, Wilson taught English Literature, which is reflected in Oprah's Book Club.

14

Halle Berry as the Reincarnation of Dorothy Dandridge; An Affinity Case

In doing reincarnation research over the years, I noted that sometimes, people were attracted to their own past life personas. I had observed this frequently enough that I gave this type of reincarnation case a name. I called them "affinity cases," where a contemporary person demonstrates a deep affinity for who they were in a previous incarnation. When Halle Berry went to great lengths to make movie about the actress Dorothy Dandridge, it was natural to hypothesize that Halle is the reincarnation of Dorothy. This theory was supported by the fact Halle and Dorothy have the exact same facial features. In a session with Kevin Ryerson, Ahtun Re confirmed the match of Dorothy Dandridge/Halle Berry.

Not only is this paring an example of an affinity case, it is an example of how a soul can reincarnate to complete a goal. Dorothy Dandridge died on September 8, 1965; while Halle Berry was born just three years later, on August 14, 1968. Dorothy and Halle were both born in Cleveland, Ohio. In 1954, Dandridge was nominated for an Oscar for her role in *Carmen Jones*, but she didn't get the award, in part because African Americans were still discriminated against in Hollywood at that time. As Halle Berry, in March 2002, Dorothy Dandridge had her goal fulfilled.

What is fascinating in this case is that a friendship has endured across two lifetimes. When Halle was making a movie about Dorothy Dandridge, she became close to Geri Branton, one of Dorothy Dandridge's close friends, who was in her seventies at the time. During an interview, Branton noted great similarities between Dandridge and Berry. She stated:

"It's amazing, and she does it [portraying Dandridge] so well." Berry appeared horrified when Branton was asked how she was most like Dandridge. "I think that Halle's personal life is shocking in that it's the same," Branton said. "Geri, shhh," Berry said. But Branton plowed on ahead. "They're beautiful people, beautiful on the outside but more so on the inside. Generous and lovely," she said. "It's unbelievable. And when I saw Halle the first time, I was taken aback, really taken aback. They're so very much akin."

Halle Berry herself has said that her life parallels Dandridge's life—"being in Hollywood, wanting to be a leading lady and feeling like a leading lady but being in an industry that has no place for us. My struggle has been very much hers, trying to carve a niche for myself as a leading lady. And, although she opened the door for me, because she was never recognized in the way that she should have been, I'm still in the exact same position she was." But after Oscar night 2002, that was no longer true. At that event, Halle Berry became the first African American to win an Oscar for Best Actress.

An interesting thing happened, regarding Halle Berry and Dorothy Dandridge, as reported in 2003. When making the movie, *Introducing Dorothy Dandridge*, Halle had obtained a dress that belonged to Dorothy, which she kept in her den. For protection, the dress was kept in paper and plastic. Let us let Halle Berry now narrate the scene:

"One night I was at home with a friend drinking tea and we heard all this rustling noise. At first I thought it was just water dripping from the teapot, then I realized it was coming from the room, and the paper on the dress was rattling - all by itself! My friend and I both hauled a*s out of there so fast!"

"Then other strange things happened in the house while I had that dress. I'd come home and the housekeeper would say she'd heard my vanity chair moving upstairs in my bathroom. And our fridge door would fly open by itself. I'm not kidding.

"When the film was over, I desperately wanted to keep her dress, but it had to go. And then everything was fine."[1]

Halle Berry interpreted these proceedings by hypothesizing that the ghost of Dorothy Dandridge was in her home. I myself don't know exactly what caused these psychokinetic phenomenons to occur, though I will ask Ahtun Re his opinion, the next time that I have a chance. Perhaps it was Halle's own soul, or that of a spirit guide, that was trying to give her a message. We will learn more about psychokinetic phenomenon in our next chapter, which features Uri Geller.

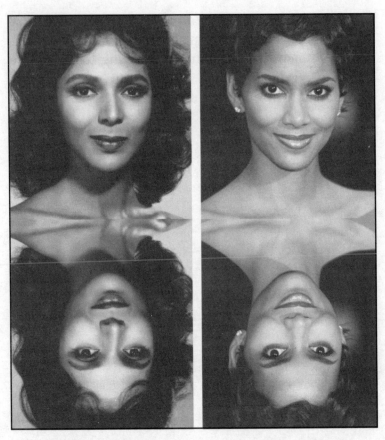

Dorothy Dandridge **Halle Berry**

Dorothy Dandridge was an actress who was denied an Oscar, in part because she was black in a prejudiced time. Halle completed Dorothy's dream by winning an Oscar for Best Actress. In making a movie about Dorothy, Halle demonstrated an intense affinity for her own past life persona, a phenomenon termed an "affinity case."

15

Uri Geller, Daniel Dunglas Home and Ariel Sharon

U ri Geller, who gained fame by bending spoons with his mind, is one of the most fascinating individuals on the planet. A friend, Jeffrey Mishlove, a parapsychologist and author of *Roots of Consciousness*, was the one who first posited that Geller is the reincarnation of Daniel Dunglas Home, a 19 century medium who was associated with psychokinetic phenomenon, much like Geller. In a session Kevin Ryerson and Ahtun Re, confirmed that Uri Geller is the reincarnation of Home.

As mentioned in the chapter involving George W. Bush, Bill Clinton and Al Gore, Uri Geller had interviewed me on his radio show in the year 2000, so I had his e-mail address and telephone number in my possession. I sent him a message with graphics comparing his facial features with those of Home's. When I didn't hear from Uri after a week or so, I telephoned him. When I spoke to him, Uri was quite excited to learn that I had a past life match for him.

He related that he had not seen my e-mail, explaining that he receives several hundred messages per day. As I tried to go through some background information, Uri interrupted me with the impatient demand, "So who was I?" I told him, "You were Daniel D. Home." Geller then exclaimed, "Daniel Dunglas Home! Oh my God, the hair just went up on the back of my neck! I know of Home, I have even written about him." I told Geller that I wanted his permission to use his case in my book. Before much more was said, Geller related that he had to go find my e-mail right away and he said a hurried goodbye. Two weeks later, Uri Geller agreed to be featured in *Revolutionaries* as the reincarnation of Daniel D. Home.

In presenting this case, I will first provide brief biographical sketches of Daniel D. Home and Uri Geller. I will then review, in detail, common features of their histories, personalities, psychic and mediumistic abilities. Let us at this point review terms that will be used. Let us define a medium as someone who acts as an intermediary, a "go between," who serves to connect spiritual beings with humans.

Psychic abilities, on the other hand, we will consider as abilities that are innate to a person, without the involvement of outside spiritual entities. An example of a psychic ability would be telepathy, in which thoughts are transmitted from one person to another. A premonition, in which a future event is discerned, is another psychic phenomenon. Remote viewing is another psychic skill in which events taking place at a distance can be viewed with the mind. An individual, of course, may have both types of talents and have innate psychic skills as well as the ability to serve as a medium. Mediums we have encountered in this book include Kevin Ryerson and Bobby Jo, who was featured in the case of Penny Peirce.

A physical medium is defined as someone who generates unusual physical phenomena, such as causing furniture to levitate. If someone is termed a physical medium, it implies that the levitation is being caused by an outside entity, such as a spirit. The medium acts as an intermediary for the spirit, so that the discarnate entity can cause levitation of objects, or other phenomenon, on the physical plane. Typically, the medium does not understand how the spirit he or she channels creates the physical phenomenon, such as levitation. Telekinesis or psychokinesis are used interchangeably and simply refer to physical effects that are caused by the mind. These two terms do not define whether the physical effects are caused by an outside spiritual entity or the human being associated with the phenomenon.

Daniel Home was born in 1833, near Edinburgh, Scotland. At the age of four, Daniel demonstrated psychic gifts, as he was able to discern events, such as the death of a family member, which had occurred geographically far away. When Daniel was nine years old, his family immigrated to the United States, settling in Connecticut. In 1850, when Home was seventeen, telekinetic events suddenly started to occur around him.

One of the first phenomenon described involved a chair, which suddenly moved up to Home on it's own power, while he was having breakfast. Home was as astonished as everyone else and commented, "What might be the cause of these disturbances to our morning meal?"[1] From that time on, furniture moving around the room, even levitating, became a regular occurrence around Home. Prominent intellectuals took an interest in Home's powers, including Judge John W. Edmonds, a justice of the New York Supreme Court.

In 1855, Home moved to London, England. Home began having séances which attracted the attention of the rich and powerful, who provided Home with lodging and food in exchange for his presence. Home never charged for séances, though he accepted gifts. When necessary, Home earned money doing public demonstrations. He became the most famous medium in the world and was sought out by the rulers of nations. Home became close to Napoleon III, the Emperor of France. Napoleon III was especially impressed by Home when spirit raps on a table answered questions that he posed mentally, rather than verbally.

When in Rome, Home met a Russian woman named Sacha, who was descended from royalty. Upon meeting her, Home had a premonition, in which he knew she would be his wife. Alexander II, the Tsar of Russia, personally gave permission for the wedding to take place and the Tsar became a close friend to Home. In 1859, Sacha and Home had a son named Gregoire, who was nicknamed Gricha. Alexander II, the Tsar, became Gricha's godfather. As his son grew, Home noted that the psychokinetic phenomena were enhanced in Gricha's presence.[2]

Unfortunately, Home was infected with tuberculosis and his wife, Sacha, caught the disease. Home lost his loving wife to tuberculosis after only four years of marriage. After her death, Home went to Rome to study sculpture, hoping to achieve financial independence as an artist. In 1863, he published the first version of his autobiography, *Incidents of my Life*, though much of the book was actually written by his attorney. In 1869, Alexander Aksakoff, a Professor of Chemistry at the University of St. Petersburg and a friend of Home's through the Russian court, introduced him to Sir William Crookes. Crookes is the prominent British scientist who was introduced earlier in this chapter, in the section pertaining to Kate Fox. Sir William Crookes studied Home in 1870.

Among the phenomenon documented, Crookes witnessed Home levitating on two occasions and saw a spirit flying around the room playing an accordion (the spirit disappeared after Crookes' wife screamed in fear). In séances, Home frequently would hold one end of an accordion with one hand, while an invisible spirit hand played the keyboard of the instrument. Oftentimes, the music played was described as extremely beautiful, as if it came from another world. At other times the tunes were quite ordinary, such as "God Save the Queen."

To ensure that this was not a trick, Sir William Crookes constructed an iron cage, in which the accordion was placed. Home held one end of the accordion through the top of the cage while the invisible hand played tunes on the imprisoned instrument. After a series of experiments such as this, in 1871, Crookes declared that Home was genuine. Crookes and Home became close friends as a result of their work together. The scientific community was close minded about spiritualism and Crookes endured criticism for his study of Kate Fox and Daniel Home. Nonetheless, years later, Crookes was elected as President of the British Association for the Advancement of Science.

During the period of time in which the experiments with Sir William Crookes were being conducted, Daniel Home met Julie de Gloumeline, another member of the Russian aristocracy. She noted that upon their introduction, a voice told her that here was her husband. They married in October 1871. Julie was devoted to Home and she eventually wrote two books about him. Home continued demonstrating psychokinetic phenomenon in the ensuing years, befriending other worldly figures such as Mark Twain. Home died of tuberculosis on June 21, 1886, in Nice, France.

Uri Geller was born in Israel on December 20, 1946, approximately 60 years after Daniel D. Home died. The first unusual incident in Geller's life occurred when he was 3 or 4 years old. The episode is described in his autobiography, entitled *My Story*. While playing in an Arabic garden across the street from his home, a silvery light as bright as the sun descended upon him. He experienced a loud ringing in his ears, a pain in his forehead and then he lost consciousness.

When Uri awoke, he knew something important happened to him, though he didn't comprehend what it was. In the years that followed, Uri discovered that he possessed telepathic skills, such as the ability to read minds. He relates an example involving his mother, who enjoyed playing cards with her friends. Uri found that he knew exactly how much money his mother had won or lost, before she had a chance to say a word about the matter. When he was 9 years old, Uri was innocently eating mushroom soup at home when his spoon spontaneously bent and hot soup was dumped in his lap. A moment later, the bowl of the spoon fell off, as if its attachment to the handle of the spoon had just melted away. Uri was as astonished as his mother.

Uri Geller's father was a tank sergeant in the Israeli army and his mother made money as a seamstress. They eventually divorced and Uri and his mother moved to the Mediterranean island of Cypress, where the psychokinetic and telepathic phenomenon continued. As a teenager, Uri Geller had an inner knowing of his destined path in life. In the 1950s, Uri told his teacher, Julie Agrotis, that scientists would study him and that he would be working for world peace. Uri and his mother subsequently returned to Tel Aviv and when he reached the compulsory age, Uri entered the Israeli army. The Six Day War broke out in June 1967 and Uri, a paratrooper, saw active combat near Ramala. In battle, he was wounded, suffering injuries to both arms and his head.

As Geller was recovering from his wounds, he was invited to work as a counselor at a resort camp for kids. At the camp, Geller entertained the children by doing demonstrations involving telepathy and spoon bending. Uri soon met Shimshon Shtrang, a 12 or 13 year old boy, whose nickname was Shipi. The two resonated and Geller noticed that the telepathy and metal bending phenomenon were enhanced around Shipi.[3] The two became close friends. Shipi is the one who arranged for Geller to do his work in front of large, public forums and eventually became his manager. Shipi also introduced him to his sister, Hannah. Years later, Uri Geller would marry Hannah. The entertainer, Michael Jackson, served as his best man.

A medical doctor from the United States, Andrija Puharich, had an interest in psychic phenomenon and came to Israel to meet Uri Geller. An immediate affinity was noted, and Uri wrote in his autobiography, "The moment I saw Andrija, I knew by instinct that I could work with him."[4] Geller also observed that Shipi and Hannah also liked Puharich. After preliminary studies were done in Israel, Puharich wrote to scientists at the Stanford Research Institute (SRI), recommending that they formally study Geller's abilities. Geller's talents were tested at SRI in 1972 and 1973. The scientists who conducted the experiments included Apollo astronaut Edgar Mitchell, Ph.D.; Russell Targ, Ph.D., a laser physicist; and Hal Puthoff, Ph.D., a quantum physicist. While experiments were being conducted at SRI, Geller also met Werner von Braun, the rocket scientist. Geller caused von Braun's wedding ring to bend, while the ring was being held in von Braun's own hand. The focus at SRI was telepathy experiments and in the end, a scientific paper was published in the prestigious British journal, *Nature*, which supported Geller's telepathic abilities as being genuine.

Geller was then tested in June 1974, at King's College, London. Professor John Taylor supervised the experiments and in contrast to the work at SRI, Geller's psychokinetic abilities were examined. Under laboratory conditions, a metal wire was observed to bend by itself and a piece of brass moved a distance of 20 feet under its own power. A piece of copper then saw fit to join the piece of brass and flew over to join it. A straight iron rod moved by itself and landed at Professor Taylor's feet, where it was found bent. In the laboratory at Kings College, Geller was also able to make a compass move 40 degrees by just concentrating on it and he activated a Geiger counter with his mind. Instruments used to monitor the phenomena revealed that no electrical force, magnetic fields or radiation were generated during Geller's feats.

Professor David Bohm, a scientist at Birkbeck College, which is part of the University of London, was the next academic scientist to evaluate Geller. Bohm was described as a brilliant and sensitive man by Geller and a special relationship existed between the two. Bohm was as quantum physicist who worked with Albert Einstein and Neils Bohr, and he was one of the people involved in the first efforts to split the atom. Several guests were invited to witness the experiments at Birkbeck, including fiction writer Arthur C. Clarke, who created *2001: A Space Odyssey.*

At Birkbeck College, under laboratory conditions, Uri Geller made keys bend and he once again activated a Geiger counter with his mind. Geller also made half a vanadium carbide crystal, which was sealed in a plastic enclosure, dematerialize. In the end, Professor John Taylor and Professor David Bohm both wrote in support of Uri Geller, acknowledging that his psychokinetic abilities are genuine. They also noted that the phenomena demonstrated by Geller completely undermine the known laws of physics.

The experiments at Stanford Research Institute, Kings College and Birkbeck College were done in the

1970s. Since then, Uri Geller has continued to conduct demonstrations of his psychokinetic abilities, has befriended world leaders and entertainers, and has persisted in broadcasting his message throughout various media. His message is that these powers signify something wonderful and unexplained about the human mind. Uri's hope is that humanity will study these powers to further explore human potential. At the same time, he repeatedly states that his greatest wish is for world peace and that he will use the forums provided to him by these powers to be a spokesperson for tolerance and understanding.

COMPARISON OF THE PHENOMENA OF DANIEL D. HOME AND URI GELLER

It is my premise that Uri Geller is the reincarnation of Daniel D. Home. I will now review the various telepathic and psychokinetic abilities of Daniel D. Home and Uri Geller, in an effort to show that the talents of the two men are similar. Subsequently, I will compare personality traits. In this way, I hope to provide another example of how talents, abilities, interests and personality traits remain consistent from lifetime to lifetime. Let us now address talents shared by Daniel Home and Uri Geller.

Premonitions, Telepathy, and Remote Viewing

Home: At age 4, Daniel Home first started describing events occurring at a distance. Whether this was a telepathic phenomenon, where ideas are transmitted, or a form of remote viewing is not clear. At age 17, Home accurately predicted that his mother would die at age 42. After his mother passed away, it was reported that Home was in regular contact with her in the spirit realm. This communication can be viewed as a telepathic phenomenon involving a spiritual entity. Home had a visual telepathic message at age 13, in which a boyhood friend named Erwin appeared and made three circles with his right hand. Erwin and Home had made a pact years before that the first one of them to die would try to communicate with the other. Home accurately interpreted the vision to mean that Erwin had died three days before.[5] Later in life, Home had a vision of his brother's death in the Polar Seas. Home's brother, Adam, indeed had died while bear hunting with officers from a ship that was exploring the polar region.

Geller: One of Uri Geller's earliest manifestations of psychic gifts was his ability to read his mother's mind. As a child, Uri was able to repeatedly know how much money his mother had won or lost at cards. Later on, Uri telepathically knew that his mother was in a car accident. In Cypress, he found that he could complete school examinations, without studying, by telepathically gleaning answers and entire essays from classmates.

Uri Geller has had many premonitions of danger and death. As a child, on a trip to the zoo, Uri sensed that a hazardous situation existed and had the urge to leave immediately. It was then learned that a lion had escaped from its cage and had chased a number of visitors around the zoo. As a teenager, Uri also telepathically knew that his stepfather had been hospitalized for a medical emergency. He walked to the hospital and went directly to the 4th floor, where his stepfather was being monitored. Uri had found his stepfather without any external notification of the situation or the stepfather's location. He also knew that his stepfather would die.

When his father took Uri on a ride in a half-track military vehicle and they started to ascend a steep embankment, he had a premonition that danger was at hand and Uri insisted that his father get off the embankment. Seconds later, one of the caterpillar treads broke off, which would have made the vehicle overturn if it was still on the embankment. When the Six Day War broke out and Uri was preparing to go into combat, he had the premonition that something would happen to him, such as incurring a wound, yet he also knew that he would not die. This indeed came to pass. When he saw a friend named Avram on top of an armored vehicle, Uri had the premonition that Avram would die in battle, which occur a day or so later.

When Uri Geller conducted demonstrations at the children's camp after the war, telepathy, such as correctly guessing numbers held in the children's minds, was one of the talents he exhibited. As described previously, Uri Geller's telepathic abilities were scientifically verified at the Stanford Research Institute. Tests at SRI included replicating pictures hidden from view. This ability may be considered visual telepathy, though the term remote viewing may also be applied.

Movement, Levitation, and Manipulation of Objects

Home: One of the most common phenomena that Home produced was the movement and levitation of objects, including heavy pieces of furniture. An interesting feature was that objects placed on top of a table, that was levitated and turned horizontally, would remain on the tabletop as if glued. Candle flames would maintain a perpendicular orientation to the rotated tabletop. As such, the flames would appear to defy gravity. Chairs, lamps, and other household objects would move of their own accord, and accordions and pianos would play as if operated by invisible hands. Luminous hands would appear, touch participants or pick up objects, then disappear. Vaporous clouds would appear spontaneously and then be gone. Sir William Crookes observed many of these manifestations under controlled conditions. Due to these phenomena, one observer made the comment regarding Home, "His great featured attraction was the mysterious rapport he had with inanimate objects."[6]

Geller: Under controlled laboratory conditions at King's College, objects were observed moving across the room of their own accord, a compass hand was deviated 40 degrees and a Geiger counter was activated. At Birkbeck College, under controlled conditions, keys were bent, a Geiger counter was activated, and half a vanadium carbide crystal dematerialized. When Uri Geller was at actor Jimmy Stewart's home, a stone carving of a hippopotamus from Stewart's library suddenly materialized outdoors.

At a female friend's home, an Egyptian statuette dated from 1000 B.C. materialized in locked cabinet.

When Uri Geller was in an airplane en route to England, his camera, which was stowed under his seat, spontaneously levitated in front of him. At the home of Dr. Andrija Puharich, in Uri Geller's presence, a heavy grandfather clock dashed across the room of its own accord, much in the style of a Home's manifestation. Geller also describes an ashtray jumping off a table onto the floor and a vase moving in from another room and settling on a table. These manifestations are identical to those produced by Home.

Uri Geller's trademark, of course, is the bending of spoons and other metal objects with his mind. Though metal bending was not reported as one of Home's usual phenomena, a common trait between the manifestations of Home and Geller is the alteration of the usual laws of physics. Home's and Geller's phenomena both involve suspending the law of gravity, movement of objects without an external force applied to them and materialization/dematerialization.

In sum, the comment, "His great featured attraction was the mysterious rapport he had with inanimate objects," could be applied equally well to Home or Geller.

Room Shaking

Home: Home had regular séances for the Napoleon III and the Empress of France. At one of these events, it was noted that the entire room shook. Elizabeth

Browning, the British poetess, also noted that during a séance the room shook as in an earthquake.
Geller: When the grandfather clock spontaneously moved across the room at Dr. Andrija Puharich's home, Uri Geller also noted that the "room rocked."

Levitation/Translocation of Living Beings

Home: Home was observed to levitate at séances on multiple occasions. Sir William Crookes observed two of these episodes. Home's most famous levitation occurred on December 16, 1867, at Ashley House in London, which was owned by the Adare family. Home was levitated horizontally out a window in one room and then floated outside the building over to window of another room, thus reentering the structure. When Home was levitating outside the building, he was approximately 50 feet above the ground. Multiple witnesses were present.

Geller: Standard levitation has not been part of Uri Geller's repertoire, though he appears to have been involved in a more advanced version of this feat. On November 9, 1975, Uri Geller describes an incident in which he was translocated from the East Side of Manhattan to Dr. Andrija Puharich's home in Ossining, New York, almost instantaneously. The distance between Manhattan and Ossining is approximately forty miles. In his autobiography, *My Story*, Geller relates that he was walking down a street in Manhattan, on his way home, when all of a sudden he felt himself being sucked upward. The next thing he knew, he was crashing through the upper panel of a porch screen. Geller landed on a glass table, shattering the glass top. Witnesses had seen Geller in Manhattan shortly before the incident and Puharich was home in Ossining, where he found Uri Geller bruised and stunned.[6] In another incident, Puharich's dog was translocated from the kitchen floor to the driveway outside the house, which occurred in Geller's presence.[7]

Ability to Stimulate Mediumistic Abilities in Others

Home: It was noted that in the presence of Daniel Home, Prince Luigi, the brother of the King of Naples, developed mediumistic abilities himself.

Geller: One of the most remarkable features of Uri Geller's radio interviews, in the 1970s, is that listeners in the thousands reported metal bending occurring in their own homes during Geller's broadcasts. In addition to metal bending, clocks and watches that hadn't run in years spontaneous started working again. The same phenomena occurred when a newspaper article on Uri Geller was published, in which readers were encouraged to bend metal at a designated and synchronized time. This phenomenon of inducing metal bending and clock repair in people's homes also occurred in London, Germany, Denmark, Sweden, Finland, and Japan. In Denmark, a woman who was listening to a Geller broadcast, complained that nothing had happened. Moments later, the metal frame of her glasses curled up on her nose. In an even more impressive demonstration of how psychokinetic abilities could be awakened in others, radio broadcasts led to the to the identification of 15 children who were found to have abilities similar to Geller's. Professor John Taylor then studied these children at King's

College. He found that these children could produce metal bending 80% of the time, a rate similar to Geller's.[8]

Powers Were Perceived to Stem Outside of the Medium/ Variable in Effectiveness

Home: Home repeatedly stated that the powers came from outside of him and that he did not have control over them. At séances, he could not guarantee that phenomenon would manifest and he noted that the strength of the powers could vary. Home was once advised by his spiritual guides or "controllers" that his powers would leave for exactly one year, which is exactly what occurred. It is interesting to note that Home was often as surprised at the phenomena he produced as anyone else. At times, when Home was awakened from a trance after a séance was completed and was told what occurred while he was in trance, he wouldn't believe that the cited phenomena actually took place. The American author Nathaniel Hawthorne wrote of Home that he was "as much perplexed by his own preternatural performances as any other person, he is startled and affrighted at the phenomenon which he produces."[9]

Geller: Uri Geller has repeatedly stated that his powers come from outside of him. Geller has written, "I feel these powers come from far outside me, that I am like a tube that channels them."[10] "Also, I always keep in mind that the forces or energies are not really mine: they are just on loan from the cosmic forces that have been sending them my way."[11] Geller also has noted that the strength of the forces can vary and that he cannot predict when they will be strong or weak. Though Geller has not received verbal instructions from his "controllers" to the same extent as Home did, such instructions have occurred. For example, once in the middle of the night a voice awoke Geller and stated, "Andrija must write a book."[12] As with Daniel Home, Uri Geller is also often shocked by the very phenomenon he produces.

Powers Could Be Mischievous

Home: During one séance that Home was trying to conduct at a table, his own chair, with Home in it, was moved backwards several feet. Home was as surprised as anyone. As he sheepishly moved his chair back to the table, he explained to his guests that the powers were being "mischievous" that evening.

Geller: Uri Geller can relate to the situation described by Home. Geller has written, "It is almost as if these intelligences or energy forces or powers— whatever they are, are clowns out in the Universe. They often do things I don't expect at all."[13] As an example, when Geller being evaluated at Stanford Research Institute, he, Edgar Mitchell, and other researchers were having lunch. As he was eating ice cream, Geller found a miniature metal arrowhead in his mouth. His first reaction was to complain to the management of the restaurant. Later, the tail of the arrow materialized on a floor. Edgar Mitchell then realized that the two pieces together formed an arrow shaped tiepin that he had lost years before.

Powers Can Be Protective

Home: It was noted that at least on one occasion, the powers protected Home from injury. Specifically, Home was levitated away from the path of a falling tree.[14]

Geller: Uri Geller describes several incidents, in which he believes that the intelligences that control his powers, have rescued him from danger or trouble. One of the most striking involves a military exercise. During his army training, Geller was supposed to carry a heavy machine gun on an extended march. Since the exercise did not involve firing the weapon, he removed a heavy, internal part out of the machine gun and left it in his quarters. Unexpectedly, a surprise drill was ordered in which Geller had to fire the gun as quickly as he could set it up. Geller went through the motions of setting up the machine gun knowing that it couldn't fire without the internal mechanism. He anticipated that he would be severely punished for his stunt. When he pulled the trigger, Geller was amazed to find that the gun fired properly. When he returned to his quarters, he found the internal part exactly where he had left it. The only difference was that he had left the part clean, whereas when he returned, the part was dirty and oily, as if it had been used in firing the gun. It thus appears that the part was translocated to the site of the military exercise, then returned to Geller's quarters after firing of the machine gun was completed.[15]

Two other instances of protection are reported in Uri Geller's autobiography. When he was a teenager living in Cypress, Uri got lost in a pitch-black cave.

Right when he gave up hope of getting out alive, his dog, who Uri had left at home several miles away, mysteriously appeared in the cave. Uri's dog then led him out to safety. In another episode, Geller was scuba diving in the Mediterranean. A shark appeared and began circling him. Just as the shark was about to attack, Geller closed his eyes and fired blindly at the shark with a spear gun. When he opened his eyes, the shark had disappeared from sight.

Visions of Holocaust

Home: It is reported that Home would have terrible visions, which made him weep and shudder.[16]

Geller: While in a trance state, Uri Geller wrote a poem called "The Day." The poem is about a time when "the wind grew yellow," "the dust fell," "they opened up the skies," and "I knew the end."[17] Geller interprets the poem to be about a terrible catastrophe that falls upon the Earth. Though he does not understand the poem completely and he admits that his poems are not literary gems, Geller has related, "I feel them deeply."[18]

Sense of Mission and Belief in God

Home: Though Daniel Home did not understand where his abilities came from, he sensed that his demonstration of these powers was extremely important for humanity's future. When they first met, Home told Sacha, his future wife, "Mademoiselle, I trust you will ever bear in mind that I have a mission entrusted to me. It is a great and holy one."[19] Home also consistently expressed a great believe in God. After he performed a psychokinetic feat, Home stated, "Is not God good? Are not his laws wonderful?"[20]

Geller: Uri Geller, who also does not fully understand where his powers comes from, also feels that it is vitally important for him to spread the word regarding these mysterious forces. Geller has written, "One thing I do know for sure is that I feel compelled to demonstrate these phenomenon, not only to make a living, but because I know something important will come out of this, even if I don't know what it is."[21] Geller has also made the following related statement: "I tried to analyze why I was being pushed from inside my mind to communicate with as many people as I could. . . . I am compelled to let people know more, to educate them somehow."[22]

Uri Geller also has frequently expressed his innate belief in God and that world peace is his greatest desire. He has written, "And I believe very much in the power of love and in people everywhere. I also believe completely in God. . . . And I believe very much that we must have peace in this world if we are to survive."[23]

Though is it speculation, I wonder if the apocalyptic visions of Daniel Home and Uri Geller underlie the sense of mission that both men have expressed. It is as if the powers they have demonstrated to humanity will somehow help avert a holocaust, which potentially looms over the horizon. I also wonder if a similar vision was experienced by John of Revelation, which led to the apocalyptic visions contained in the New Testament. Perhaps the visions are not a prediction of what will happen but rather what could happen, if mankind does not evolve past a stage where violence is used for conflict resolution. Perhaps the visions of holocaust, so consistent with the fury of nuclear war, can be averted if we better understood who we are as spiritual beings. This appears to have been the mission of Daniel Home, as well as the continuing mission of Uri Geller. For what it is worth, my own spiritual consultant in the sky, Ahtun Re, concurs with the analysis provided above.

Reverence for Established Religions

Home: Though Home was the most famous physical medium of the 19th century, he maintained a respectful attitude towards organized religion. Home became a Roman Catholic at one point and even had an audience with Pope Pius IX. When Home married Sacha, he converted to the Greek Orthodox Church. After her death, Home returned to Rome to study sculpture. Despite his prior conversion to Catholicism, the Papal Government had him expelled from Rome for sorcery. Home viewed this incident with sadness, as he felt an enlightened church should be interested in his work. The expulsion came with a comical touch. When Home met with Rome's police chief to hear the charges against him, the spirits or powers that worked with him rapped on the police chief's desk in support of Home. Despite the display, Home was still forced to leave.[24]

Geller: Despite being the most famous physical medium of the 20th century, Uri Geller has maintained a respectful attitude towards organized religion. Geller is grounded in his Jewish heritage and had a traditional Jewish wedding when he married Hannah. Recently, Geller has sought and received a blessing from Pope John Paul II. At the time of this writing, the pope's blessing was proudly displayed on Uri Geller's web site, www.urigeller.com.

Personality Traits in Common

Daniel D. Home and Uri Geller share a large number of personality traits in common. One similarity involves the titles of their autobiographies. Home called his book *Incidents in My Life*, while Geller called his *My Story*. The phrases "My Life" and "My Story" are remarkably similar. Regarding career, both Home and Geller have had no professions outside of being physical mediums, a vocation each adapted to quite well. Both Home and Geller have demonstrated qualities of showmen. For example, Home was described as liking an audience, even as a young child. Uri Geller relates that ever since he was a child, he wanted to be a performer or movie star. When he first started doing public demonstrations, Geller found that he thoroughly enjoyed it. He observed that he was a "natural ham."

Both Home and Geller have demonstrated musical and artistic inclinations. Home played the piano with skill, while Geller picked up the piano naturally, learning to play by ear. Home studied sculpture; Geller is a painter and has had exhibitions over the years. Home was considered handsome and he was very much a people person, as he enjoyed meeting and conversing with various people. The same can be said for Uri Geller. Home and Geller also demonstrate similar appetites for travel, as well as geographical preferences. Home was born in Scotland, immigrated to the United States, then gravitated to London as a home base. From there, he traveled widely throughout Europe. Uri Geller was born in Israel, lived for a time in Manhattan, then settled in England, near London. From there, like Home, Geller has traveled widely, demonstrating his skills.

Writing style is also consistent. For purposes of comparison, I have selected a letter that Home wrote to his son, Gricha, as well as two passages from Uri Geller's book, *My Story*. Home's letter was written when he was acting, curiously, as a newspaper correspondent for the *San Francisco Chronicle*, covering the siege of Paris during the Franco-Prussian War. The "voice" of Uri Geller is clearly apparent in this letter written by Daniel Home, at least to my ear and mind. The King in this passage refers to the Prussian King Wilhelm I, who was waging war against Home's old friend, the Emperor of France, Napoleon III. Home's letter is followed by Uri Geller's description of Cypress, as remembered from his boyhood days. In the second passage, Geller is setting the stage for a incident in which he and a group of passengers apparently immobilized a cruise ship, by bending a metal fuel line with their minds. In the passage, Geller calls this a borderline incident, as he is not completely sure that a psychokinetic event caused the pipe the bend. Let us now turn to Daniel Home's letter to his son.

Oct. 25, 1870
My Darling Gricha,

I have not heard a word from you as yet, but I know it is the fault of the post.

The post has been, and is still, delayed by the siege guns being brought to the front. Very terrible work all this is; and I will be right glad to be home again. We had a terrible battle on the 21ˢᵗ. I was in the very midst of it, and aided in bringing home the wounded. It was a fearful sight, and even now seems like some dreadful dream. I will tell you all about it soon.

On the 20ᵗʰ, I went to visit a beautiful chateau some three or four miles distant from Versailles; and while there, the King came and had a long chat with me.

I write on some paper which was taken in Strasburg the day it capitulated. . . . I wish much to see you all, and count the hours when I can be free.[25]

The following passages are from *My Story*, published in 1975, approximately 100 years after Home's wrote his letter to Gricha.

Like any typical boy, I used to go out of my way to find adventure. Cypress is an island, and the sea always fascinated me. The sea around Cypress is beautiful. I fell in love with it. It's so clear, you can drop a coin in water 8 meters deep and see it on the bottom. I learned about snorkeling from a friend at school and became a fanatic. With the water around Cypress so crystal clear, you could see all the beautiful patterns of the sea animals and plants, all of it an exciting new world.[26]

Some incidents are on the borderline. One occurred when two of my closest friends, Byron and Maria Janis, invited me to accompany them on a cruise from Bordeaux

*to Italy on the liner Renaissance. Byron is the
internationally known concert pianist, and his wife,
Maria, who is Gary Cooper's daughter, is a wonderful
artist. It was a musical cruise. Byron was performing
on the piano, and on board were the members of the
Hungarian String Quartet.*[27]

Daniel Home and Uri Geller have a similar writing
style in that both tend to use short sentences, filled
with colorful adjectives such as "beautiful,"
"wonderful," "terrible," and "dreadful." Home and
Geller both like to cite the prestigious credentials of
their friends and associates. In these three passages, a
sense of adventure is conveyed and a quality of boyish
innocence is discerned.

KARMIC CONNECTIONS AND REVELATIONS

In studying Daniel D. Home and Uri Geller, I came
up with hypothesized past life connections between
the associates of Home and the people surrounding
Uri Geller. Ahtun Re has confirmed these matches. I
will not discuss most of these past life connections in
detail, though I will briefly address the one involving
Napoleon III.

Home's first wife, Sacha, has been identified in
contemporary times as Hannah, Uri Geller's wife.
Daniel Home and Sacha had a son name Gricha. In
contemporary times, Gricha is Shipi, Hannah's brother
and Uri Geller's young friend and manager. As such,
a married couple had been rejoined and Sacha's son
has returned to play the role of Sacha's/Hannah's

brother. The reader will recall that Home's mediumistic abilities were enhanced when Home's son, Gricha was present. This phenomenon has recurred, as Uri Geller's abilities of telepathy and metal bending were enhanced when Gricha/Shipi was present. Home's second wife, Julie de Gloumeline, in this lifetime is a woman named Yaffa, who Uri Geller fell in love with just after his involvement in the Six Day War. Though a long-term relationship never evolved between the two, Uri Geller wrote that he would always love Yaffa.

Home was close to an artistic couple named Mr. and Mrs. D. Jarvis. In this lifetime, the Jarvises are Bryron and Maria Janis, the artistic couple mentioned in the cruise ship passage. Uri Geller noted that he resonated with the Jarvises upon their first meeting. Judge John Edmonds was the New York Supreme Court Justice who encouraged Home to continue exhibiting his mediumistic abilities, when Home lived in Connecticut. In this lifetime, Edmonds is Amnon Rubinstein, an Israel law school dean who suggested to Uri Geller that he pursue scientific assessment of his powers.

Another promoter of the scientific investigation of Home's abilities was Russian chemistry professor, Alexander Aksakoff, who eventually introduced Home to Sir William Crookes. In this lifetime, the reincarnated Aksakoff has played a similar role, introducing Uri Geller to the scientists at the Stanford Research Institute. Aksakoff in this lifetime has been identified as Dr. Andrija Puharich. The most eminent scientist to study Home was, of course, Sir William Crookes. Crookes also reincarnated in the 20th century, to study Daniel D. Home/Uri Geller once again. Sir William

Crookes has been identified as the late Professor David Bohm.

Daniel D. Home was especially close to two heads of state. One was Alexander II, the tsar of Russia, who became the godfather of Home's son, Gricha. In contemporary times, Alexander II reincarnated as another head of state, who again became close to Daniel Home/Uri Geller. Alexander II reincarnated as Jose Lopez Portillo, a former President of Mexico. The other head of state that Home was close to was Napoleon III. The reincarnation of Napoleon III involves one of the most intriguing and significant past life matches that we have encountered. Napoleon III has been identified in contemporary times as an Israeli leader that Uri Geller knows and has been photographed with. Napoleon III in this lifetime is Ariel Sharon.

The physical resemblance between Napoleon III and Ariel Sharon is quite striking and personality features are almost identical. Napoleon III, like Ariel Sharon, was a military strongman, who could be perceived by some as a tyrant. He destroyed any adversaries that opposed him. At the same time, Napoleon III cared greatly about his people, particularly the peasants, and he tried to improve their lot. Napoleon III, like Ariel Sharon, was also a supporter of democracy. Because of these characteristics, the populace supported Napoleon III and elected him into power. The balance between democratic reforms and autocratic rule, though, was a delicate one for the Emperor. Napoleon III eventually was exiled from France when the Franco-Prussian War was lost.

When Ahtun Re confirmed the match between Napoleon III and Ariel Sharon, I asked him how did it occur that Napoleon III reincarnated in Israel in contemporary times? What is the karmic logic of Napoleon III becoming a leader of the Israeli people? I also asked why Napoleon III and Ariel Sharon have had such militaristic tendencies over two incarnations. The question may by also be raised of why did Daniel D. Home reincarnate in Israel, in the persona of Uri Geller? I will address the questions regarding Sharon in the paragraphs that follow. The question of why Daniel Home reincarnated in Israel will be discussed in a subsequent chapter. Let us now turn to Ahtun Re's responses regarding Ariel Sharon.

Ahtun Re told me that in the French Court, there was a significant level of anti-Semitism. To remove that prejudice, members of the court chose to incarnate into a Jewish culture. In response to the question of militarism, Ahtun Re stated that Sharon was not always that way. In fact, in prior incarnations, Sharon was more of a pacifist. The turning point occurred in the 13th century, during a lifetime in Asia, in which Sharon was a Taoist. In one of the campaigns of Ghenghis Khan, Ariel Sharon's village was used as a shield to protect Khan's troops. The forces that opposed Ghenghis Khan destroyed the village that Sharon belonged to and everyone in it was killed. It was after that lifetime that Ariel Sharon gave up pacifism and he decided that in the future, he would protect his people, his group, from attack. According to Ahtun Re, this is how Sharon's militarism was born.

Though the lifetime in the era of Ghenghis Khan cannot be objectively confirmed, the lifetime as

Napoleon III appears to be valid. If it is a true past life match, much can be learned from this case of Napoleon III and Ariel Sharon. I have stated repeatedly that we change religious and ethic orientation from lifetime to lifetime. Well, Napoleon III was Christian, while Sharon is a Jew. The advantage of having diverse religions and ethnic groups is that in successive incarnations, we can experience variety in our lives. Life would not be as interesting if we did not have various ways to worship God and live life. Religions and ethnic cultures are indeed beautiful creations, the product of the work of multiple generations. Unfortunately, rather than being creations to enjoy, religions and ethnic cultures have become foci of separation and division.

The mistake we make is that we forget our true nature, that we are souls that reincarnate many times into many different religions and cultures. We forget who we are and then we over identify with one particular religion, one ethnic group, one race, one culture, or one nation. This is the great misunderstanding of humanity, which leads to misguided action, to violence and war. It is a great waste of life.

For the shadow of holocaust to be lifted, we must change our sense of identity from within. We must not think of ourselves as Jews, Muslims, Christians, Taoists, Buddhists, or Hindus. We must think of ourselves as Jews, Muslims, Christians, Taoists, Buddhists, and Hindus, for we have been all of these in lifetimes past. Until we make this shift in identity, there will never be peace, there will only be separation and war. Let us raise humanity to a greater level of maturity, let us make this shift in identity. Only then will the visions of holocaust endured by John of Revelation, Daniel Home, and Uri Geller be dispelled. Only then will they weep no more. It is in our power to do so. In fact, it is a shift in identity that is so simple. Let us shout from our houses and places of worship, from mountaintops and from the valleys, that it will be so. Let us teach our children of this shift in self-awareness. Let us decide to have Peace.

D. D. Home   **Uri Geller**

Courtesy of Uri Geller

Uri Geller   **Daniel Dunglas Home**   **Uri Geller**

D.D. Home was the most famous physical medium of the 19th century, who produced levitation of objects, experienced telepathy and had accurate premonitions, much like Uri Geller. Personalty traits and even the writing style of Home and Geller correspond.

Uri Geller supports this past life match for himself, in which he identified as the reincarnation of D.D. Home

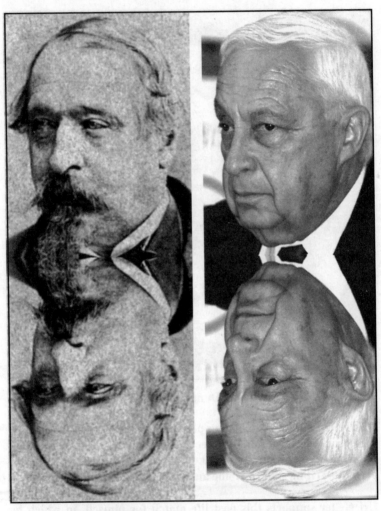

Napoleon III

Ariel Sharon

Napoleon III was very impressed with D.D. Home's physical manifestations and psychic abilities, epecially when qustions that Napoleon posed mentally, not verbally, were answered.

16

The Reincarnation of Nostradamus and Rabelais

"Earthshaking fire from the world's center
Will cause tremors around the New City."

"The sky will burn at 45 degrees
Fire approaches the Great New City
Immediately a huge scattered flame leaps up."

These lines were written by Nostradamus in 1555. When the New York World Trade Center was attacked on September 11, 2001, many interpreted the event as the fulfillment of this prophecy made by Nostradamus almost 500 years ago. What made the prediction seem to fit, in an uncanny way, was the fact that the second suicide plane struck the second tower with wings tilted at a 45 degree angle. Due to this prediction, new interest arose in Nostradamus. I will now assert that Nostradamus is reincarnated, in the persona of veteran professional psychic, Hans Christian King.

I met Hans Christian King on December 7, 2003, when I attended a presentation entitled *Three Mediums*. Hans was, of course, one of the three mediums featured in the program. My plan was to ask each speaker whether they would give permission for me to try to derive a past lifetime for them, through my work with Kevin Ryerson and Ahtun Re. It was my experience that sometimes, when I asked Ahtun Re about a past life match, he will refuse to give me information. Perhaps the case was too sensitive, or perhaps the person in question was not ready to know about a past lifetime. I found, though, that if I received an individual's permission to derive a past lifetime for them beforehand, then it was more likely that Ahtun Re would cooperate.

When I introduced myself to Hans, he greeted me in a warm manner. When I extended my hand to shake his, he grasped my hand with both of his. He struck me as a very loving soul. When I asked if I could ask Ahtun Re for past lifetime for him, one that could identified historically, he immediately agreed to the proposition.

When I inquired about a past incarnation for Hans, Ahtun Re refused to give me any information. I protested, stating that Hans had given me permission, so why wouldn't he give me a past life match. Ahtun Re replied, "We will tell Mr. King directly." Ahtun Re added, "It is an interesting one, though."

I tried to arrange a session for Hans with Kevin Ryerson, as we were all scheduled to be in Las Vegas, in January 2004, over the same weekend. Though logistics for a session didn't work out, we all managed to have dinner together on a Saturday night. I sat Hans and

Kevin together, so that they could talk. I overhead Hans pose the following inquiry to Kevin: "Why won't Ahtun Re give Walter a past lifetime for me?" Kevin replied, "It usually means that there is something important that Spirit wants to tell you directly."

The evening and weekend ended uneventfully. Though I didn't manage to arrange a session for Hans with Kevin, I myself did have a session with Hans, which I will describe below. A week or two later, I was pondering the situation. "Why won't Ahtun Re give me a past lifetime for Hans?" It always struck me as unusual that Hans used a three word name, Hans Christian King. I knew that when people reincarnate, they often choose to use versions of their names that have the same cadence from previous lifetimes, though I wasn't consciously thinking of the correlation of names at the time. I continued pondering the case of Hans Christian King and who he might have been in a past lifetime. I silently repeated the name "Hans Christian King" in my mind and suddenly, the name "Michel de Nostradame" popped into my awareness. I realized that Michel de Nostradame, the real name of Nostradamus, had the same cadence as Hans Christian King.

I quickly checked the Internet for a portrait of Nostradamus and found that there was only one historically accurate portrait of the prophet, which was done by his son, Cesar Nostradame, and that Hans's face matched exactly with the face of Nostradamus. In a subsequent session with Kevin Ryerson, Ahtun Re confirmed that Hans Christian King is the reincarnation of Nostradamus.

When I received this confirmation, I telephoned Aaron Hunt, Hans's Executive Personal Assistant, to tell him of the news. Aaron was pleasantly shocked. I asked Aaron to tell Hans of the match. When Aaron telephoned Hans to inform him of his past life identity, guess what program Hans was watching on television? Hans was watching a program on Nostradamus.

Hans has made a living by giving psychic readings for over 40 years. He has been named one of the top five psychics in America by the Miami Herald, and Hans has been endorsed by Yale trained psychiatrist Brian Weiss, MD, author of *Many Lives, Many Masters*. In performing psychic readings, Hans works with four spirit guides. After he was informed of his past life match with Nostradamus, Hans asked his spirit guides if this was true, that he is the reincarnation of Nostradamus. Hans's guides told him that it was true. Later, when I asked Hans if I could disclose his past life identity as Nostradamus publicly, Hans gave me permission to do so. When I reflected, "People could ridicule you for this," Hans simply replied, "Truth is Truth."

Objective evidence of reincarnation demonstrates that people have the same personality characteristics, and often times the same gifts, from lifetime to lifetime. When I was in Las Vegas in January 2004, prior to the time that I came up with the hypothesis that Hans was Nostradamus, I had a session with Hans. Interestingly, the session was all about my future. I later ordered CDs that Hans produced, which featured sample sessions which he had with various clients. In all these sessions, Hans is observed forecasting the future for his clients.

There is a difference in the public image of Nostradamus, though, and persona of Hans Christian King. Nostradamus, due to his prophecies, is known as the "Prophet of Doom." One the other hand, I perceive Hans as a "Prophet of Light and Love." It is my contention that Nostradamus, who was trained as a medical doctor, a man who risked his life treating victims of the Black Plague in France, was misunderstood. Nostradamus was as much of a humanitarian as is Hans Christian King. His written work, *Les Propheties*, which established him as the "Prophet of Doom," simply overshadowed the man, Michel de Nostradame.

The Hans Christian King/Nostradamus case led to an interesting secondary case. Nostradamus went to medical school with a man named Francois Rabelais. Though trained as a doctor, Rabelais became one of the cleverest writers in French history. He is known for writing a fantasy epic about two giants, Gargantua and Pantagrue. In studying Rabelais, I had the spontaneous intuitive hit that Rabelais has reincarnated in contemporary times as another physician and author, who also has written a fantasy epic involving giants. My hypothesis that Rabelais has reincarnated as Michael Crichton, author of *Jurassic Park*, was subsequently confirmed by Ahtun Re.

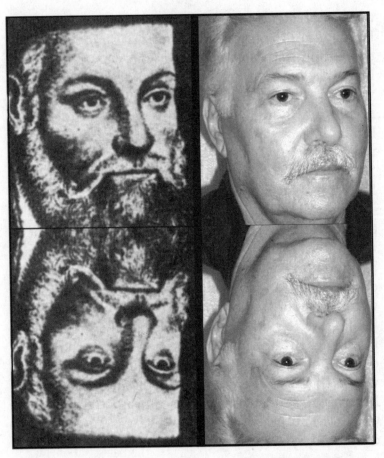

Nostradamus **Hans Christian King**

Hans Christian King has worked as a psychic since he was 19, his readings deal with the future and he has been rated as one of the top five psychics in America.

Mr. King supports the premise that he is the reincarnation of Nostradamus

17

The Reincarnation of
Laurel and Hardy

As mention in previous chapters, after working with Kevin Ryerson for a period of a few months in late 2001 and early 2002, I realized that Ahtun Re, the spirit guide that he channels, was able to make what appeared to be accurate past life matches. At this point, I began asking about celebrities across time. For contemporary figures I asked about past lives, for historical figures, I inquired whether they had reincarnated in contemporary times.

One pair I had asked about early on was Laurel and Hardy, one of the most famous and loved comedy teams in history. I, in particular, was a great admirer of the duo and always loved their movies. Further, I was quite sentimental regarding Laurel and Hardy was because they would make my father laugh. My father was a kind, generous and loving man, but he endured various medical problems throughout his life, and a melancholy and serious mood prevailed over him. This would change, though, when we watched Laurel and Hardy movies. It was so wonderful to hear my father laugh out loud.

Starting in 2003 or so, I asked Ahtun Re whether Laurel and Hardy had reincarnated in contemporary times. Ahtun Re told me that they had, but he would not reveal to me who they were, which peeved me. When I inquired why he could not divulge their identities to me. Ahtun Re simply replied, "We cannot tell you at this time." Over the next year, I tried to circumvent his decree by hypothesizing matches. I would inquire whether various slim contemporary comedians may be the reincarnation of Stan Laurel and whether various chubby comedians may be Oliver Hardy reincarnated. To all my hypothesized matches, Ahtun Re would tell me that the proposed match was incorrect and he still refused to tell me who Laurel and Hardy were in contemporary times. Having exhausted all the possibilities for matches that I could think of, I gave up and forgot about the issue for about a year.

At this juncture, I would like to point out that one of the reasons I have grown to trust Ahtun Re's ability to make matches is that he does not "rubber stamp" proposed past life matches. To the contrary, most matches that people propose, when I ask about them, are deemed inaccurate by Ahtun Re. When I myself try to derive a past life match, many times Ahtun Re will tell me that I am inaccurate, but when the true match is found and then confirmed by Ahtun Re, it uniformly turns out to be a very compelling case.

For example, I have a deep affinity for the composer Chopin and I was trying to derive his identity in contemporary times. I made several hypothesized matches and Ahtun Re dismissed them all. When I finally made the correct match, confirmed by Ahtun Re, it made enormous sense and the facial features matched more precisely than in any of the previously hypothesized matches. Further, at times, when contact can be made with the person who is the subject of the match, this individual would validate the match independently. In other words, the confirmed match would relate that they already knew that he or she is the reincarnation of the person in question; either though direct memories or other means. It is my experience with Ahtun Re over a period of five years, 70 sessions and a database of over a thousand reincarnation cases that gives me perspective on his ability to make accurate past life matches.

Let us now return to the case of Laurel and Hardy. As Ahtun Re would not reveal the contemporary identities of Stan and Ollie and he refuted my numerous hypotheses regarding their contemporary identities, I gave up on making these past life matches. A year or two passed when I my interest was suddenly rekindled by seeing an old cover of *Rolling Stone* magazine, brought into our medical clinic by our nurse, which had on it a small headline on it, "Best New Comedy Team." This nurse had always been very interested in the reincarnation research I have had been doing and she has, in the past, served as a "scout" for me, finding reincarnation cases in the media, etc., which I would later pursue. She didn't know anything, though, about my interest in Laurel and Hardy. I couldn't find anything in the magazine about a new comedy team, but I had the very, very strong intuition that I would search the Internet for new comedy teams. As described in previous chapters, intuitive guidance has served me well in establishing past life matches.

This occurred in November 2005 and when I searched the Internet, I found an web site advertising a show entitled, ***The Funniest Show in the World About the History of***

Comedy, Performed by Two Brothers, in Less Than Two Hours, For Under Twenty Bucks, which would be performed in January 2006 in New York City. I saw a picture of the two brothers, Josh and Danny Bacher, and a broad smile appeared on my face. Not only were these two brothers naturally funny looking, they were funny looking like Laurel and Hardy were funny looking. I intuitively and deeply knew that I had found them. Josh, the older brother, was the skinny Stan Laurel character and Danny was the slightly chubby Oliver Hardy. In fact, the only major difference in appearance between Stan and Ollie and Josh and Danny is that Oliver Hardy was much heavier than Danny is.

In my next session with Kevin Ryerson, after refuting all the previous proposed matches that I had made for Laurel and Hardy, Ahtun Re confirmed that Josh and Danny Bacher are the reincarnated comedy team of Stan Laurel and Oliver Hardy. Stan Laurel was born in 1890, in Ulverston, England, while Oliver Hardy was born in Harlem, Georgia, in the United States. Stan worked as a comedian in Glasgow and eventually came to the US, where he joined a touring group that included Charlie Chaplin, which led him to Los Angeles. Oliver started performing as a boy in a minstrel show and as an adult, migrated to California and signed with the producer, Hal Roach. Leo McCarey, a director working for Roach, wanted to create a comedy team for film shorts made up of a skinny guy with a fat guy. McCarey brought Stan Laurel and Oliver Hardy together for the project and the comedy team that would last over 20 years was born.

With the belief that I had found the reincarnation of Laurel and Hardy as two brothers, I wondered at the mechanism of how reincarnation and life works. If the cases of Stan and Ollie/Josh and Danny are valid, then a comedy team that came together from across the Atlantic Ocean in 1926 was now reunited as two brothers, who were performing comedy once again, in New York City, 80 years later.

I called the *Theater for the New City,* where the Josh and Danny would be performing, and purchased tickets for their show. I also asked that the Bacher Boys, as they are known, contact me, indicating that I could make some connections for them in Hollywood. Danny Bacher contacted me within a couple days. After discussing ways I could possibly help them in their careers, I told Danny about my book and then carefully explained to Danny the principles of reincarnation that were emerging from independently researched cases, and of the work that I was doing with Kevin Ryerson. I asked Danny if he had any particular spiritual leanings and he replied, "We were raised Jewish." I could tell that Danny was starting to wonder where this was going and what all this had to do with their comedy work. I then delicately blurted out, "You and Josh have been confirmed to be the reincarnation of Laurel and Hardy by Ahtun Re, the Egyptian spirit guide channeled through Kevin Ryerson."

After a moment, Danny replied, "I don't know about this reincarnation stuff, but what you say is very interesting because by far, the biggest influences on our lives, in terms of our comedic development, have been Laurel and Hardy." Following our conversation, I sent Josh and Danny a copy of my book and a videotape of Barbro Karlen telling her story of being the reincarnation of Anne Frank, which for me, is one of the most compelling of past life cases. I made plans to attend their show in New York because one, I wanted to meet the reincarnation of Laurel and Hardy, and two, I wanted to see if Josh and Danny could make people laugh like Laurel and Hardy did.

I then worked on arranging a reincarnation presentation while in New York, as a way to maximize the usefulness of my trip to the East Coast. I had recently spoken at the New Life Expo in New York City in October 2005, where I was approached by Harriet Wagniere, the Director of the Metaphysical Center of New Jersey, who asked if I would consider speaking at their center in Wayne, New Jersey, in the future. At the time, I told her that I would love to, but I had no idea of when I would be back in the area, since I lived in California. Now, since I would be in New York to see the Bacher Boys, I called Harriet to see if I could speak at their center on that same weekend in January 2006. Though I had told Danny that I would keep the Laurel and Hardy match quiet until the brothers had time to digest it, I couldn't resist sharing the secret with Harriet. I told her that I was coming to New York to see the reincarnation of Laurel and Hardy. Harriet was surprised and asked, "Can I know who they are."

After a fleeting moment of attempting to keep the matches confidential, I advised Harriet that I would tell her only if she would not divulge the matches to anyone. Harriet agreed and so I let out the secret identities of the reincarnated Laurel and Hardy. Harriet then exclaimed, "I know Josh and Danny Bacher, I used to teach high school in Wayne and they were my students!" When Harriet said that, I was a bit flabbergasted at the coincidence, yet at the same time, I have come to expect synchronistic events to occur as part of the reincarnation research project. In the end, this opportune coincidence resulted in the Metaphysical Center of New Jersey hosting my presentation at a venue in Wayne, New Jersey, located five minutes from where the parents of Josh and Danny live.

I saw Josh and Danny perform on January 14, 2006 and I found myself laughing out loud, much as I had laughed at the antics of Stan and Ollie. Though they are of a different generation, they are just as funny and they relate to each other just as did Stan and Ollie. Josh, the skinny brother, plays the role of the innocent, sometimes confused one, who can break down whimpering when a plan goes wrong, while Danny, the slightly chubby brother, plays the role of the more sophisticated, intelligent and worldly one, who inevitably gets tripped up by Josh's antics.

What was the highlight for me in their show was a silent movie that Josh and Danny created for their performance. It was as humorous as any silent movie that Hal Roach ever created, filled with slapstick, a gorilla on the loose, a Keystone cop and a blind girl who evokes empathy and at the same time, accidentally gives Danny a wicked whack to his private parts with her white cane. In that silent film, and indeed, in the entire show, Josh and Danny, reenacted the comedic development of Laurel and Hardy, much as Peter Teekamp replicated the artistic development of Paul Gauguin and Alexandra Nechita, at a very young age, replicated the work of Picasso. Reflect on the fact that not many modern day comics create a 1920's style slapstick silent movie as part of their act. I myself had never seen a modern day silent movie, until I saw the one that Josh and Danny created.

I was honored to have Josh and Danny, as well as their parents, Joel and Jane, attend my presentation on reincarnation research the following day, in Wayne, New Jersey. One can view the bringing of us together by Harriet Wagniere as a coincidence, but it also can be perceived as the work of spiritual guidance. Recall the case of Captain Robert Snow and how he was brought to New Orleans by his wife, where he found the portrait of the hunchback woman, as well as his past lifetime as Carroll Beckwith. Though Captain Snow's wife and Harriet Wagneire may not have had a telepathic voice tell them what to do, intuitions and desires can be just as effective in coordinating events.

Though the Bacher Boys and their parents do not claim that Josh and Danny are the reincarnation of Laurel and Hardy, they do note very intriguing correspondences. Josh was born on August 22, 1976, eleven years after Stan Laurel died. When Josh was born, he was given a set of Laurel and Hardy dolls by his cousin Sally. Sally and Jane Bacher, Josh's mom, are close friends and they themselves formed a Laurel and Hardy type pair, as observed by Sally's husband. Joel and Jane Bacher relate that their son, Josh, loved the Laurel and Hardy dolls and they became his very favorite toys.

Danny was born on January 15, 1978, about twenty years after Oliver Hardy died. Over the preceding years, Josh had played with the Laurel and Hardy dolls so intensely that when Danny was born, only the rubber heads still survived. Throughout their childhoods, Josh and Danny continued to play with the Stan and Ollie heads and they still have them, 29 years later.

Josh and Danny would often imitate Laurel and Hardy; Josh was always Stan and Dan was always Ollie. Danny would draw Oliver like mustaches on his toys and he himself would wear an Ollie mustache made out of black felt, which he would affix to his upper lip with transparent tape. While Danny wore his Ollie mustache, Josh would imitate Stanley, scratching the top of his head.

Josh and Danny acted like Stan and Ollie whenever they could and Joel and Jane Bacher reflect that it was challenging, though entertaining, going out into the world, doing shopping and chores, along with little Laurel and Hardy. (Hopefully not too much property, such as pianos and automobiles, were destroyed in the process.) Further, Mr. Bacher, a trial attorney, relates that at their birthdays, the boys would insist on showing Laurel and Hardy silent films, which were borrowed from the local library. As they grew up, Josh and Danny would develop comedy routines based on Laurel and Hardy, as well as other comedians old and new, which has culminated in their recent January 2006, New York, Off-Broadway debut.

Though the Bachers do not assert that Josh and Danny are the reincarnation of Stan Laurel and Oliver Hardy, they find it plausible. For me, Josh and Danny Bacher represent affinity cases, where individuals are drawn to their own past life personas. As noted, one of the most dramatic affinity cases is that of Halle Berry, who has been identified as the reincarnation of her own heroine, Dorothy Dandridge. Halle has fulfilled Dorothy's dream of winning an Oscar and she passionately continues performing in her acting career.

In the same way, in my assessment, Stan Laurel and Oliver Hardy have reincarnated as Josh and Danny Bacher. Their self proclaimed mission, as related by Joel Bacher, is to: "Bring joy and laughter to a world in need of a good laugh." Stan and Ollie, I joyously proclaim, "Welcome back." I sincerely hope that your comedic dreams will come true and that in the future, in your twilight years, you will reflect on your lives and acknowledge that you have, once again, created "another fine mess."

Josh (left) and Danny (right) Bacher have been identified as the reincarnation of Stan Laurel (middle left) and Oliver Hardy (middle right). As such, the comedy duo of Laurel and Hardy have reincarnated as two brothers.

As children, Josh and Danny imitated Stan and Ollie whenever they could, with Danny affixing an "Ollie" mustache to his upper lip.

As adults, Josh and Danny have become a comedy team and in their Off Broadway debut, they replicated the comedic development of Stan and Ollie, even creating their own silent movie.

Josh and Danny's parents find the proposition that they are the reincarnation of Laurel and Hardy plausible.

Stan Laurel   **Josh Bacher**   **Danny Bacher**   **Oliver Hardy**

Laurel and Hardy, © Bettmann/CORBIS

Josh and Danny Bacher : Courtesy of Josh and Danny Bacher

Born Again

SECTION THREE

Reincarnation Cases Involving Political Legends of India and Film Stars

Note to the Reader:
The cases presented in this section were derived through the work of Walter Semkiw, MD, trance medium Kevin Ryerson and the spirit guide that Kevin channels, named Ahtun Re, who has demonstrated an ability to make what appear to be accurate past life matches.
To learn more about this process please refer to Chapters 10-17

18

President APJ Abdul Kalam as the Reincarnation of Tipu Sultan, Vikram Sarabhai as Haider Ali Reborn and the Missile Men of India

APJ Abdul Kalam is considered a father of the Indian missile program and as such, he is often referred to as the "Missile Man." The father of the Indian space program is Vikram Sarabhai and, in tribute, the Indian Space Research Organization's largest facility is called the Vikram Sarabhai Space Center. Let us learn about these two leaders of Indian rocket research.

APJ Abdul Kalam grew up in the Madras island municipality of Rameswaram in the South of India. As a boy, he and his best friend, Jallaludin, would take walks at the close of the day, discussing God and spiritual matters. Though Abdul was raised a Muslim,

he and Jallaludin would visit the Hindu temple of
Lord Shiva. As a ritual, they walked around the temple
in reverence and as they did, Jallaludin and Abdul
"felt a flow of energy" pass through them.[1] Later in
life, when visiting the Sivananda Ashram near the
Ganges river, Abdul described "feeling intense
vibrations" when he entered the ashram.[2] In another
episode, Kalam described a scene in which his father
arranged for a ceremony at a mosque to celebrate an
advancement in his career: "I could feel the power of
God flowing in a circuit through my father to me and
back to God; we were all under the spell of the
prayer."[3]

A sense of the spiritual has never left APJ Kalam
and he has never seen science and spirituality as
conflicting interests. Indeed, Kalam has stated that
for him, "science has always been the path to spiritual
enrichment and self-realization." [4] Further, the fire of
Shiva, the transformer, seems to flow through his veins.
Fire is prominent in the writings of APJ Abdul Kalam.
His autobiography is entitled, *Wings of Fire*, and
another book he has written is called, *Ignited Minds*,
which refers to the children of India and the potential
they have to make India a more sophisticated and
developed nation.

As a boy, Abdul dreamed to fly, and like Leonardo
da Vinci, he studied the flight of birds. Later in life,
as a young man, Abdul entered the Madras Institute
for Technology (MIT) to become an engineer. Here
too, he noted a fascination for flying machines. In his
autobiography, he describes his admiration for aircraft
and their systems that were on display at MIT. He
writes, "I felt a strange attraction towards them, and

would sit near them long after other students had gone back to their hostel, admiring man's will to fly free in the sky, like a bird."[5] Indeed, Kalam's greatest ambition and desire at the time was to become an officer in the Indian Air Force. Kalam went through the application process and it was a terrible disappointment to him when he was rejected by the Air Force Selection Board, just missing the cutoff for becoming a flyer.

Though his dream of becoming a pilot was thwarted, APJ Abdul Kalam took a post with the Ministry of Defense, where he became a Senior Scientific Assistant for the Directorate of Technical Development and Production (DTD&P). Kalam would not be flying aircraft, but he would be involved in designing them. In one project, Kalam lead a team that developed a battlefield hovercraft and Abdul indeed flew in this devise, though only a few inches off the ground. His next developmental step involved an interview with Professor Vikram Sarabhai, as the Indian Committee for Space Research was interested in hiring Kalam for the post of "Rocket Engineer."

An immediate rapport developed between Kalam and Sarabhai. Kalam was impressed with Sarabhai's warmth, perceptive nature, contagious optimism and vision. Sarabhai, Kalam observed over time, was an innovator, experimenter and leader who inspired the people under him by demonstrating faith and trust that they would succeed. Rather than giving directions, Sarabhai encouraged the exchange of ideas which led to a collective solution to a problem. The tone in which Kalam writes of Vikram Sarabhai reveals that over the years, Abdul developed a deep love and admiration for Sarabhai, much more so than with any other professional colleague. He was deeply saddened when Vikram Sarabhai suddenly and unexpectedly died of a myocardial infraction at the age of 52, at the prime of his career. Kalam later referred to Vikram Sarabhai as the Mahatma Gandhi of Indian Science.

In addition to his fascination with flight, APJ Abdul Kalam has maintained an ardent passion for India to become self sufficient and that societal advancements be made through the development of indigenous technology, not from technology imported from the Western world. Indeed, one of his most treasured experiences derives from a Western power's acknowledgement of India's pioneering contributions to the field of missile technology. The setting for this experience is NASA's Wallops Flight Facility, in Maryland. As a leading engineer in India's missile program, Kalam had been invited by NASA to participate in a six month training program on rocket launching techniques.

At the Wallops center, Kalam observed a painting that was hung in the reception lobby, depicting a battle scene in which rockets are being launched against oncoming troops. Curiously, the soldiers launching the rockets were all dark skinned, while the targets of the rockets were white skinned troops in what appeared to be British uniforms. Kalam took a closer look and realized that the painting was of a battle between Tipu Sultan's army and colonial British troops on Indian soil. Tipu Sultan is considered, along with his father, Haider Ali, as a pioneer of rocket development. Kalam was quite amazed that an Indian was being honored at a NASA facility, while back home, most of his fellow Indians had forgotten about Tipu Sultan.

Though the Chinese were the first to invent rockets, which they used for ceremonial purposes, it was Haider Ali and Tipu Sultan who are accredited with developing rockets for military purposes. The innovation that made the rockets used by Haider Ali and Tipu Sultan more effective was the use of iron casings, which allowed the attainment of greater chamber pressures and accordingly, greater range. Some of these rockets could fly 1000 yards. The base of the rocket consisted of an iron tube that was eight inches long and 2-3 inches in diameter. The warhead of the rocket consisted of a bamboo shaft four feet in length, though the design was altered for specific purposes and effects. For example, some of Haider Ali's rockets had pierced metal cylinders which would emit sparks as the rocket flew, which would set fire to objects along its path. Two of Tipu Sultan's rockets on display at the Woolwich Museum Artillery in London have sword blades as warheads. Tipu Sultan also developed wheeled rocket organs which could fire multiple rockets simultaneously. It is estimated that the army of Tipu Sultan had 27 brigades, which were called Kushoons. A company of 200 rocket men, called Jourks were assigned to each brigade. Tipu Sultan authored a military manual, entitled *Fathul Mujahidin*, in which the structure and functions of his military units were delineated.

We have seen in independently researched reincarnation cases, such as in the cases of Paul Gauguin/Peter Teekamp, Alexandra Nechita/Pablo Picasso and Francesco Foscari/Wayne Peterson, how

interests, passions and talents can extend across
lifetimes. We now observe this phenomenon in the
case of APJ Abdul Kalam, for in my work with Kevin
Ryerson, Ahtun Re, the Egyptian spirit guide who has
demonstrated an ability to make accurate past life
matches, has confirmed that Kalam is the reincarnation
of Tipu Sultan. Ahtun Re has also confirmed that APJ
Kalam's great mentor, Vikram Sarabhai, is the
reincarnation of Haider Ali, the father of Tipu Sultan.
As father and son, Haider Ali and Tipu Sultan built
the Indian nation of Mysore, while as mentor and
student, Vikram Sarahai and APJ Abdul Kalam built
the Indian space and missile program, greatly
enhancing India's stature among the world's nations.
Indeed, APJ Kalam credits India's space and missile
program as India's ticket into the league of world
superpowers.

Let us learn more about Haider Ali and Tipu Sultan,
who ruled the region called Mysore for a period of 38
years.

Mysore is a district in South India 140 kilometers
from Bangalore. Haider Ali was born around 1722.
Sources differ slightly regarding his exact year of birth.
Haider Ali's father was Fateh Mohammad and he had
a brother, Shabiz, who became a soldier in the Mysore
army. Haider Ali joined his brother on a campaign
and distinguished himself in military service. He also
demonstrated an interest in military engineering,
visiting French troops in Pondicherry, where he
admired the skill of the French engineering officers.
Haider Ali was noted to have "a most retentive
memory" and "keen penetration."[6]

Due to his military skills, in 1755, Haider Ali was appointed as military commander of Budikot, in Mysore. Haider Ali demonstrated significant organizational skills. He realized that the colonial powers of England and France had developed efficient systems of military command and he organized his own army in a similar way. Haider Ali even manufactured military equipment based on English and French weaponry. Eventually, the entire Mysore army was placed under his command in 1757. When Haider Ali defeated an invading force of Marathas, a rival Hindu group of people, the Hindu Maharaja of Mysore gave him the title of Fateh Bahadur. Haider Ali was made Chief Minister of Mysore in 1761 and when the Maharaja died in 1766, Haider Ali himself became the ruler of Mysore.

In this capacity, Haider Ali proved to be a great administrator. It was documented that he had the "faculty of giving his attention to several subjects at the same time, so that he could hear a letter read, dictate orders, and witness a theatrical exhibition all at once, without being distracted by any one of these occupations."[7] During his reign, Haider Ali improved the infrastructure of Mysore, building roads and gardens. The fortifications of Bangalore and Seringapatam were constructed by Ali. He was tolerant to other faiths. Haider Ali was also diplomatic with people and it was noted that he did not generate personal enemies.

Unfortunately, military campaigns continued through out his period of rule. The First Mysore War was started in 1767 when the British formed an alliance with the Marathas, who controlled northern and central

India, and the Nizam of Hyderabad. Nizam was the name of the ruler of a dynasty, which maintained Hyderbad as its capital. Haider Ali controlled the Madras territory and southern India. Despite this alliance made up of the British, the Marathas and the Nizam, Haider Ali was able to defeat the British led forces. In the peace treaty that followed, the British were required to assist Haider Ali if Mysore was attacked by other powers.

When the Marathas again attacked Mysore in 1771, the British reneged on their promise and refused to assist Haider Ali. This caused Ali to make an alliance with the French. The Second Mysore War started in 1780 when the British planned to attack French troops in the region and Haider Ali refused to assist the British. The English then made an alliance, once again, with the Marathas and Nizam of Hyderbad and declared war on Haider Ali and Mysore. In the Second Anglo-Mysore war, at the Battle of Pollilur (September 10, 1780), Haider Ali and Tipu Sultan achieved a grand victory. One factor that helped them in their win was that one of the British ammunition carts was set on fire by Mysorean rockets.

Haider Ali led 80,000 men and 100 guns on campaign and in October 1780, he scored a victory in capturing Arcot. In 1781, though, he was defeated near Madras. It is reported that Haider Ali developed a suppurative tumor of the back, which led to his death at this camp outside Chittur, on December 7, 1172, in the midst of this campaign. When he received the news of his father's death, Tipu Sultan marched to Chittur with 90,000 troops and took command of the Mysore army. Tipu Sultan then moved on to the British held fort at the seaport of Mangalore and with the help of French engineers, began a siege. The battle coincided, though, with the time that the British and French came to a peace accord, following the American Revolutionary War. The French engineers who were helping Tipu Sultan were thus bound to withdraw their assistance. Tipu Sultan, indignant at the withdrawal of the French, was forced to convert the siege into a blockage. Tipu eventually secured victory over the British in 1783, winning the Second Mysore War. Through the treaty that was signed in January 1784, the territory that Tipu Sultan now controlled was vastly expanded.

Let us now review the life of Tipu Sultan. He was born on December 10, 1750 at Devanhalli. Tipu was trained as a military leader from his boyhood years and starting at the age of 15, he would join his father on military campaigns. Tipu Sultan loved to learn and had a library of 2000 books. In particular, Tipu studied maths and science. He was described as very dynamic.

After his father died, Tipu Sultan took control of Mysore and he was considered a benevolent and enlightened ruler. He worked dynamically to advance the welfare of his people. For example, to promote agriculture, Tipu Sultan constructed dams and tanks to water crops, as well as roads to transport goods to the market. Tipu Sultan created industries, building factories in Cutch, Masquat, and Jedda. He encouraged commerce with neighboring countries, such as Oman, Persia and Turkey. Tipu built forts and palaces. A Muslim, Tipu forbade liquor in Mysore, but he treated his non-Muslim subjects well. He invited foreign know-how to build factories to produce glass, mirrors and ship-building. He aimed at making his kingdom the most prosperous state of India. Tipu Sultan also sought information on the latest scientific developments from around the world.

Tipu Sultan was a great supporter of the independence of his nation from colonial powers and in this light, was wary of the British East India Company's plans to expand its influence across India. In order to strengthen his position against the British, Tipu made alliances with the French, Sultan of Turkey and the Amir of Afghanistan. In 1787, Tipu even sent a delegation to Paris, which met with Louis XVI, in an effort to strengthen his alliance with the French.

The British, aware of Tipu Sultan's growing power, after making alliances once again with the Nizam of Hyderabad and Marathas, started the Third Mysore War in 1790. In January 1791, Lord Cornwallis took command of the British troops at Vellore, determined to undertake the siege of Bangalore. When Cornwallis moved through the Mugli Pass, they were attacked by Tipu Sultan's rocket men.[8]

In reflection, perhaps the painting displayed in the lobby of the NASA Wallops Flight Facility, in Maryland, which gave APJ Abdul Kalam such a feeling of validation, was stirring an unconscious memory or knowing in Kalam, that it was a battle that he once led. If APJ Kalam is indeed the reincarnation of Tipu Sultan, at Wallops, he received recognition of his own contributions to rocket technology, made over 200 years ago.

In the end, though, Tipu Sultan was defeated in the Third Mysore War. In a treaty signed in

Seringapatam, his capital city, on March 22, 1792, Tipu Sultan had to give up half his kingdom and pay damages to the British and their allies of 33 million rupees.

After his defeat in 1792, Tipu Sultan rebuilt his military with the assistance of the French. The British considered this a violation of the treaty of Seringapatam, which led to their attack on Mysore in 1798, which signaled the start of the Fourth Mysore War. Tipu was eventually cornered in his capital, Seringapatam. Once again, Tipu Sultan's rocket men were involved in the battle. Tipu tried to evade capture by riding through the combat zone on his horse, but took a gun shot to the breast. He incurred a second wound in the right side as his horse fell from under him. Tipu Sultan's attendants picked him up and implored him to surrender to British officers, knowing that he would be spared. Tipu Sultan refused. One British soldier tried to grasp Tipu's jewel encrusted sword belt. Tipu, though himself wounded, struck out with his sword and cut a gash in the soldier's knee. In retaliation, the British soldier pulled out his musket and shot Tipu Sultan in the head, which caused instant death. This occurred in May 1799. Tipu Sultan later was entombed in the "Gumbaz," a mausoleum which he himself built, where he rests with Haider Ali and his mother, Fatima Begum.

In a moment, we will observe how character traits have remained consistent in the cases of Vikram Sarabhai and APJ Abdul Kalam. First, I would like to just comment that other karmic ties have also been renewed in contemporary times and that many of the engineers and scientists that Sarabhai and Kalam worked with in developing missile technology were also with them in the era of Haider Ali and Tipu Sultan, as confirmed by Kevin Ryerson's spirit guide, Ahtun Re. For example, it is thought that Haider Ali's minister Muhamed Sadik reincarnated as Brahm Prakash, the first Director of the Vikram Sarabhai Space Center. Even the great rocket scientist, Werner Von Baun, was with Tipu Sultan, perhaps in the persona of Sultan's trusted commander, Burhan-ud-din.

Let us now review personality traits that Vikram Sarabhai and Haider Ali have in common.

- Colorful Clothing-Haider Ali was fond of bright colored clothes, as was Vikram Sarabhai, who wore loud colored shirts.

- Talent in Administration-As described above, Haider Ali had a powerful memory and keen perception. He was able to multitask easily in performing the duties required to run his domain. Vikram Sarabhai was also a gifted manager, who not only ran India's space program, but at the same time directed operations of his family's pharmaceutical, chemical, glass, agricultural and engineering companies. Like Haider Ali, Vikram Sarabhai was frequently observed multitasking, running industrial operations, while mentoring students at the same time.

- Resourcefulness-Haider Ali was a very resourceful military commander, finding opportunities in a creative manner. Abdul Kalam has also that noted Vikram Sarabhai was a resourceful, at times unconventional manager, who successfully ran India's space program that was lacking sufficient funds and staff.

- Replicated Foreign Military Equipment-Haider Ali was reported to copy French and English military equipment. Vikram Sarabhai obtained a Russian RATO motor, used to assist jets in taking off in adverse conditions, which was used to engineer an Indian RATO motor. Abdul Kalam participated in this effort.

- Accessible-Haider Ali was said "to be accessible to all and to have conversed with great readiness."[9] Vikram Sarabhai was also reported to look upon all men as equals. It was noted that even a servant could approach him freely and converse with him in an open manner.

Let us now review common features in the personalities of Tipu Sultan and APJ Abdul Kalam.

- Simple habits-Tipu Sultan ate common food and slept on coarse canvas. Abdul Kalam has maintained simple quarters and has, at times, refused to accept more privileged living quarters, when offered to him, such as when he was leading the Satellite Launch Vehicle 3 team in Thumba.

- Casual Dress-Tipu Sultan preferred very simple dress, in contrast to his father, who liked colorful dress. Abdul Kalam has always preferred casual dress and when invited to meet Prime Minister Indira Gandhi after the first successful launch of an Indian Satellite Launch Vehicle, he only had casual dress and slippers for the meeting.

- Abstinence-Tipu Sultan maintained abstinence from alcohol, for himself and his domain. It has been described that Tipu Sultan was not swayed by women. Abdul Kalam abstains from alcohol, is a vegetarian and has practiced celibacy.

- Poetry-Tipu Sultan was known as a decent poet. Abdul Kalam likes to write poetry and his verses are found in his biography, *Wings of Fire*. Abdul Kalam also has published poetry books entitled, *My Journey* and *The Life Tree*.
- Spiritual Scientists-Tipu Sultan enjoyed religious books, yet he was also greatly interested in the latest scientific discoveries and inventions. Abdul Kalam is a scholar of several holy texts and is even familiar with the clairvoyant philosopher Rudolf Steiner, who is well known for advocating the development of a spiritual science
- Innovation-Tipu Sultan was known to have a "rage" for innovations. Tipu created new measures, a new calendar, coinage and a manual on military matters. Tipu created a shipbuilding facility and as part of this project, he developed a new non-magnetic alloy for shipbuilding. Abdul Kalam has also demonstrated an interest in material science and has admitted a fascination with composites, which can be seen as akin to alloys. A very specific parallel involves Tipu Sultan's development of wheeled rocket organs which could fire multiple rockets simultaneously. In his book, *Ignited Minds*, Abdul Kalam notes with some pride that India has produced a modern multi-barrel rocket

launcher called the Pinaka. Like Tipu Sultan, Abdul Kalam is an acknowledged innovator.

- Daring-Tipu Sultan often said, "It is better to live one day like a lion than a hundred years like a sheep". Abdul Kalam has stated, "I prefer a dash of daring and persistence to perfection."
- Hardworking-It has been said that Tipu Sultan worked from dawn to midnight for the welfare of his subjects. Abdul Kalam is known to work 18 hour days and is an admitted workaholic.
- Dedication to the Advancement of Country-Tipu Sultan worked effortlessly to advance his realm in terms of technological advancement and economic development. He even came to call himself, "Citizen Tipu Sultan", to reflect his social consciousness. Abdul Kalam has similarly striven to make India a developed, prosperous nation and a world power, as outlined in his book, *India 2020, A Vision for the New Millennium.*
- Pride of Indigenous Achievement and Independence-Tipu Sultan greatly resented the British presence in India and strove to push the British and the East India Company out of the region. Tipu made alliances with France in this effort, though he was disappointed by the French when they pulled out of combat when a peace treaty with Britain had been signed. Abdul Kalam is an ardent supporter of indigenous production of needed technology and products, in large part due to Kalam's understanding that dependence on foreign technology and products leads the nation of India to be vulnerable. Kalam, by the way, was

involved in a missile project with the French which ended when, similarly, the French suddenly pulled out. It is almost as if Abdul Kalam brought with him the experiences of Tipu Sultan, which resulted in his insistence of India being independent, not only politically, but technologically.

Of course, the trait that Tipu Sultan and Abdul Kalam have in common, that is most striking, is their mutual fascination with rocketry. As indicated in his experience at Wallops, APJ Abul Kalam has shown great interest in Tipu Sultan. On a recent visit to Bangalore in 1991, Kalam expressed a desire to visit Tipu Sultan's court in Srirangapatna. It was also noted that Kalam wistfully related that Tipu Sultan's legacy as a pioneer of rocketry has largely been forgotten, even in Tipu Sultan's own region, though a "Tipu Sultan Shaheed Memorial Lecture" is regularly held in Bangalore. Abdul Kalam, ironically, was the speaker at this forum in November 30, 1991. Kalam has also visited the Woolridge Artillery Museum near London and related that he felt thrilled when he saw Tipu's rockets. In this light, the case of Tipu Sultan/Abdul Kalam is indeed another "affinity case," in which an individual is attracted to their own past life persona.

Haider Ali   Vikram Sarabhai

Haider Ali and his son, Tipu Sultan, ruled Mysore for 38 years. Ali was interested in military equipment, rocketry and he was a skillful administrator. Ali reincarnated as Vikram Sarabhai, father of the Indian space program and mentor of Abdul Kalam.

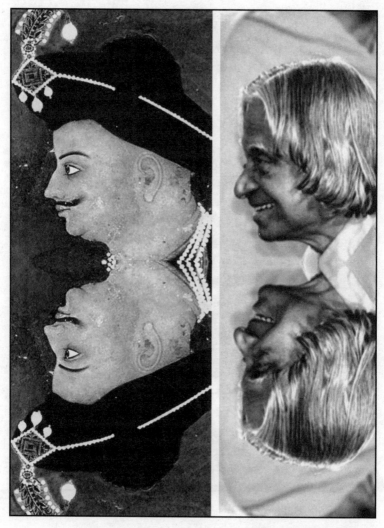

Tipu Sultan　　　　**APJ Abdul Kalam**

Tipu Sultan, with his father, pioneered the use of rockets in the battlefield. Dr. Kalam, the "Missile Man" of India, has been identified as the reincarnation of Tipu Sultan.

19

Indira Gandhi, Jawaharlal Nehru and the War of Independence of 1857

I ndia has been subject to foreign domination though much of its history. This is a reality that has pained Abdul Kalam and which has motivated him to urge the development of indigenous technology, so that India can remain self-reliant. British domination of India has led to many conflicts, such as those recounted in the history of Haider Ali and Tipu Sultan. Much brutality has been witnessed and many atrocities have been committed in these struggles. After India attained independence in 1947, conflicts based on ethnic and religious differences have fueled internal struggles and bloodshed.

It is hoped that the evidence of reincarnation that is found in the chapters of this book will help quell violence between nations and people of different

origins. In the cases that follow, we shall see how
souls can change national, ethnic and racial affiliation.
With this knowledge, let us no longer try to dominate
one another. Let us use our energies to build a
harmonious planet, rather than to destroy our
accomplishments and ourselves.

In investigating past lifetimes of prominent figures
of India, one person who I was interested in was Prime
Minister Indira Gandhi, daughter of Jawaharlal Nehru.
Prior to my session with Kevin Ryerson, I had read
about Ms. Gandhi and was struck by what a powerful
figure she was. It occurred to me that she must have
also been a formidable person in the past. It occurred
to me that she was most likely a male in a past lifetime,
as in distant history, generally only men could rise to
positions of power. Before discussing a past lifetime
for Indira Gandhi, as well a past incarnation of her
father, let us first briefly review the lives of Jawaharlal
Nehru and his daughter, Indira.

Jawaharlal Nehru was born on November 14, 1889.
Nehru came from a prominent political family, as his
father had served as a President of the Indian National
Congress. Nehru was attracted to the work of
Mohandas Gandhi. In 1924, Nehru was elected
President of Allahabad Municipal Corporation and was
city's Chief Executive for 2 years. He later served as
the General Secretary of the All India Congress
Committee. Nehru was one of the first Indian political
leaders to conceive of India as an independent and
sovereign state. With the support of Gandhi, on
January 26, 1930, Nehru asserted India's independence,
which led to his arrest and imprisonment. After his
release, Nehru was elected President of the Indian

Congress in 1936. World War II complicated and delayed the agenda of those who sought independence from Britain, but on August 13, 1942, the Indian Congress demanded that India be free from Britain. Following strikes and boycotts of British establishments, British authorities arrested the Congress Working Committee and thousands of Indian independence protesters were imprisoned and killed by police.

After World War II ended, India became an independent nation on August 15, 1947, with Nehru as the Prime Minister. He remained in that position until he died, on May 27, 1964.

Indira Gandhi, the daughter of Jawaharlal and Kamala Nehru, was born on November 19, 1917. Indira grew up in the backdrop of national politics and at one point; she became a young national heroine for carrying her father's plan for political revolution in her schoolbag, under the nose of British surveillance. In 1936, her mother died of tuberculosis. In 1942, she married Feroze Gandhi, a political activist, but not of family relation to Mahatma Gandhi. Shortly thereafter, Indira and Feroze Gandhi were arrested for participating in Mahatma Gandhi's Quit India Movement, which was intended to free India from British rule. In 1944, Indira gave birth to her first child, Rajiv Gandhi, followed two years later by Sanjay Gandhi. As her boys matured, Indira became especially close to Sanjay.

Indira later settled in New Delhi to assist her father. In 1959, Indira herself was elected as President of the Indian National Congress. In 1964, she was elected to Parliament and then, in 1966, Indira Gandhi followed in the footsteps of her father and became the third Prime Minister of India. Though others thought that she could be swayed by others, Indira proved to be an extraordinarily strong politician. She wielded political power in a way that was quite unexpected. In 1971, her esteem among the people of India was at its peak when India defeated Pakistan in regional war.

Under Indira Gandhi's tenure, in 1974, India conducted an underground nuclear test. APJ Abdul Kalam supported this venture and though it led Pakistan to develop its own nuclear capability, Kalam has insisted that mutual nuclear deterrent has maintained peace in the region. During Indira Gandhi's term, India also expanded its agricultural production in what was called a Green Revolution and India became an exporter of food. A crisis occurred in 1975 when a court found her guilty of campaign practices that were against the law and the court ordered that she resign. Rather than submitting, Indira Gandhi declared a state of emergency. Indira acted in an authoritarian and heavy handed manner in dealing with her enemies, including having her adversaries arrested. Indira allowed her son Sanjay to have increasing power in her government, which earned the enmity of the Indian people, particularly when he spearheaded unpopular programs such as forced sterilizations. Consequently, Indira Gandhi was voted out of office in 1977. Subsequently, the new government arrested Indira and Sanjay on charges of corruption. The prosecution was unsuccessful in attaining a conviction, which led to popular sympathy for Indira.

1980 marked the year that Indira Gandhi was returned to office as Prime Minister of India, but it was also the year of great tragedy for her, when Sanjay Gandhi died. He was in a private plane that was performing a dangerous stunt when it crashed. Sanjay had been elected as a Member of Parliament and when he died, Indira encouraged her other son, Rajiv, to run for Sanjay's seat, which he succeeded in winning.

Another crisis occurred in 1984, which involved a Sikh leader named Jarnail Singh Bhindranwale, who was pressing of equal treatment of Sikhs in India. There was also the proposal for a separate Sikh state, an independent Khalistan, which would be formed from territory from the Punjab region of India. Violence had broken out between Sikhs and Hindus in the area. At one point, Bhindranwale decided to take refuge in the Golden Temple, the holiest place of the Sikh religion. Indira Gandhi gave the order to the Indian army to remove Bhindranwale. In this operation, called Blue Star, in addition to many deaths of army personnel and Sikh militants, the temple itself was damaged, which was viewed as a desecration of the Sikhs' most holy temple. In the aftermath of Operation Blue Star, on October 31, 1984, Indira Gandhi was assassinated by her own Sikh bodyguards. Her death was followed by anti-Sikh riots, in which thousands of Sikhs were killed.

It appears that Indira Gandhi had a premonition of her own death. Just a few days before her assassination, she reflected, "If I die a violent death as some fear and a few are plotting, I know the violence will be in the thought and the action of the assassin, not in my dying......and each drop of my blood will give birth to new India!" Following her death, Rajiv

Gandhi, assumed the office of Prime Minister of India. The War of Independence of 1857

Indira Gandhi was indeed a powerful leader, who was at times authoritarian and who had no aversion to using political or military power. In a session with Kevin Ryerson, when I asked for a past lifetime for Indira Gandhi, Ahtun Re, the Egyptian spirit guide who was last incarnated over 3000 years ago, told me that Indira Gandhi was a prominent leader of the Sepoy Rebellion. Ahtun Re later confirmed that Indira Gandhi is the reincarnation of Nana Sahib. To better understand Nana Sahib, let us review the history of Britain's entrance onto the Indian continent via the East India Company.

In 1600, a company was formed by British merchants, who were given exclusive rights by the British Crown to trade in India. This East India Company first had ships land in 1608 and in 1615; Sir Thomas Roe secured permission to build a factory in Surat, from Jahangir, the Mughal Emperor. The Mughal Empire, which was a Muslim dynasty, had ruled the Indian subcontinent since 1526. The East India Company grew throughout India and developed with its own military, which began challenging territorial control over various regions of India. In 1773, Lord North's India Bill gave Britain's government greater control of the East India Company and a British Governor-General was installed in India.

From this point, Britain's expansion of military control over India accelerated and campaigns against native rulers, such as Haider Ali and Tipu Sultan, were undertaken. In addition, the British instituted the "Doctrine of Lapse," which asserted that when a state or region's ruler died without a direct male heir, or if the ruler was deemed incompetent by the British, then the British had the right to seize that ruler's territory. In the eight years that preceded the rebellion of 1857, Governor-General James Broun-Ramsay claimed 250,000 square miles of land, adding it to the territory of the British East India Company. When the company seized properties, they would also auction off heirlooms belonging to the deceased heir, which further increased hostility towards the British. Indeed, by the time of the rebellion, Britain controlled all of India. These events were accompanied by taxation of the natives by the British and enforced economic policies which caused hardships to farmers.

In addition to the British controlling the country administratively and militarily, Western customs were also introduced, which caused further consternation and resentment. Further, Indians perceived that the British judicial system was unfair to them, with accusations that the British did not police their own, when torture and brutality was used against the Indian natives. Evidence of this was provided to the House of Commons in 1856 and 1857.

Against this backdrop, the War of Independence of 1857, also known as the First War of Independence, took place. The British, though, did not see this as a war of independence, rather, to the British the turn of events was known as the Great Mutiny, the Indian Mutiny, the Sepoy Rebellion and the Revolt of 1857. The British clearly felt that they were the rulers of India, though of course, native people generally don't like to be ruled. It is quite sobering to reflect that

Indian independence from Britain would not ultimately occur until the mid twentieth century.

The most immediate cause of the First War of Independence was the introduction of a new rifle, the 1853 Enfield (P/53), which used a cartridge that had to be bit before loaded for use. These rifles were dispensed to the Sepoys, who were native Indian soldiers who had enlisted into the service of the East India Company. The Sepoys were under the command of British officers trained in England; at the companies own military college. There were three main divisions of Sepoys, headquartered in Bengal, Madras and Bombay, whose numbers totaled 257, 000. The Sepoys had various grievances against their British superiors, a situation that made fighting against their own countrymen, when the British deployed Sepoys against natives, even more difficult.

Introduction of the new rifle and cartridge caused a new level of distrust as a rumor began to circulate that the paper of the cartridge was greased by pig or cow fat. For Muslim soldiers, it was unacceptable to bite into a cartridge treated with pig fat, while for Hindu Sepoys, was against their religion to bite into a cartridge manufactured with the fat of a cow. Though the British tried to use reason and have the Sepoys use beeswax or vegetable oil for the cartridges, the Sepoys could not be swayed and in response, the British Commander, George Anson took a hard line, disciplining those who refused to use the rifles.

In February 1857, the 19th Regiment at Behrampore mutinied, as did the 34th regiment at Barrackpore in March. Also in March, a Sepoy was hanged for attacking a British officer. A month or so later, 85

Sepoys who refused to use their new cartridges and rifles were imprisoned. The revolt began full force on May 10, 1857, when Sepoy cavalry in Meerut turned on their commanders and were then joined by additional regiments. The Sepoys reached Delhi on May 11 and captured the Red Fort, where Bahadur Shah Zafar II, the last Mughal Emperor, resided. The Sepoys convinced Bahadur Shah Zafar to reclaim his throne and become the leader of this war for independence. This Bahadur Shah Zafar was declared Emperor of India and he produced coins in his name to assert his sovereignty.

NANA SAHIB AND THE FIRST WAR OF INDEPENDENCE

Teerek Dhunu Punt was born in a small village at the foot of the Ghats mountain range, some thirty miles east of Bombay. Dhunu Punt, later known as Nana Sahib, was adopted by Baja Rao II, the last Brahmin Peshwa (Mayor of Palace), a regional ruler of the Marathas confederation. In 1817, a battle that took place at Kirkee, where Baja Rao's troops were defeated by British East India military forces. Baja Rao surrendered and as part of treaty of peace, he was given a pension from the East India Company. In exchange, Baja Rao had to give up any claim to power and regional governance. Baja Rao and his family were escorted to Bithoor, a small town 12 miles up the river from Cawnpore, where they were to reside.[1]

Baja Rao died in 1851. Nana Sahib, who was about 32 years of age at the time, petitioned the British authorities for the pension be continued. Nana even sent an emissary to London, but the stipend was discontinued. Though historical sources cite the loss of the pension as the reason that Nana participated in hostilities against the British, the pension in truth was a relatively minor issue. The greater issue was that Nana Sahib was the adopted son of a Hindu Peshwa, a leader of the Maratha people, who, along with his father, had become exiles in their own land due to British control of India.

Though Nana Sahib resented British rule, as had his father, Nana could be gracious and social with the English. In Cawnpore, he befriended the British magistrate, a Mr. Hillersdon. When news of the rebellion by the Sepoys reached Cawnpore, Nana Sahib advised Hillersdon to evacuate to Bithoor, where Nana could guard the Hillersdon, his wife and treasury of Cawnpore. The treasury and associated parties moved to Bithoor and on May 22, 1857, Nana Sahih took up a position there with 200 armed Marathas. [2]

When rebellious Sepoy regiments entered Bithoor, a delegation of Sepoy officers from the Second Cavalry and First Native Infantry approached Nana and stated: "Maharaja, a kingdom awaits you if you join our cause, but death if you side with our enemies." Nana replied, "What have I to do with the British? I am altogether yours."[3]

For Nana, who the Sepoy now saluted as their Raja, joining the Sepoys was a way to regain his father's throne and to restore power to the Maharata confederacy. His plan was to take Cawnpore and extend his territory to the sea.

On June 6, 1857, Nana led the Sepoy rebel force of over 10,000 into the city of Cawnpore, where Nana proclaimed himself ruler of the Marathas. A new government was installed, with Nana at its head, and those opposed to Nana were put in irons. That same day, Nana Sahib sent a letter to the British commander, General Hugh Wheeler, who was encamped with a force of 900 English soldiers outside of Cawnpore, that Nana Sahib and the Sepoy were ready to attack them.

Not long thereafter, Wheeler saw stretched across the plain, the rebel infantry in battle array, forming a crescent, with banners flying, bugles blowing and cavalry at the ready. The infantry parted to allow Nana Sahib to take his place at the front of the formation. The battle and carnage then began and lasted for days. Nana Sahib was victorious and installed a court at Cawnpore.

In was during this time that the incident which has been called the Cawnpore Massacre occurred. About a thousand British soldiers and their dependents sought protection from the Sepoys in a fortified magazine in Cawnpore near the Ganges River, in the hope that British reinforcements would rescue them. The Sepoy laid siege to the magazine for three weeks and on June 25, 1857, the inhabitants, now only numbering 400, surrendered. The survivors were promised safe conduct via boats, which were brought to the shore of the Ganges.

When the British entered the boats, the Sepoys opened fire, killing all of the men except three. Nana Sahib historically has been blamed for the Cawnpore Massacre, but at last one British author, G. W. Forrest, suggests that the Sepoy troops acted on their own accord. Forrest writes that "Whilst that massacre was taking place at the ghat a trooper galloped to the

Savada House, where the Nana was staying and informed him that his enemies, their wives and children, were being slain...The Nana then answered, 'for the destruction of women and children there was no necessity, and directed the sowar to return with and order to stay their slaughter."[4]

So, it appears that Nana Sahib himself was not present at the siege and that the Sepoys acted on there own accord, for whatever consolation that may bring. Following the incident at the shore, the survivors, estimated to be 73 British women and 124 children, were taken into building called the Bibighar. On July 15, 1857, a mob returned and killed those inside.

In the end, the British regained control of their Indian territories and they were equally brutal in seeking revenge for British deaths. New Delhi was recaptured in September 1857. Bahadur Shah Zafar surrendered and was arrested. On September 22, 1857, British Major William Hodson, acting on his own, shot Bahadur's sons Mirza Mughal, Mirza Khizr Sultan, and Mirza Abu Bakr at the Delhi Gate. Their heads were presented to their Bahadur the next day. Sepoys who participated in the rebellion were strapped to artillery cannon and blown to death. Nana Sahib was routed from Cawnpore and it is thought that he escaped to Nepal.

' The brutality of the times is hard to contemplate, though brutal acts continue to be perpetrated today. As I have stated many times in these pages, it is my greatest wish that evidence of reincarnation will help quell barbarism, for indeed, from the point of view of karma, violence begets violence. In studying reincarnation cases, it is discouraging to observe how behavior and patterns repeat. If we can become aware of these patterns, which are repeated unconsciously, then we change our behavior. When we realize that we can be born to any nationality, race, religion and ethnic affiliation, then we will understand that it is foolish to fight one another over these differences. We will also realize that it is wrong for one group to rule, to exploit another group. Short profit made with selfish intent will only boomerang back and cause hardship in another incarnation.

Let us return to the reincarnation cases of Nana Sahib and Bahadur Shah Zafar. Recall that Ahtun Re, the Egyptian spirit guide channeled through Kevin Ryerson, revealed the Nana Sahib reincarnated as Indira Gandhi. Analysis of the facial features does reveal that the facial architecture between Nana and Indira is consistent. In reviewing the personalities of Nana Sahib and Indira Gandhi, certain character traits are also consistent. In particular, both Nana and Indira demonstrate a tendency to be authoritarian and to use military force. When Nana took control of Cawnpore, he placed his foes in irons, just as when Indira Gandhi called a state of emergency in 1975, she had her adversaries arrested. Nana used military force to regain his throne and reign. Indira Gandhi put into action Operation Blue Star to deal with militants. Violence, though, just begets violence.

When I read about Bahadur Shah Zafar and saw his image, he immediately reminded me of Jawaharlal Nehru. People do incarnate in groups and can reincarnate to continue work started in another lifetime. George W. Bush, Al Gore, Bill Clinton and Ralph Nader all were part of the American Revolution and they reincarnated to participate in American presidential politics in contemporary times. Ahtun Re later confirmed that Bahadur Shah Zafar did indeed reincarnate as Nehru. What was the character of Bahadur Shah? Little is known, though Forrest said of Bahadur Shah, "He was a quiet reflective man, fond of letters."[5]

In this way, two leaders of the First War of Independence reincarnated, as father and daughter, to be part of the attainment of Indian Independence in 1947, 90 years after the Sepoys initiated the process in 1857.

Nana Sahib   **Indira Gandhi**

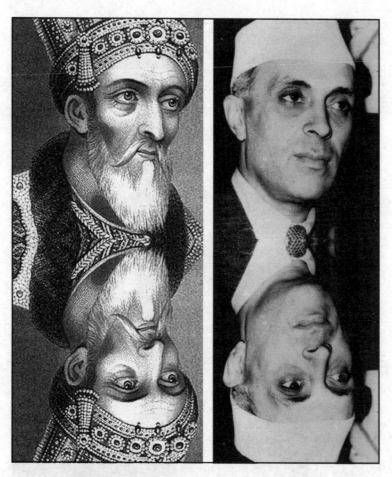

Bahadur Shah II   **Jawaharlal Nehru**

20

Benazir Bhutto as the Reincarnation of Jawaharlal Nehru; with Dr. Bhimrao Ramji Ambedkar Reborn in America

Knowing that I would be speaking in New Delhi at the Second World Congress on Regression Therapy in 2006, I worked on reincarnation cases that would be of interest to people in India. One of the leaders of Indian independence who I asked about in a session with Kevin Ryerson was Jawaharlal Nehru. I was pleasantly surprised when Ahtun Re, the Egyptian spirit guide that Kevin channels, told me that Nehru is incarnate at this time. Ahtun Re told me that Jawaharlal Nehru has reincarnated as the most prominent woman politician in Pakistan, Benazir Bhutto. After the session, I quickly found images of

Bhutto and noted that her facial architecture did indeed match that of Jawaharlal Nehru.

If this case is accepted, it demonstrates, much like in the cases of Barbro Karlen/Anne Frank, James Wilson/ Oprah Winfrey and Pablo Picasso/Alexandra Nechita, how talents from a prior lifetime can emerge early in a subsequent lifetime. Also as demonstrated in the Wilson/Winfrey and Picasso/Nechita cases, we see how gender can change from one incarnation to another, yet facial features, and in particular bone structure, remains consistent. Cosmetic changes occur in these cases, but underlying facial architecture remains the same.

This case is also interesting in light of another past lifetime that was identified for Jawaharlal Nehru/ Benazir Bhutto in the preceding chapter, that of Bahadur Shah Zafar. Bahadur Shah Zafar was the last living Mughal ruler, who was made powerless by British control of India. During the War of Independence of 1857, Bahadur Shah Zafar was made Emperor of India by the Sepoys, though his new reign was destined to be short lived. So in this series of three lifetimes, where in each roles involving national leadership were assumed, we witness a soul traversing incarnations as a male Muslim, a male Hindu and a female Muslim. That we would find three incarnations for the soul of Bahadur Shah Zafar/Jawaharlal Nehru/Benazir Bhutto should not be surprising. Please keep in mind that in independently researched reincarnation cases, including those studied by Ian Stevenson, MD at the University of Virginia, souls can reincarnate very quickly, even within a matter of days.

In the case of Jawaharlal Nehru/Benazir Bhutto, a talent for political matters is observed early in life in both incarnations. Nehru was born on November 14, 1889. His father, Motilal Nehru, was involved in politics, which allowed Nehru to get a head start in his own political career. Nehru, as a young man, was sent to Europe and received schooling at Trinity College, at Cambridge. He had the opportunity to experience Western culture before returning home to enter his own country's political scene. In time, Nehru became the first Prime Minister of India.

Benazir Bhutto has followed a very parallel path. Bhutto's father was Zulfikar Ali Bhutto, a former Premier of Pakistan. At the young age of 16, Benazir Bhutto was admitted to Radcliffe College, at Harvard University. After graduating at Harvard with a degree in Political Science, Benazir Bhutto went on to Oxford University, where she graduated with a degree in Philosophy, Politics and Economics. While at Oxford, in 1977, Benazir Bhutto was elected President of the Oxford Union, which is considered the most prestigious debating society in the world. Upon her return to Pakistan, after a very difficult period of time in which her father was imprisoned and executed, Benazir Bhutto, became the first woman Prime Minister of Pakistan at the age of thirty five. Bhutto was indeed the first female to head the government of a predominantly Muslim state.

So we see precise parallels in the development of Jawaharlal Nehru and Benazir Bhutto. Both were born into political families, both were educated at premiere Western universities where they demonstrated great talent and both became political leaders early in life. The phenomenon of Nehru/Bhutto incarnating in political families in two lifetimes is not an accidental one. Souls can plan to incarnate in circumstances that will help them achieve their intended goals for a particular incarnation. A good example involves the case of Dr. Bhimrao Ramji Ambedkar.

Ambedkar is remembered for being a chief architect of The Constitution of India, as well as being an advocate for human equality, championing the effort to eliminate the caste system in India. Ambedkar was born in 1891. He received a doctorate from Columbia University, in New York, and continued his education at the London School of Economics. In 1923, Ambedkar founded the Bahishkrit Hitkarini Sabha to improve the living conditions and civil rights of the disadvantaged, including the Untouchables. One focus was to provide education to these people, so that they could obtain better jobs. In 1927, he initiated a movement to allow the Untouchables to take water from Chawdar Lake. Throughout his life, Ambedkar struggled to eliminate the caste system in India and help elevate those born into poverty. He died in 1956.

When I asked Ahtun Re, the Egyptian spirit guide channeled through Kevin Ryerson, about Dr. Bhimrao Ramji Ambedkar, I was happy to hear that Ambedkar had also already reincarnated. Ahtun Re told me that he has returned as a grandchild of Robert F. Kennedy and that Ambedkar was already starting to work in international affairs. Recall that it was during the time of John F. Kennedy and Robert F. Kennedy that the civil rights movement in the United States hit its peak. The Kennedys supported Martin Luther King in his efforts to dismantle segregation in America. The segregated South, a vestige of slavery, was the equivalent of a caste system in the United States. By incarnating in the

Kennedy family, the soul of Dr. Bhimrao Ramji Ambedkar was laying the foundation for its work in contemporary times.

Ambedkar has reincarnated as Maeve Townsend, who bears a striking resemblance to Ambedkar. Maeve even wears glasses that are very similar in style to those worn by Bhimrao. Maeve is the daughter of Kathleen Kennedy Townsend, who is the eldest daughter of Robert F. Kennedy. Kathleen Kennedy Townsend herself is a politician and she served as Lieutenant Governor of Maryland. Maeve was born on or around the year 1980. She is the first Kennedy to join the Peace Corps, an organization that was founded by John F. Kennedy. In her service in the Peace Corp, she has traveled to Mozambique, Africa, where she has been raising money to build a library in the town of Quissico, which has population of about 2000. In Quissico, Maeve has lived in a small cement room, she has learned the native language and she has taught in the local school. In these actions, Maeve is replicating the work of Dr. Bhimrao Ramji Ambedkar, who raised the living conditions of the underprivileged through education. It will be interesting to follow the progress of Maeve Townsend in coming years.

In closing, I would like to make two observations. The first deals with the issue of caste. The reincarnation research presented in this book demonstrates that souls of great experience and skill can be born into any race, religion, socioeconomic class or caste. An excellent example involves Oprah Winfrey, who as James Wilson belonged to the highest socioeconomic class of Revolutionary America. In her lifetime as Oprah, though, she was born into a poor African American family, in difficult circumstances. Still, the talents that she demonstrated as Wilson came through when she was still a small child, which led her to become one of the most powerful women in the world. It is the soul's experience in earth existence that determines one's gifts and place in the world, not the caste that one is born in.

Secondly, I would like to point out that the case of Jawaharlal Nehru/Benazir Bhutto represents another case of split incarnation, in which a soul has split itself and has inhabited two bodies at one time. Jawaharlal Nehru died on May 27, 1964, while Benazir Bhutto was born on June 21, 1953. As such, the lifetimes of Nehru and Bhutto overlapped by almost eleven years. Though at first, the phenomenon of split incarnation is difficult to comprehend, in reality, it is not unusual. Ahtun Re has indicated that about five percent of souls on earth today are capable of this phenomenon. Also, an overlap of 11 years, as seen in the Nehru/Bhutto case, is not excessive. Recall that in the very compelling case of Penney Peirce, her lifetimes as Alice Carey and Charles Parkhurst overlapped by 29 years.

So we see, even on the earth plane, the soul is much more powerful than the human mind has imagined.

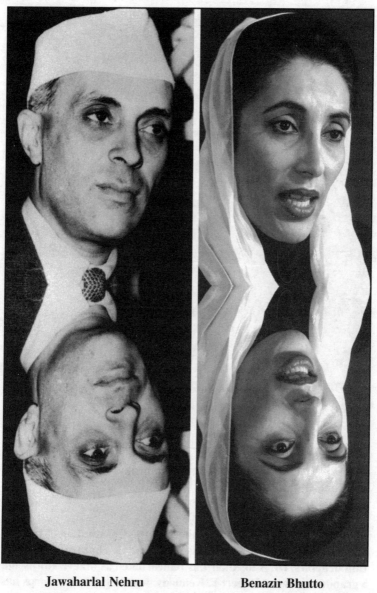

Jawaharlal Nehru

© Bettmann/CORBIS

Benazir Bhutto

© Reuters/CORBIS

Bhimrao Ramji Ambedkar

Bhimrao Ambedkar was an architect of The Constitution of India, a crusader against the caste system and a champion for the Untouchables. Dr. Ambedkar has reincarnated as Maeve Townsend, a granddaughter of Robert F. Kennedy, who in the Peace Corps has worked to help the underprivileged of Mozambique.

21

Shah Rukh Khan as the Reincarnation of Sadhona Bose

In addition to investigating past lives of India's political legends, I also was interested in reincarnation cases involving in the performing arts and in particular, of Indian movie stars. As described in previous chapters, I had established a working relationship with Kevin Ryerson, the trance medium who has worked with Shirley MacLaine for over 20 years and who is featured in three of her books, including *Out on a Limb*. Kevin channels a spirit guide named Ahtun Re who has demonstrated an ability to make accurate past life matches. In sessions with Kevin, I asked about Shah Rukh Khan, who has been described as India's heartthrob.

In the case of Shah Rukh Khan, Ahtun Re confirmed that Mr. Khan is the reincarnation of Sadhona Bose, who lived from 1914 to 1973. Sadhona was an actress and dancer from Calcutta. Sadhona was trained in classic Indian dance, but she also performed ballet. In

1929, she even worked with Anna Pavlova on a stage version of Alibaba. Her best known movie is *Raj Nartaki*, which was released in the United States as *Court Dancer*. Sadhona Bose also produced the show, *Rhythm of Victory*, an extravaganza which featured 40 dancers.

In the case of Sadhona Bose/Shah Rukh Khan, a strong resemblance in facial features is evident. As a boy, Shah Rukh Khan was described as an extrovert with a mischievous streak. At school, he liked to entertain classmates with imitations of their teachers and celebrities. Shah Rukh Khan was attracted to the theatre early on and eventually earned a Masters degree in film and journalism.

If this reincarnation case is accepted, then the dancing talent of Sadhona Bose was expressed early on in the career of Shah Rukh Khan, who performed as a dancer under Barry John, an internationally known director and actor. John was producing *Annie Get Your Gun* with his Theatre Action Group in Delhi. Shah Rukh Khan asked John for a role and was cast as a male dancer in the production. Barry John has remarked on Shah Rukh Khan's abilities: "His ability to mime and clown, his dancing skills and his gymnastic skills were remarkable."[1] Shah Rukh Khan performed in other musicals, including *Wizard of Oz*, and continues to engage in musical productions. In 2004, he went on a two month song and dance tour which included venues in Europe and North America.

An interesting part of Shah Rukh Khan's story is his romance and marriage with Gauri Chhiba. Shah Rukh Khan is Muslim, whereas Gauri Chhiba is Hindu. As such, their romance has a Romeo and Juliet quality, in that their different religions created complications in the relationship. At one point, Gauri Chhiba went to Mumbai for solitude, without informing Shah Rukh Khan. This unexpected separation led to Rukh Khan's realization that he must be with Gauri. Though he did not know her specific whereabouts in Mumbai, he went there to search for her.

Knowing that Gauri liked beaches, on the last day of his expedition to Mumbai, he asked a cab driver for a recommendation regarding a beach he might go to in order to find his lady. The driver told Shah Rukh Khan to try Aksa Beach, where he indeed found Gauri. The couple embraced and knew that they were meant to be with one another. Generally, when there is such a strong pull between people, such as demonstrated in the relationship of Shah Rukh Khan and Gauri Chhiba, there is usually a past life connection. It would be interesting to investigate the relationship history of these two people over the eons, over many lifetimes. The phenomenon of a couple returning together in two eras is indeed demonstrated in our next case, which involves Amitabh Bachchan and his wife, Jaya.

One last point that needs to be made is that the case of Sadhona Bose/Shah Rukh Khan represents another case of split incarnation, where a soul is observed animating two physical bodies at one time. Sadhona Bose died in 1973, while Shah Rukh Khan was born in 1965, which represents an overlap of eight years. Other cases which demonstrate split incarnation include those of Jawaharlal Nehru/Benazir Bhutto and the very important and compelling past life cases of Penney Peirce, in which lifetimes are observed to overlap by 29 years. Though the phenomenon of split incarnation is a bit mind-boggling at first, it is not that unusual. Ahtun Re, the spirit guide channeled through Kevin Ryerson, has indicated that about five percent of the souls incarnate on earth today have the ability to animate more than one physical body at a time.

Sadhona Bose   **Shah Rukh Khan**

22

Amitabh and Jaya Bachchan, Rekha, Sonia and Rahul Gandhi and the American Civil War

A phenomenon that I observed in researching cases related to Amitabh Bachchan is that souls that love the theatre can incarnate in different countries to pursue developing their skills as thespians. Historically, theatrical souls incarnated most frequently in England and France, as the European courts and large cities provided a venue for actors. In more recent times, India and the United States are popular destinations for theatrical souls, due to the film industries that have burgeoned in these countries. Indeed many of our favorite movie stars in contemporary times were actors on the Elizabethan stage, affiliated with William Shakespeare.

The level of accomplishment and public recognition is often consistent, from lifetime to lifetime, which should be expected. Reflect on the cases of Pablo Picasso/Alexandra Nechita and Paul Gauguin/Peter Teekamp and how talent and career progression were mirrored in successive incarnations. In a similar manner, great actors return as great actors across the centuries, though the venues, the countries and languages spoken, can change. In the paragraphs that follow, we shall see how the souls of great actors incarnate in nineteenth century America, in the era of the Civil War; have returned on contemporary stages, many in India and some in the United States.

When in a session with Kevin Ryerson, I asked who Amitabh Bachchan was in prior lifetime, I was surprised by the answer that I got. Ahtun Re revealed to me that Amitabh Bachchan is the reincarnation of Edwin Booth, an American who was considered one of the finest Shakespearian actors of Victorian times. Edwin's fame as a world class actor, though, has been overshadowed by the notoriety of his brother, John Wilkes Booth, who assassinated Abraham Lincoln. When Ahtun Re told me that Amitabh was Edwin, I quickly researched images of Booth and Bachchan and found that in certain photos, the resemblance is quite extraordinary. In studying their personalities, perhaps the trait in common that is most striking is that despite being famous actors, both can be characterized as painfully shy. Amitabh Bachchan readily admits that he can feel very awkward in social settings and he has been observed at functions standing alone in a corner, nursing a soda.

The following quotes pertain to Edwin Booth, though they could be equally applied to Amitabh Bachchan. Edwin was described to be shy boy, "who stood to one side when his more active brothers and sisters played games and engaged in horseback riding contests. He didn't say much during family discussions, either. Instead he was content to stand back and listen, observing the others with his large dark eyes.[1] Further, "Edwin was shy at social gatherings. He often sat in a corner and spoke to no one...Those who knew him well said Edwin suffered from stage fright everywhere except on stage."[2]

Later on, in researching Edwin Booth and Amitabh Bachchan, I found that Edwin Booth's entire family has reincarnated with Amitabh Bachchan. For example, Amitabh's wife, Jaya Bhaduri, was later confirmed by Ahtun Re to be Mary McVickers, Edwin Booth's second wife. Further, Edwin Booth's children are again his offspring in contemporary times. The Indian actress Rekha, who has made 20 movies or so with Amitabh Bachchan, has been identified as Edwin Booth's first wife, Mary Devlin.

Let us review the lifetime of Edwin Booth. Edwin was born on November 13, 1833, in Maryland. His father, Junius Brutus Booth, originated from London and became a successful actor. It was outside of the Covent Garden Theatre where Junius met his future wife, Mary Ann Holmes, who was selling flowers. Mary had seen Junius acting at Covent Garden not long before their meeting. The couple decided to immigrate to America, where they settled in Maryland. In the summertime, Junius Brutus Booth stayed with his family at their farm, as theatres became too warm and stuffy in the summer heat, and then toured across America in the fall, winter and spring. Such was the life of a theatre star in Victorian times. Rather than having an entire troupe tour the country, only the star would travel, who would be supported by resident actors in each city. The star and supporting players all knew the standard plays by heart and they put on shows with little rehearsal.

When at home, Junius loved to read to his children, making selections from his extensive library. Though he did not have the benefit of a higher education, Junius loved literature and was familiar with all the classics. There was almost a Hindu like spirituality about Junius Brutus Booth, as he raised his children to be strict vegetarians and he would not allow any animals on their farm to be killed. He hired workmen to help run the farm, rather than own slaves. Maryland was a border state between the North and South, and slave owning was allowed.

Junius traveled from city to city, theater to theater, from the spring through the fall. Perhaps to help deal with the loneliness that came with being separated from his family, Junius had a tendency to drink alcohol in excess when on the road. Mary's solution was to send young Edwin on tour with his father, first acting as personal assistant and chaperone, later taking on supporting roles in theatrical productions.

Shakespeare was performed by Junius and Edwin wherever they went. Junius seemed to sense Edwin's innate talent as an actor and one day told his son that he was not feeling well and asked him to play the title role in Richard III. Whether Junius's illness was real or feigned is not entirely clear. The audience, though, loved Edwin's performance and the theatergoers was even more appreciative when they learned that the actor playing Richard was not Junius Booth, but his son Edwin, who was only 17 years of age.

In 1852, Junius and Edwin decided to travel to San Francisco, as they heard that with the Gold Rush taking place in California, actors could make a fortune entertaining mountain men and the newly rich. After a West Coast tour that was only marginally successful, Junius Brutus Booth decided to return home, while Edwin opted to remain in San Francisco to establish an acting career of his own. It was while Edwin was working in the mining towns of the Sierra Mountains that Edwin, who frequently experienced premonitions, sensed that something terrible had happened to his father. A fellow actor had received a message for Edwin from San Francisco, indicating that Junius had died, and ran for Edwin to give him the sad news. Edwin, though, had intuited the message moments before. Junius had developed a febrile illness while on a paddleboat going up the Mississippi and he perished on his way back to Maryland.

Amitabh has also been noted to have premonitions. In *Amitabh Bachchan, The Legend*, his biographer, Bhawana Somaaya, describes a scene in Toronto, where Amitabh is rehearsing a show: "As you dance to the tune of 'Jhumma Chumma,' nobody can tell what's on your mind. Your heart is sinking and your premonition is not without foundation. Back at the hotel, bad news awaits you. Your father slipped in the bathroom and has been hospitalized. For the next fortnight, you make weekly trips to India, spend five days in Mumbai, and weekends in America. These are days of jet lagging, anxiety and pressure."[3]

Let us now return to California of Gold Rush days.

In 1854, Edwin met an actress from England, Laura Keene, who was making her name known in the United States, and who, we shall see, was destined to play a dramatic role in lives of Edwin Booth, James Wilkes Booth and Abraham Lincoln. Of interest, according to Ahtun Re, Laura Keene has reincarnated in contemporary times as Nicole Kidman. Though the facial match at first glance may not be obvious, analysis of portraits of Keene and Kidman in the right pose does reveal matching bone structure and facial architecture. The Keene/Kidman match was actually made a year or so before my study of Amitabh Bachchan, which I will discuss later in this chapter.

As a young woman, Laura Keene made her living as a barmaid, though she had an innate love of literature and would quote Shakespeare as she served drinks. Her patrons gave her the name "Red Laura," due to her hair, a physical trait shared by Ms. Kidman. Keene became married to a British Army Officer named John Taylor and the couple had two daughters. In a sudden turn of events, Taylor was arrested, tried, convicted and deported on a prison ship. Laura was never told where her husband was shipped to, though she suspected he was sent to the British colony in Australia. With her husband gone, Laura tried to make a living as an actress and her talent was soon recognized. After a tour in England, she performed in New York, later making her way to San Francisco, where she and Edwin Booth played the leads in *The Love Chase.*

A new international opportunity now tempted the troop. An acting couple returned to San Francisco from Australia, reporting that they had great financial success performing there. Laura Keene intuited an opportunity of finding her husband, and Laura, Edwin and a few others sailed to Australia on July 1854. Laura found that her husband indeed was imprisoned in Melbourne, serving a life sentence with no possibility of parole. To her great disappointment, she was denied visitation rights. The Australian tour was equally disappointing financially, though Edwin, who had turned 21 on the trip, received rave reviews for his performances. Nonetheless, Edwin, Laura and the others sailed for home, arriving in 1855. Edwin spent another year in California and in September 5, 1856, he sailed home to visit his mother and siblings in Maryland.

At this point, the actor Joseph Jefferson enters the scene. Tom Cruise has been confirmed, by Ahtun Re, to be the reincarnation of Joseph Jefferson, and we shall see how the lives of Nicole Kidman and Tom Cruise, who were husband and wife in contemporary times, were intertwined in the time of Lincoln. Joseph Jefferson was born in 1829 in Philadelphia. As such, Joseph was only a few years older than Edwin, who as born in 1833. Joseph's parents were both actors and the family traveled around the country performing at various venues. With this background, Joseph began appearing on stage at an early age, which parallels the career path of Tom Cruise.

When Jefferson was still young, following a tour of Iowa, the family had the opportunity to settle down when his father found a partner to build a theatre in Springfield, the capital of Illinois. A problem arose when the city council, whose members perceived a theater as a source of trouble, tried to block the opening of the venue by charging an exorbitant license fee. Religious parties considered the theater as the "devil's workshop," and they didn't want such a place in Springfield. A young lawyer, who loved the theatre, came to the rescue by agreeing to take the case to court. The young lawyer, Abraham Lincoln, prevailed and the theatre was opened. This incident is thought to have occurred in 1839, when Joseph Jefferson was ten years old, who documented Lincoln's rescue of the theatre in his subsequent autobiography. It would be very interesting if Tom Cruise would read this autobiography, which we are positing is his very own, to see if similarities in thought and style are found.

By 1857, Joseph Jefferson, still struggling as an actor, was managing a theatre in Richmond, Virginia, where Edwin, 24 years of age, was about to play the lead in Romeo and Juliet. Jefferson and his wife, Margaret Clements Lockyer, had taken into their home a young actress, Mary Devlin, who was at that time sixteen years of age. When the Edwin and Mary played starring roles in *Romeo and Juliet*, they fell in love for real. Edwin left Richmond to continuing his tour and acting career, but in 1860, Edwin and Mary were wed.

In 1858, Joseph Jefferson/Tom Cruise and his wife moved to New York, where Laura Keene/Nicole Kidman, had opened her own theatre on Broadway. Keene had hired Joseph Jefferson to play a lead role opposite her. So we see, in contemporary times, Nicole Kidman and Tom Cruise replicated a professional relationship from the nineteenth century. The relationship between Keene and Jefferson could be tumultuous. Though it was Keene who opened the theatre, Jefferson perceived that her choice of plays was poor, which resulted in small audiences. Joseph Jefferson, on the other hand, had a knack for sensing what an audience wanted and the plays he convinced Keene to put on, such as the Revolutionary War drama, *Blanche of Brandywine*, became hits. Joseph Jefferson, in the persona of Tom Cruise, has continued to demonstrate a nose for financially successful productions.

Another play Jefferson recommended, with himself in the lead, was *My American Cousin*, written by the English playwright, Tom Taylor. In this comedy, Asa Trenchard, who was played by Jefferson, inherits a fortune and sails to England to meet his aristocratic relatives. The production was a smash and it gave the careers of Joseph Jefferson, as well as fellow actor E.H. Sothern and his actress wife, Virginia Harned, major boosts. There must have been affinity between Joseph Jefferson and Virginia Harned, because in contemporary times, Harned reincarnated as Tom Cruise's former wife, Mimi Rogers.

Though the Laura Keene Theatre enjoyed capacity audiences, Keene and Jefferson's relationship became increasingly antagonistic. Joseph Jefferson finally decided to resign from the troupe at the end of the season. Before leaving, he asked Keene, who had bought the American rights, if he could produce *Our American Cousin* elsewhere. Keene refused and Laura and Joseph drifted apart.

By the way, Tom Taylor, the author of *Our American Cousin*, has been identified as being reincarnated as the Pulitzer Prize winning dramatist, David Mamet. Taylor was born in 1817 and at a very early age, displayed an affinity for theater, creating dramatic pieces with his childhood playmates in the loft of a stable. As young man, Taylor studied at Cambridge and became a professor of English Literature at University College, in London. Taylor is known for dialogue in his plays that is very natural and fast paced. His works include *Still Waters Run Deep* (1855); *Victims* (1857); *Contested Election* (1859); *Overland Route* (1860); *Ticket of Leave Man* (1863); *Anne Boleyn* (1875); *and Joan of Arc* (1871). Taylor died in 1880.

David Mamet, born in 1947, is also known for impeccable, dramatic, fast-paced dialogue. He won a Pulitzer for *Glengarry Glen Ross*, and he is the author of a number of successful screenplays, including *The Postman Always Rings Twice, The Verdict, The Untouchables* and the Steve Martin movie, *The Spanish Prisoner*. It would be very interesting for scholars to analyze the work of Tom Taylor and David Mamet to assess for similarities, as well as differences, in literary style.

Having digressed, let us return to the story of Edwin Booth/Amitabh Bachchan. Edwin and Mary Devlin were married on July 7, 1860. Later that year, Abraham Lincoln, who was opposed to the extension of slavery in the developing western states, was elected President. On December, 20, 1860, the succession of southern states from the Union began. Lincoln was inaugurated on March 4, 1861 and with the attack on Fort Sumner in South Carolina by supporters of the Confederacy, on April 12, 1861, the American Civil War broke out.

Unlike his brother John Wilkes Booth, a political activist and who hotly supported the South, Edwin Booth supported the North, as he was against slavery.

Though Edwin was solidly behind Lincoln and on the side of the Union, which caused a rift between the two brothers, Edwin was also admittedly apolitical. Politics simply didn't interest him which is also consistent with Amitabh Bachchan, who despite serving for a period of time as a Member of the Indian Parliament, states that entering politics was a mistake for him. As for Edwin Booth, politics for Bachchan is foreign territory.

In 1861, Edwin and Mary went to England, where Edwin would do a series of performances. From London, the couple had the interesting vantage point of observing the American Civil War though the eyes of the English press. Edwin was surprised to find that the *London Times* supported the South. Edwin speculated that this was due to the aristocratic ways of the British, which was mirrored by the American South more than the North. On December 9, 1861, a daughter, Edwina, was born in London.

The couple returned to the United States and Edwin learned that his good friend, Richard Cary, was killed at the Battle of Antietam, where 24,000 perished or were wounded. Recall that Jeff Keene, in his incarnation as John B. Gordon, was also severely wounded in that battle. Lincoln used Antietam to make the Emancipation Proclamation, which freed slaves in the rebel states, but not in the border states that were loyal to the Union, which included Edwin's home state of Maryland.

Though the Civil War was continuing, Edwin's career was on the rise and his income and wealth increased. In November 1862, Edwin was doing a run at the Boston Museum, where he received extraordinary reviews. Mary and Edwina were staying in a rented country home in nearby Dorchester, outside of Boston. Edwin then went on to New York, where he played Hamlet to capacity crowds. While in New York, he received word that Mary was sick back in Dorchester. While on the train going from New York back to Boston, he had another premonition, as he later described in a letter to a friend: "I saw every time I looked from the window Mary dead, with a white cloth tied around her neck and chin, I saw her distinctly, a dozen times at least."[4] When he arrived in Boston a friend came to pick him up and update Edwin on Mary's condition. Just as in the case with his father, Edwin already knew Mary's fate and when he got home and entered Mary's room, Edwin saw her exactly as he had in his vision, on the bed with a white cloth secured around her neck and chin, to keep her warm. Following Mary's death, Edwin resisted returning to the stage, not performing again until September 21, 1863.

Recall that Amitabh Bachchan also has had premonitions and the Mary Devlin, Edwin's first wife, has been identified in contemporary times as Rekha, who has played leading lady in many of Amitabh's films. The physical resemblance between Devlin and Rekha is quite extraordinary. So we see that a couple, in marriage and on stage, separated by premature death, can return in a subsequent era and resume performing together once again. It is interested to note that Rekha was born on October 10, one day before Amitabh, who was born on October 11, and they both started their acting careers on the same year, 1969.

In New York, Laura Keene lost her theatre and to maintain an income, Keene took her popular production, *Our American Cousin*, on the road. In April 1865, she would be opening in Washington, DC, at Ford's Theater. The mood was celebratory in the capital city, as on April 9, the South had surrendered. The war lasted four years and left 620,000 dead. On April 14, 1865, Abraham and Mary Lincoln attended *Our American Cousin*, sitting in the presidential box. Previously, John Wilkes Booth had performed at Ford's Theater and Abe Lincoln had been in the audience when John performed *The Marble Heart*. Lincoln admired John Wilkes Booth's performance and sent word that he would like to meet actor, but John refused. After the South had surrendered, John blamed Lincoln for the destruction of a culture that he admired. As a boy, John went to a boarding school along with the South's elite. He developed lasting friendships with members of the South's young aristocracy. John Wilkes Booth, in fact, considered himself a Southern actor. After the fall of the South, John decided to seek revenge by killing Lincoln, thinking that he would become a hero to those who had been part of the Confederacy.

Tragically, love had just bloomed in the hearts of John Wilkes Booth and a beautiful young woman named Lucy Hale, the daughter of John P. Hale, a former Senator from New Hampshire who was an ardent Abolitionist and supporter of Lincoln, who had just been made Ambassador of Spain. The Hale family was staying in the same Washington hotel as was John Wilkes Booth and Lucy and John met there in January 1865. The couple fell in love and Lucy professed that when they returned from Spain, they would wed. At that point, their love was three months new, yet Lucy was sincere. John had dinner with Lucy on April 14, 1865 and upon leaving her, he quoted from *Othello*, "Nymph, in they orizens [prayers], Be all my sins be remembered."[5]

After making final preparations, which included plans for escape, John went to the Ford's Theater. Knowing the theatre staff, John easily gained entrance and walked up to the presidential box, shooting Lincoln in the head at close range. He then jumped on the stage, yelled "Sic semper tyrannis" ("Thus always to tyrants") and fled. The audience was in shock and then panic. It was Laura Keene/Nicole Kidman who tried to bring order, as she called out from the stage, "For God's sakes have presence of mind and keep your places and all will be well."[6] When someone from the presidential box called for water, Laura Keene brought a picture to Lincoln, who lay bleeding, surrounded by two doctors who were assessing his wound. When one of the physicians instructed that Lincoln be given a sip of brandy, it was Laura who held the President's head while the liquid was administered to Lincoln.

Nicole Kidman was identified as the reincarnation of Laura Keene in 2004, long before I became interested in past lives of Amitabh Bachchan. I had been trying to derive past lives of Hollywood celebrities and asked Ahtun Re about Nicole. At that time, Ahtun Re told me, "Ms. Kidman was on stage when Lincoln was shot." I didn't know my history well enough then to identify the actress by name, but after I researched Lincoln's assassination, Ahtun Re confirmed that Kidman was Keene. After the Keene/Kidman match was made, the identification of Tom Cruise as Joseph Jefferson followed.

Lincoln was transferred from Ford's Theater to a nearby house on Tenth Street. Secretary of War, Edwin H. Stanton arrived at this location and took command. Stanton made the needed notifications to General Ulysses S. Grant, Vice President Andrew Johnson and Chief Justice Chase. It was Stanton, too, who took charge of the investigation of John Wilkes Booth, the suspected assassin.

While these events took place, Joseph Jefferson/ Tom Cruise was sailing on a ship headed for South America. Jefferson had been on tour in Australia and New Zealand for most of the Civil War. He would not learn of Lincoln's death for another month, when he reached Peru. Edwin Booth/Amitabh Bachchan was performing at the Boston Theater the evening that Lincoln was shot.

In the dark, early morning hours of April 26, 1865, Union troops found John Wilkes Booth hiding in a barn outside Bowling Green, Maryland, where he was subsequently shot and killed. The Secretary of War, Edwin Stanton, ensured that Booth's body was secretly taken to the Old Arsenal Penitentiary, where it was buried under the floor of a storage room. Stanton, who was concerned that Booth's body in Southern hands could serve as a rallying point for resumed conflict, personally kept the key to room where Booth was buried. Stanton too, was in charge of the military tribunal against those who were charged as Booth's co-conspirators.

Edwin Booth, who was horrified at his brother's act of assassinating Abraham Lincoln, went into seclusion for 18 months before returning to the stage. During this period of exile, he worked on his mother's behalf in the attempting to have his brother's body released for proper burial. In this effort, he wrote directly to Edwin Stanton, though he did not receive a reply. When Edwin prepared to return to the stage in New York in January 1866, rumors had spread that revenge would be taken out on Edwin. But when he appeared as Hamlet at the sold out Winter Garden Theater, he was given ovations.

Edwin continued on to Chicago, where he performed at the McVicker's Theatre. Once again, professed love on stage evolved into a marriage. Edwin played the lead in *Romeo and Juliet*, opposite Mary McVicker, the theater owner's daughter. Mary enamored Edwin with her sense of humor and her "heart shaped face."[7] There is a person in Amitabh Bachchan's life too with a "heart shaped face," his wife, Jaya. As previously noted, Jaya has been confirmed by Ahtun Re, Kevin Ryerson's spirit guide, as being the reincarnation of Mary McVicker. Jaya starred with Amitabh Bachchan in *Zanjeer*, which became a hit in 1973. In December of that year, Amitabh's leading lady became Jaya Bachchan. After their marriage, Jaya took a sabbatical from films to focus on family life.

After his run at McVicker's theater, Mary joined Edwin on his continuing tour. During this time, Edwin was in the process of building a state of the art theater in New York City. The Booth Theater had its grand opening on February 3, 1869, when Edwin was only 35 years old. On opening night, Edwin and Mary again played the roles of Romeo and Juliet. It was during this period of time that Edwin proposed to Mary and they were wed on June 7, 1869. Like Jaya, Mary retired from the stage following their marriage to make ready for a family. Mary became pregnant and a boy, Edgar, Jr., was born on July 4, 1870. It was a difficult birth and little Edgar incurred brain damage, living for only a few hours.

Following the death of their son, Mary went into a deep depression, which plagued her periodically for the rest of her life. In modern times, antidepressant medications would have been used, in Victorian times, available treatments were ineffective. Still, Mary would tour with Edwin, demonstrating incredible endurance when needed. They toured the South and then traveled to San Francisco, where in 1876, Edwin, in an 8 week run earned $50,000, an enormous sum in those days. So like Amitabh Bachchan, Edwin was not only considered one of the greatest actors of his day, he was also one who could draw large audiences and profits.

In 1880, Edwin took Mary and his daughter Edwina on a tour in Europe. It was in London that Mary, who had been enduring a chronic cough, was diagnosed with advanced tuberculosis. From this point on, Mary's physical and mental health deteriorated and on November 13, 1881, Mary died.

After Mary's death, Edwina, became her father's touring companion. Ahtun Re, by the way, the spirit guide channeled through Kevin Ryerson, has confirmed that Edwina, the daughter of Edwin and his first wife, Mary Devlin, has reincarnated in contemporary times as Shweta Bachchan, the daughter of Amitabh and Jaya. Similarly, Ahtun Re has indicated that the Bachchan's son, Abhishek, is the reincarnation of Mary McVicker's son Edwin, who died as newborn. If these cases are accepted, we see how entire family units can reincarnate together again.

In 1882, Edwin and Edwina set sail for England again and in December of that year, they traveled to Berlin, where Edwin got rave reviews. After runs at four other German cites, they were off to Austria. So we see that Edwin became an international star, much like Amitabh Bachchan. When he returned home to the United States, Edwin continued to earn enormous amounts of money from this theater tours. For example, in his tour of 1886-1887, Edwin made $200,000. So we see that before he was the "Big B" in contemporary times, Bachchan was a "Big B" in Victorian times.

For his finale, Edwin Booth built a club in the Gramercy Park area of New York City called "The Players," which would be a place for actors and various professionals to spend time together and share ideas. Edwin was the master of ceremony when the Players opened on New Years Eve, 1880. In the main parlor, under a portrait of Junius Brutus Booth, Edwin gave a toast in his father's honor: "Let us drink from this loving cup, this souvenir of long ago, my father's flagon. Let us now, beneath this portrait, drink to the Players perpetual prosperity."[8]

Ahtun Re has revealed that Edwin's beloved father Junius Brutus Booth reincarnated as the Amitabh Bachchan's beloved father, the late Harivanshrai Srivastav Bachchan. This claim is supported by a strong match in facial features and common passions for Shakespeare and literature. Junius died in 1852, while Harivanshrai Bachchan was born in 1907. Harivanshrai received a doctorate in English Literature at Cambridge, writing a dissertation on Yeats. In Delhi, he worked for the government in efforts aimed at making Hindi as the official language of India. Harivanshrai is famous for writing the poem *Madhushala*, as well a numerous other volume of poetry. He was also the first person to translate Shakespeare into Hindi, specifically *Macbeth* and *Othello*. For his literary contributions, he won the Padma Bhushan in 1976.

Junius Brutus Booth also loved English literature. Though he did not attend college, he was self taught in the classics and at his farm in Maryland, would read to his children selections from Milton, Dante, Keats and Shelley. Junius, of course, was one of the most famous Shakespearian actors of his day and as noted, Harivanshrai was the first to translated Shakespeare in Hindi and he dedicated the volume to Amitabh. Junius had a deep spirituality in which he saw all life as scared, maintained a vegetarian diet and wouldn't allow animals to be killed on his farm. Junius mentored his son Edwin, who became the Big B of the Victorian stage, while Harivanshrai mentored today's Big B.

One difference is that Junius is best known as an actor, while Harivanshrai is remembered as a poet. Souls can concentrate on different areas of life, though usually a common passion exists. In this case, the passion is literature. A second difference is that Junius had episodic problems with alcohol, while Harivanshrai was a teetotaler. This is a phenomenon that I have observed in several reincarnation cases, that when an individual has an problem with substance abuse in one lifetime, in a subsequent lifetime, the soul will have nothing to do with intoxicating substances.

Amitabh's mother, Teji Bachchan, has also been confirmed by Ahtun Re to be the reincarnation of Edwin Booth's mother, whose maiden name was Mary Anne Holmes. A physical resemblance exists. Edwin had a sister named Asia, who had a close relationship to her brother, John Wilkes Booth, though she was aligned with the North and did not share his political passions. Still, after John died, Asia wrote a book about her relationship with him, in an attempt to share some of his good qualities with posterity. In contemporary times, Asia Booth has also written a book about her sibling, though a sibling from a past lifetime. Asia has been confirmed by Ahtun Re to have reincarnated as Bhawana Somaaya, who wrote the biography, *Amitabh Bachchan, The Legend*, which was cited above in reference to premonition,

The Bachchan family, I came to understand, has had a close relationship with the family of Indira Gandhi. In particular, I have been told that Teji and Indira were friends. If this is the case and if Bachchan family members lived in America during the time of the Civil War, it begs the question of whether Indira Gandhi was incarnate in that era too. When I asked Ahtun Re this question he replied, "She was Edwin Stanton, the Secretary of War, you will see the resemblance." This, of course surprised me. I checked images and indeed, a resemblance in facial features can be seen in certain images of Indira Gandhi and Stanton. I also found that character traits were similar.

One trait in common is the willingness to use force to achieve an end. Stanton believed that the purpose of the war was to end slavery and military force should be used until this was accomplished. This attitude is reminiscent of Indira Gandhi's authorization of Operation Blue Star, as described in the previous chapter. Stanton acted boldly in his actions and when he was appointed Secretary of War he took charge of all telegraph lines and censored the press, to control information that went to the public. This is reminiscent of Indira Gandhi's actions, when she was faced with political crisis and opposition.

Parallels to Indira Gandhi's proposed past lifetime as Nana Sahib can also be seen, in the in Stanton's support of the abolishment of slavery is consistent with the attempt to create an independent India. In Nana's time, the oppressors were the British, while during the Civil War, the slave holders were the oppressors. The trait of the willingness to use force can also be applied to Nana Sahib.

At this point, I would like to emphasize the observation that our modus operandi usually does not change much from lifetime to lifetime, the reincarnated Picasso paints like Picasso, the reincarnated Laurel and Hardy still like to make people laugh. Similarly, souls who like to operate in circles of national power like to return and work into these roles. Let us recognize, though, that karmic cycles are placed in motion by violence, that violence begets violence and that he who lives by the sword dies by the sword. In the long run, it is in nobody's long term interest to create war against one another. Most violence is based on a misunderstanding of how life works and on perceived differences in terms of national, racial or ethnic affiliation. Cases such as the Anne Frank/Barbro Karlen case, and many other cases cited in this book, demonstrate that we can change these affiliations from lifetime to lifetime. With this knowledge that evidence or reincarnation brings, let us end these cycles of violence.

If these cases are valid, why would Edwin Stanton/ Indira Gandhi, Mary Anne Holmes Booth/Teji Bachchan, Harivanshrai Edwin Booth/Junius Brutus Booth and Edwin Booth/Amitabh Bachchan reunite in India? I believe that karmic bonds were forged between these souls in the time of the Civil War. The Booths were the eminent Shakespearean actors of the era and Stanton was one of the most important political figures of that very emotional time. Stanton was responsible for the capture of James Wilkes Booth and he maintained control of Booth's body. It was to Stanton that Edwin Booth wrote, on behalf of his mother, to request that John's remains be returned. In this physical world, we tend to be judgemental and unforgiving. In the spiritual world, I believe that forgiveness and reconciliation prevail and with seeds of emotion that are generated on the other side, an intricate web of destiny is laid for a group's future incarnation.

The beautiful Lucy Hale, by the way, who fell in love with John Wilkes Booth and became engaged to him just a few just months before he died, has been identified in contemporary times as Sonia Gandhi, the wife of the late Rajiv Gandhi. Rahul Gandhi, the son of Sonia, has been confirmed to be the reincarnation of Lucy's father, the Abolitionist senator from New Hampshire, John P. Hale.

There is one last reincarnation connection that Amitabh Bachchan has with a contemporary cinema legend, which is derived from the lifetime of Edwin Booth that I will share. This involves Robert Todd Lincoln, the son of Abraham and Mary Lincoln. This incident occurred in 1863 or 1864, prior to Lincoln's assassination. Robert Todd Lincoln was standing on a platform next to a train. When the train unexpectedly started to move, Robert was knocked off balance and began to fall off the platform. Suddenly, his coat collar was forcefully grasped and he was pulled to safety. His savior was Edwin Booth, who Robert recognized immediately and thanked him by name.

A year or two before I started researching past lifetimes for Amitabh Bachchan, in the course of my work with Kevin Ryerson the reincarnation of Robert Todd Lincoln was revealed to me. I had asked Ahtun Re for a past lifetime of the Hollywood director, Steven Spielberg, and Ahtun Re told me that Spielberg was Abraham Lincoln's eldest son, Robert Todd, which surprised me. I later noted a strong facial resemblance between Robert Todd Lincoln and Steven Spielberg. Though the match had taken me aback at first, it did make some sense upon further reflection. The Lincoln family did love the theater and what better forum is there to influence mass consciousness, in contemporary times, than cinema? Think about all the socially meaningful movies that have been made by Spielberg.

With further research and additional sessions with Kevin Ryerson, it was derived that all four of Lincoln's sons are reincarnated and active in Hollywood. In fact, my understanding is that two of these sons are contemplating producing a movie on Lincoln. Mary Lincoln, Abe's wife, has herself become an attorney in contemporary times and has a role in the filmmaking industry. Honest Abe is back with us too.

Edwin Booth died in 1893. After he passed, Joseph Jefferson became the second President of the Players Clubs, in Gramercy Park. Jefferson died in 1905. The soul of Laura Keene was waiting for Edwin and Joseph on the other side, as she had passed in 1873. These souls, though, we know have emerged in new places. The curtain will now be closed, our story having been told.

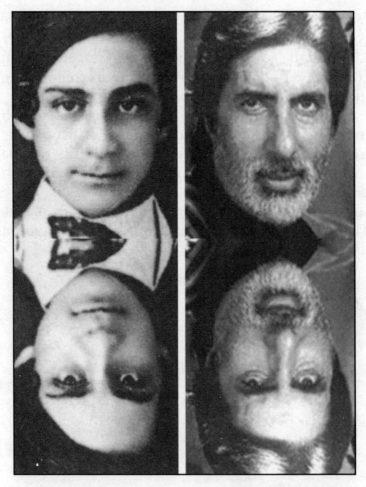

Edwin Booth

Amitabh Bachchan

Edwin Booth became one of the greatest Shakespearean actors of the Victorian stage. The young Booth and Bachchan bear great resemblance. Bachchan has been described as a gifted actor in a Shakespearean way.

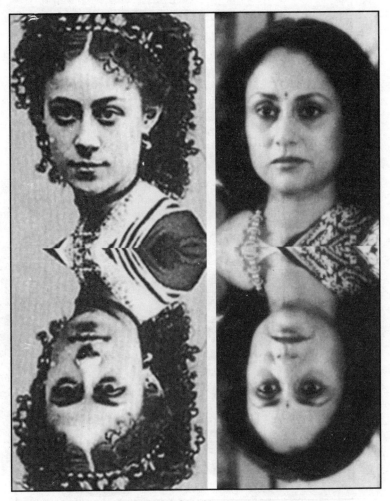

Mary McVickers

Jaya Bachchan

Edwin Booth met Mary McVickers when he performed in a theater that her father owned. Edwin and Mary played the leads in "Romeo and Juliet," fell in love and later married. Mary has reincarnated as Jaya Bachchan.

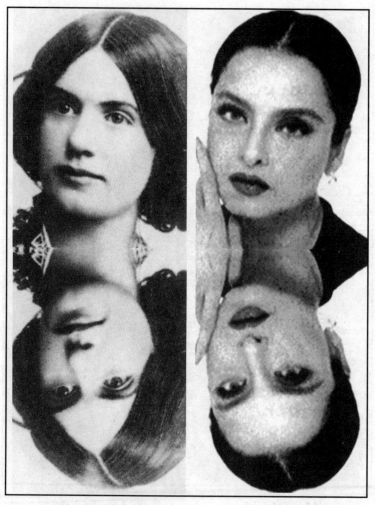

Mary Devlin Booth   **Rekha**

Edwin married Mary Devlin, an actress. When they first met, they played the lead roles in "Romeo and Juliet." Mary died a few years after they wed.

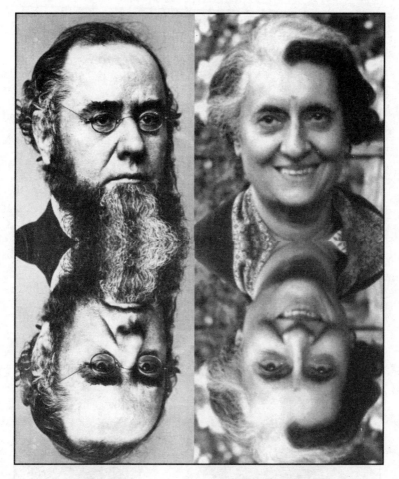

Edwin Stanton

© CORBIS

Indira Gandhi

© Bettmann/CORBIS

According to Ahtun Re, Indira Gandhi was Edwin Stanton, the Secretary of War under Lincoln during the American Civil War. After John Wilkes Booth, Edwin Booth's brother, shot Lincoln, Edwin Stanton took charge of the situation. After J.W. Booth was killed, Stanton took possesion of the body.

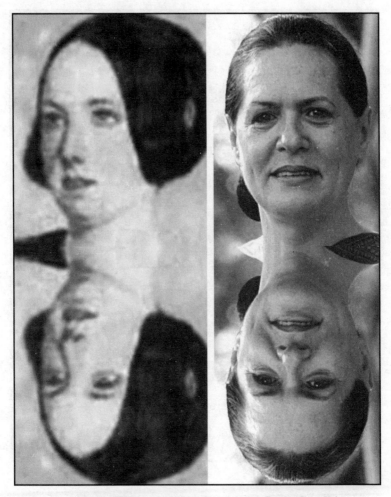

Lucy Hale

Hale House Museum, Woodman Institute,
Dover, New Hampshire

Sonia Gandhi

© Harish Tyagi/epa/epa/CORBIS

Lucy Hale met and became engaged to J.W. Booth a few months before he assassinated Lincoln. Her father, John P. Hale, was a US Senator, an abolitionist and supporter of Lincoln. John P. Hale has reincarnated as Sonia Gandhi's son, Rahul Gandhi.

23

Siva Baba and his Past Lives of Agastyar and Vallalar; With the Reincarnation Edward de Vere and William Shakespeare

Yoga is the science of attaining merger of the individual soul with Divinity or God. Yoga comes from a Sanskrit word that means "yoke" or "unite." Many in the West think of yoga as a set of physical exercises and postures, which is just one discipline of yoga called Hatha Yoga. In its truest sense, though, yoga refers to union with God consciousness. There is a lineage of saints who brought a form of yoga, Kriya Yoga, to the world, who originated from a region of India known as Tamil Nadu, which is located on the Bay of Bengal near the island country of Sri Lanka.

Tradition has it that one of the first of these saints or "siddhas" was Agastyar, who subsequently initiated Babaji, who is considered the greatest of the Kriya Yoga saints. Babaji was born in the Tamil region of India in 203 AD, and his teachings have been transmitted over time. In addition to Agastyar and Babaji, there were 16 other saints who contributed to the body of knowledge contained in Kriya Yoga. Recently, the teachings of Babaji and the science of Kriya Yoga have been popularized by Paramahansa Yogananda, who wrote *Autobiography of a Yogi* and who founded the Self Realization Fellowship.

Today, there is a living saint or siddha from the Tamil region of India who has also traveled to the West to share the wisdom of Kriya Yoga, which is the science of attaining union with the Divine. This siddha's name is Siva Baba, though he has also been known as Sri Siva, Sri Guruji, Guruji and Brzee. Siva Baba has served as a spiritual teacher to Dr. Wayne Dyer, whose book, *Manifest Your Destiny*, is based on Siva Baba's teachings. Indeed, Dr. Dyer dedicated this book to Baba as "Guruji."

In this narrative, several past lives of Siva Baba will be discussed. Siva Baba himself affirms these past life matches. These reincarnation cases presented below involving Baba have also been confirmed by Ahtun Re, the spirit guide channeled through Kevin Ryerson, who has demonstrated an ability to make accurate past life matches. I am very pleased to relate that Siva Baba supports my work and he has validated that I am the reincarnation of John Adams. We share a common belief that objective evidence of reincarnation can help create greater world peace.

Indeed, Baba Sri Siva has announced that Kali Yuga or the Age of Darkness, is ending and that an Age of Miracles, or Age of Truth, has arrived. I believe that the objective evidence of reincarnation, which is now streaming into the world, will help usher in this new Age of Truth. Let us now review Siva Baba's past lifetimes as Agastyar and Ramalingam, also known as Vallalar.

AGASTYAR/SIVA BABA

Tradition has it that Agastyar received his own initiation from Lord Shiva, an aspect of God, on Mount Kailash in the Himalayas of Tibet. Of importance, Ahtun Re has also confirmed that Siva Baba is currently in the process of merging his consciousness with this aspect of God known as Lord Shiva. Agastyar later traveled from Mt. Kailash south to the Tamil region of India. It was in the Tamil city of Courtrallam that Agastya initiated Babaji, whose birth year, we noted, was 203 AD.

Agastyar, considered one of the most famous holy men in India, was a dynamic fellow. In his book, *Babaji and the 18 Siddha Yogi Tradition*, M. Govindan, relates that Agastyar, "though less than five feet tall,..was a fighter, a famous hunter and an archer, who triumphed over barbarous enemies, and whom, like Hercules of ancient Greece, none could approach in eating and drinking." The life of Agastyar is detailed in the epic, Mahabharata. Siva Baba differs from Agastyar, in that he is no longer a great hunter, eater or drinker. Instead, compassion for all life is the greatest virtue for him. There are interesting similarities, though, between Agastyar and Sri Siva. Let us examine these:

Interest in Language/Literature

Agastyar is considered the father of Tamil language, as demonstrated by his treatise on Tamil grammar, which is cited to have 12,000 statements on the principles of language.

Siva Baba, whose secular name is Baskaran Pillai, received his formal education at the Univerity of Madurai, in India, where he was a Research Fellow and earned a Master's Degree in English literature, as well as a Master of Letters in Comparative literature.

Interest in Ancient History, Religious History, Theology and Meditation

Agastyar wrote *Canda Pooranum*, a work on ancient history which contained 1000 stanzas. He also wrote several treatises on religion and theology, including *Calikianum, Poorna Soostru* and *Agastyar Dundakum Nooroo*. Agastya was also a master in meditation and, as described, became enlightened on Mount Kailash in the mountains of Tibet.

Siva Baba received a Ph.D. in Religious Studies at the University of Pittsburg. He then served as coordinator of Indian Studies within the Asian Studies Program at the University of Pittsburg, and taught Buddhist meditation. Baba Sri Siva was also an invited speaker on Hinduism at the United Nations World Religions conference and served as an editor for the Encyclopedia of Hinduism. Siva Baba is a master of meditation and has attained enlightenment.

INTEREST IN RELIGIOUS RITES AND RITUALS

Agastyar wrote *Deekshavedy*, a work that deals with magic, enchantment and the use of the rosary. Siva Baba dares his students to "live an outrageously wonderful life," and teaches them how to manifest their desires in reality. Indeed, this process encompasses the message of Wayne Dyer's book, *Manifest Your Destiny*, which was dedicated to Baba. Siva Baba has interest in rituals of various kinds.

I recently had a scientific insight on how rituals may work. Meta analysis of a large number of research studies regarding the ability of people to affect the output of random number generators has been statistically proven by large studies. In other words, when people focus on random number generators and try to influence whether these devises produce more 1s or 0s, it has been scientifically demonstrated that people can actually alter the outcome of mechanical, electrical events. These experiments show that intent can truly affect that physical world. In this light, perhaps one can view a ritual as a physical exercise that focuses intend concretely, which has the goal of bringing the desired outcome into manifestation.

INTEREST IN MEDICINE, PHARMACOLOGY AND BOTANY

Agastyar wrote numerous treatises on medicine, surgery, pharmacy and the use of plants and herbs in the treatment of various illnesses. Indeed, he is considered the Hippocrates of the Tamil region of India.

For the past two decades, Siva Baba has been involved in the study and use of herbs for healing, and plans to make available herbs from all over the world available through a web site he will manage. Baba has sponsored several conferences on siddha medicine and he is conducting seminars to help AIDS patients enjoy better health.

INTEREST IN SCIENCE

Agastyar wrote hundreds of treatises on various aspects of science, including medicine, chemistry and astronomy.

One of Siva Baba's foremost goals is to integrate spirituality and science. He is trained in neuropsychology, which he has used to interpret yogic and tantric wisdoms pertaining to psychobiology, the interface between mind and body. Just as Agastyar was interested in astronomy, Baba is an expert in Vedic astrology. Siva Baba has participated in many university conferences and has been included on panels with Nobel Laureates, including Eugene Wigner of Princeton, who won a Nobel Prize in physics.

COMMON LEADERSHIP QUALITIES

Agastyar was a leader of the Tamil region of India and was described as a fierce warrior, who defended his people against invaders. He is also attributed as the first Tamil Siddha, or saint, who help found the Kriya Yoga tradition.

In addition to his spiritual aspect, Siva Baba has served as a consultant to leading industrialists on business development and leadership skills. He heads a computer company in New York City and has founded the Tripura Foundation, whose purpose is to help eliminate hunger in the world. Currently, the Tripura Foundation is feeding 1500 people in India daily.

In sum, we see that Agastyar and Siva Baba share many qualities. Though an accurate image of Agastyar is not available, Baba Sri Siva has been confirmed to be the reincarnation of Agastyar by Ahtun Re, the spirit guide channeled through Kevin Ryerson.

RAMALINGAM/VALLALAR

Let us now examine the very interesting life of Ramalingam, also known as Vallalar, which is another past lifetime of Siva Baba

Ramalingam is one of the favorite saints or siddhas of southern India. He underwent a Divine Transformation and wrote 40,000 verses describing this achievement. Every day, millions of school children sing verses written by Ramalingam.

Ramalingam was born on October 5, 1823, in the Tamil village of Marudur. His family name was Pillai. At five months of age, Ramalingam was taken to a Hindu temple for sanctification. During the ceremony, a great atmosphere of sacredness descended upon the temple, so noticeable, that the chief priest ran up to the Ramalingam and declared that he was a child of God.

Ramalingam was a child prodigy and at five years of age, after a few lessons from a tutor, he began composing ecstatic verses to God. At nine years of age, in the family's home at 9 Pillai Street in Madras, India, Ramalingam gathered writing materials and isolated himself in his room. He then wrote what was termed a "torrent of psalms and hymns."

At twelve years of age, his elder brother, who taught religion, asked Ramlingam to substitute for him due to an illness. The congregation was so impressed by the teaching of this young boy that they choose to have Ramalingam complete the lecture series. Throughout his formative years, he continued writing verses, yearning for "descent of the divine grace."

By 1846, when Ramalingam was 26, he had already attracted disciples. At that time, a scholar named Velayutha Mudalier became his principle disciple, who over the next 25 years documented the life of Ramalingam.

In 1860, at 37 years of age, Ramalingam moved to the village of Vadalur and founded a house to feed the poor. During the inauguration ceremony, which lasted for three days, 10,000 people were fed. Ramalingam taught compassion for all things, condemned the killing of animals, and converted many to vegetarianism.

Ramalingam composed many of his spiritual verses at night. His principle disciple, Velayutha Mudalier, persuaded Ramalingam to allow him to publish his verses to God, which were issued in 1867 as *The Divine Song of Grace*. Written in poetic form, in *Divine Song*, Ramalingam describes the attributes of God and the soul, and of the spiritual transformation that he was going through.

As Ramalingam evolved spiritually, his physical body took on a golden hue, as he developed a "body of love." As he continued to sing in praise of God, he later developed a "body of light." At this point, his physical body was no longer perceptible to touch and further, this light body cast no shadow. With this transformation, Ramalingam had merged with God.

Not only was Ramalingam's light body imperceptible to touch, it also could not be photographed. The famous photographer of Madras, Masilamany Mudalier, was summoned by Ramalingam's disciples to capture Ramalingam and his light body. Masilamany Mudalier tried to photograph Ramalingam on 8 separate occasions, but the photographic plates only revealed Ramalingam's clothes. His body was transparent to the camera. During this time, Ramalingam demonstrated telepathy, and miracles and healings were performed by him.

In 1870, Ramalingam moved into a small hut in the town Mettukuppam, three miles south of Vadalur. This hut still exists today. In Mettukuppam, Ramalingam had his disciples built a temple, which at its core had a glass box, 5 feet tall, with a flame burning in its center. The box represented the soul, merged with God, or Supreme Grace Light.

In this period of time, Ramalingam alternated spending time in seclusion with giving lectures on "universal spiritual communion," as described by M. Govindan in *Babaji and the 18 Siddha Kriya Yoga Tradition.* Madame H. P. Blavatsky, a founder of the Theosophical Society, came to know Ramalingam during this period and was so taken with him, that she wrote that

Ramalingam was the forerunner for the Theosophical Society.

On January 30, 1874, at the age of 50, Ramalingam decided to merge with God and leave the physical plane. He wrote a declaration to his disciples, "My beloved ones, I have to be out of your sight for a time...I am in this body now and after a while I shall enter into all the bodies of His creation. Close the door and lock it outside. The room, if ordered to be opened, will only be void."

Ramalingam then entered his room in the hut, in Mettukuppams, and the door was closed. His disciples remained in the hut, outside the room that Ramalingam had secluded himself in. Later that night, as his disciples chanted "Supreme Grace Light, pour down upon us," a miracle occurred. M. Govindan narrates the scene. "Suddenly, a flash of violet light emanated from Ramlingam's room, signaling the merger of Ramalingam "into all the bodies of His creation." For, when the room was eventually opened it was found to be empty. Ramalingam had disappeared without a trace."

After receiving a police report of Ramalingam's disappearance, British colonial officials conducted an extensive investigation. Villagers were interviewed and the hut was carefully inspected by officers. M. Govindan writes, "Finding no evidence which would support suspicion to the contrary, they concluded that Ramalingam was a great soul who had vanished into thin air." In 1878, an account of Ramalingam's disappearance was noted in an official British publication, the *Manual of South Arcot District*.

Ramaligam left extensive documentation of his transformation and in his writings. He related that the

Tamil saint Manikavacakar had achieved transformation into a light body before him, in the seventh century AD. Of note, Siva Baba states that he is also the reincarnation of Manikavacakar, a past life match that Ahtun Re, the spirit guide channeled through Kevin Ryerson, has also confirmed. In his lectures, Baba states that he remembers how to transform into light, as he did as Manikavacakar and Ramalingam.

TRAITS SHARED BY AGASTYAR, RAMALINGAM AND SIVA BABA

Let us now review common patterns observed in Siva Baba's series of lives, as well principles of reincarnation that are illustrated by these cases.

CHILD PRODIGIES AND REINCARNATION/ SPIRITUAL STUDY AT A YOUNG AGE

First of all, we see how the phenomenon of a child prodigy, which has also been discussed in prior chapters, can be understood in the light of reincarnation. Ramalingam was recognized as a child of God by a Hindu priest when only five months of age. Ramalingam began writing verses to God at age six and was able to teach religion to a congregation at age twelve. Ramalingam's childhood spiritual gifts can be seen as a reflection of his mastery of meditation in his prior lifetimes as Agastyar and Manikavacakar

In contemporary times, Siva Baba has demonstrated similar proclivities, for as a child, he spent most of his time as a young boy in the temple, on the island of Rameswaram where he grew up. Siva Baba has the same family name, Pillai, as did Ramalingam. Like Ramalingam, Siva Baba became immersed in spiritual study at a very early age, has attained enlightenment and has become a teacher to others.

LITTLE NEED FOR SLEEP, WORKS AT NIGHT

Ramalingam preferred to write his verses to God at night, rather than sleep.

Siva Baba likes to do his spiritual work at night and relates that he often does not sleep for several days in a row.

FEEDING THE POOR

Ramalingam founded a house to feed the poor and on its inauguration, 10,000 people were fed over a period of three days.

Similarly, Baba Sri Siva has founded the Tripura Foundation, which feeds 1500 people in India daily.

DEVELOPMENT OF LIGHT BODY

Ramalingam developed a light body, as he did in a previous lifetime as Manikavacakar.

Siva Baba states that he remembers how to enact this transformation.

Though most of us have accomplishments of lesser grandeur, the ability of Siva Baba to create a body of light in his lifetimes as Manikavacakar and Ramalingam demonstrates a phenomenon that pertains to all of us. That is, over incarnations, we tend to demonstrate the same strengths, talents and weakness; we seem to embody a consistent set of energies.

When we are created as souls, it is as if a die is cast in which we are imbued with specific qualities, which remain consistent over many lifetimes. If one is created with a great deal of aggressive energy, perhaps symbolized by the color red, was well as a generous portion of intellect, symbolized by yellow, we will tend to be an aggressive intellectual over many incarnations. If we are created with an abundance of emotion, symbolized by blue, then we will tend to be sensitive and nurturing in successive lifetimes.

If one is created with an energy pattern or energy signature conducive to merging with God, that person will have many lifetimes as a mystic, minister or guru. Over successive lifetimes, we grow by learning how to use our native energies, our energy spectrum or signature, more effectively.

In addition to being a very evolved soul, I would propose that Siva Baba has an energy spectrum that facilitates his ability to experience the mysteries of creation, and to create a body of light, in this lifetime, as well as in past lifetimes. Ramalingam's transformation into light has been extensively studied and documented in a two volume work written by T. R. Thulasiram, entitled *Arut Perum Jothi and Deathless Body*, published by the University of Madras. These two volumes, released in 1980, contain 1800 pages. Siva Baba has gifted this rare, two volume set to me, and I am very, very honored and grateful to be entrusted with this treasure.

In conclusion, Siva Baba, I contend, is a living Tamil Siddha, as he was in prior incarnations. In a conversation with him, Baba has related that he and I have a common purpose, which is to help create a worldwide Spiritual Democracy, where all people are equal and united; where divisions based on conflicting religious doctrines are washed away. In this light, let the Age of Miracles begin.

REINCARNATION CASES OF EDWARD DE VERE AND WILLIAM SHAKESPEARE

Siva Baba has always had a very deep affinity for William Shakespeare, which is consistent with his and Agastyar's love of literature and language. Baba even went to visit Shakespeare's grave in England, where he had an intense emotional experience. This connection exists, I posit, because in a past incarnation, the lives of Siva Baba and William Shakespeare were interwined. In my work with Kevin Ryerson, Siva Baba has been confirmed to be the reincarnation of Edward de Vere, the Seventeenth Earl of Oxford, who some have suggested is the true author of at least some of William

Shakespeare's plays. Siva Baba himself supports that he is indeed the reincarnation of de Vere.

Edward de Vere was born in 1550 and died in 1604, while Shakespeare is thought to have been born in 1564 and he died in 1616. As such, de Vere was 14 years old when Shakespeare was born and they were contemporaries for a period of 40 years. The interval in which de Vere and Shakespeare would have had most opportunity to interact would have been from about 1585 to 1604, a period when Shakespeare was an actor and playwright in London, the home of de Vere.

That de Vere and Shakespeare ran in the same circles is supported by the fact that Edward de Vere's daughter, Susan, was married to Philip, Earl of Montgomery, who scholars accept as a primary patron of Shakespeare. Shakespeare, in fact, dedicated the 1623 publication of his *First Folio Edition of Shakespeare Plays* to Philip, Earl of Montgomery, the son in law of Edward de Vere.

Edward de Vere and Shakepeare were considered exceptional playwrights by their contemporaries. When Francis Meres published his book in 1598, *Palladis Tamia: Wit's Treasury, A Comparative Discourse of our Engish Poets with the Greek, Latin, and Italian Poets,* Shakespeare and Edward de Vere were both cited as among England's best writers. Meres, in particular, praised de Vere's comedies, while Shakespeare was lauded for his dramas.

Let us briefly review the life of Edward de Vere, the 17th Earl of Oxford. When young, Edward grew up as a royal ward of the state, as his father had died when he was a boy. Edward lived at the Royal Court as a ward and his lands were managed by the crown until he was 21. De Vere received Masters of Arts degrees from Oxford and Cambridge and when 25, he went on a tour of Europe, visiting Italy, Germany and France. De Vere was especially fond of Italy and having returned to Britain speaking the language, he was dubbed the "Italian Earl."

De Vere was considered one of the best poets at the Royal Court by several literary authorities over a period of three decades. As mentioned, de Vere also wrote plays, though none have survived through the centuries. De Vere sponsored two theater companies, Oxford's Boys and Oxford's Men.

De Vere also seems to have sponsored scholars in philosophy, religion, medicine and literature, as many volumes on these subjects were dedicated to him. His financial support of the arts and letters may have even been excessive, as de Vere had to sell all his lands and in 1586, was given royal pension to provide for his needs. De Vere had two military commands in the 1580s. He died in 1604, in Stratford, the home town of Shakespeare, outside of London.

New interest in Edward de Vere, the Earl of Oxford, arose in 1920 when J. Thomas Looney wrote a book in which he claimed that de Vere was the true author of Shakespeare's plays. Controversy regarding this assertion has swirled about since. The majority view, though, is that Shakespeare wrote at least most of his own plays. It is intriguing to wonder, though, what the relationship between the two men truly was, given that the reincarnated Edward de Vere, Siva Baba, feels so identified with the bard of Stratford and felt so moved at Shakespeare's grave.

THE REINCARNATION OF WILLIAM SHAKESPEARE

I am not a master of mediation, as Siva Baba is, nor do I have psychokinetic gifts, as does Uri Geller, and though I do not see auras, I do, at times get intuitive, telepathic messages that bear fruit. The reincarnation cases of George W. Bush, Bill Clinton and Al Gore were all initially solved by intuitive messages that told me where to look for past lives of these men. Recall the telepathic message that I received when I was in the kitchen of my friend Igor, which led to the discovery that he speaks French in his sleep. As Igor has never learned French, this represents a form of xenoglossy, in which it is thought that language skill are accessed from a past life.

I also received an intuitive message which led to the identification of a contemporary past lifetime of Williams Shakespeare. Keep in mind that many cases that we have reviewed, including the independently researched cases of Ian Stevenson, MD, at the University of Virginia, demonstrate that people reincarnation very quickly, from a few days to a few decades following death in a past lifetime. As such, it would be expected that William Shakespeare should have had several lifetimes since he died in 1616, and it should be no surprise that he should have an incarnation in contemporary times.

The way in which a past lifetime for Shakespeare was established is as follows. In November 2005, I was minding my business doing my job as a physician in a clinic in which we treated workers who are injured on the job. An actor had fallen on a large knotted rope during a staged maneuver during a performance of a play and had bruised a rib and had come to our clinic for treatment. As soon as this actor walked into my office and started talking, I received the following intuitive, telepathic message, which seemed to come from outside of me:

"He will tell you the contemporary identity of Shakespeare."

I was taken aback by this message, just as I was taken aback when I got the message at Igor's kitchen. For one, in the past I had not even considered investigating incarnations of Shakespeare and I certainly did not have that in mind at the time when the actor walked in. Further, I had treated other injured actors from the same troupe in the past and the thought of being told of Shakespeare's contemporary identity has not arisen. Lastly, as mentioned, what was striking to me was that this intuition seemed to come from outside of me, which gave it a telepathic quality.

Sure enough, this actor was a great admirer of William Shakespeare and he was injured while doing one of his plays. The actor reflected to me, in describing the lasting nature of Shakespeare's verses, "Who else is still quoted after 400 years?" As he continued on in his soliloquy on the master playwright, I had the certainty that he would indeed tell me who Shakespeare was today and when he had finished his discourse, I asked him this question.

"Of all the contemporary playwrights, who is most like Shakespeare?

Who writes in a way that his works will endure for long passages of time?"

The actor replied without hesitation, "August Wilson, his plays will be around for a very long time." I am not a frequent patron of the theater and though I myself had never heard of Wilson, at the moment his name was mentioned, I felt an inner certainty that this fellow, August Wilson, was indeed a reincarnation of Shakespeare. Within a day or two, I checked images and found that Wilson's facial features matched those of Shakespeare's in striking way. I even found that he had been named by theater critics as an "American Shakespeare," When I had a session with Kevin Ryerson, Ahtun Re confirmed the match. Let us briefly review the lives of these two men. .

Relatively little is known about Shakespeare, the person. Shakespeare's birth date is uncertain, but records show that he was baptized on April 26, 1564. As such, it is assumed that he was born on April 23, 1564. William was the son of John and Mary Arden Shakespeare. John, his father, was a prominent town official of Stratford, a municipality a hundred miles northwest of London.

Though William grew up in Stratford, little is known about his childhood. It is thought that he was educated only through grammar school. When William Shakespeare was eighteen, he married Anne Hathaway, who was eight years older than he and already pregnant with a child. Their daughter, Susanna Anne, was born several months later in 1583. Twins, a boy Hamnet and a girl Judith, were born to the couple in 1592. Hamnet died of an illness at the age of eleven.

It is thought that Shakespeare moved to London sometime around or just after 1585. In1592 Shakespeare received an infamous and historic insult from the writer Robert Greene, who called Shakespeare "an upstart Crow," unworthy to be considered as being in the same league as other accomplished playwrights of the time. This remark indicates that even by 1592, when Shakespeare was 28 years old, he was already drawing attention as a writer.

In London, Shakespeare worked as an actor, writer and became a partner in an company known as The Lord Chamberlain's Men. When James I became the monarch of England in 1603, James became the sponsor of Shakespeare's company, which was now known as The King's Men. Shakespeare retired in 1611, producing his literary legacy from the early 1590's to 1611, roughly a period of twenty years. If Shakespeare was truly born on April 23, 1564, he timed his death well, for Shakespeare died on April 23, 1616 at the age of 52. William Shakespeare wrote his own epitaph:

> *Good friend, for Jesus' sake forbear,*
> *To dig the dust enclosed here.*
> *Blest be the man that spares these stones,*
> *But cursed be he that moves my bones.*

William Shakespeare, as noted above, reincarnated as August Wilson, as confirmed by Ahtun Re, the Egyptian spirit guide channeled through Kevin Ryerson, who as demonstrated an ability to make accurate past life matches. August Wilson, originally named Frederick August Kittel, was born in Pittsburg, Pennsylvania on April 27, 1945. Recall that record show that Shakespeare was baptized on April 26, so it seems the bard's timing was a little bit off. He was born to an African American mother, a cleaning woman whose maiden name was Daisy Wilson. His father, a German born baker named Frederick Kittel, who was an absent father. When Kittlel died in 1965, his son changed his name to August Wilson.

When his mother remarried, the family moved from the poor, African American section of Pittsburg, called "The Hill," to a predominantly white neighborhood, where in high school, August was subject to racial taunts and harassment that eventually led him to drop out. August then found a home in the Carnegie Library of Pittsburg, where he educated himself in literature, much as it is thought that Shakespeare was self taught. He spent so much time at the library; Carnegie gave him a degree, the only one that the Library has ever issued.

In 1968, with Rob Penny, August founded the Black Horizon Theater in the Hill District, whose name is reminiscent of the theatre that Shakespeare had plays performed in his later years, the Blackfriars Theatre, named after the monks who wore black robes on the monastery grounds, which eventually become the theatres home. For the next ten years at the Black Horizon, Wilson wrote and directed plays. He and Penney initiated the Kuntu Writers Workshop, which still functions today.

Wilson moved to St. Paul, Minnesota, in 1978, where he worked for the Science Museum of Minnesota, writing scripts for educational programs. With a steady job to pay the bills, in his spare time, Wilson began working on an epic series of plays that would shed light on the experience of Blacks in America, to expose the

emotional wounds and scars caused by racism, to
theatre goers who were primarily white. In retrospect,
some, such as actor Charles Dutton, have assessed that
Wilson's contributions to ending segregation in America
as equal to those of Martin Luther King.

Wilson emerged as a major playwright with is work,
Ma Rainey's Black Bottom, which earned him a Tony
Award nomination in 1985, as well as numerous other
awards. Even the *London Times* was impressed, as
reviewer Holly Hill deemed *Ma Rainey's Black Bottom*
"a remarkable first play," and who cited Wilson as "a
promising new playwright" Richard Christiansen of
the Chicago Tribune stated, following a Broadway
production of the play, "Wilson's power of language is
sensational."

In 1987, August Wilson's play *Fences* won a Pulitzer
Prize for drama. For *The Piano Lesson,* Wilson won
another Pulitzer. These are but a few of many, many
awards that August Wilson earned in his career, in which
he became to be known as a "master storyteller" and
"An American Shakespeare."

In 1990, Wilson moved to Seattle, where the weather
is akin to that of London, and he helped Seattle become
a new theater town. It was here that he completed his
ten play series on African American life. Amusingly,
one of Wilson's latter plays, called *King Hedley II,* is
entirely Shakespearian in its structure and character. In
June 2005, Wilson was diagnosed of having liver cancer
and he died, at the age of 60, on October 2, 2005, at
Seattle's Swedish Medical Center. Wilson's third wife,
Constanza Romero and his two children survive him.
In his honor, The Virginia Theatre on Broadway, in New
York, was renamed the August Wilson Theatre.

An interesting question that can be asked is why did Shakespeare incarnate into the circumstances that he did, poor and into a race that was discriminated against? I asked Ahtun Re that question and his answer rings true. Ahtun Re said that the soul of Shakespeare observed that the plight of African Americans in the twentieth century was a story that had to be told and he, Shakespeare, knew that he had the skills to tell that story.

PAST LIVES OF JOHNNY DEPP AND ROBERT ROSEN

Many other souls from the time of Shakespeare are also incarnate at this time. Athun Re, for example has confirmed that the popular actor Johnny Depp is the reincarnation of the Elizabethan thespian Nathan Field. Ahtun Re's abilities were well demonstrated when I asked him who William Camden might be in contemporary times. Camden was a contemporary of Shakespeare's, who was an antiquarian, scholar and historian. He became a leading teacher at Westminster School, where he taught aspiring and gifted playwrights.

Ahtun Re told me that Camden had reincarnated as the Dean of the University of California, Los Angeles, School of Theatre, Film and Television. Ahtun Re was referring to Robert Rosen. When I looked up Rosen, not only did his facial features match in an uncanny way, but realms of endeavor were also the same. Rosen describes himself as an educator, critic, and preservationist, who teaches young minds the crafts of drama, much as William Camden did.

So as the bard said, life is but a stage and it appears that our roles keep recurring. With consciousness of the drama, though let us move away from tragedies and create venues that we return to with joy.

A MODEL OF HUMAN EVOLUTION

As mentioned, Wayne Dyer has been a student of Siva Baba. It turns out that Dr. Dyer also agreed to be case in *Return of the Revolutionaries,* where he is identified as the reincarnation of Jonathan Edwards, a minister, orator, writer and leader of the Great Awakening in 18th century America. APJ Abdul Kalam, it turns out, is a fan of Wayne Dyer. In his book, *Ignited Minds,* Kalam cites a model of human evolution from Dyer's book, *Manifest Your Destiny,* in which man passes through four stages of development, the athlete stage, the warrior, the statesperson and spirit stage. Ahtun Re concurs with this fundamental scheme, though he has called the stages the innocent, the warrior, the philosopher and the spiritual man.

The basic idea is that once we emerge from the Godhead as an innocent, we must develop ego strength; we must forge a self sufficient and strong personality, before we can move on to more sophisticated stages. Once we are secure in our ego, in our identity, we can then move toward merging once again with the Godhead, as Siva Baba has done in the past and is reiterating today.

Problems arise for humanity in the middle stages, when ego dominates and separates itself that which is different from itself. As my friend Ahtun Re has stated:

"The Great Sin is Separation."

With the understanding that we now have regarding reincarnation, let us do away with this sin and let us all move to higher stages of human evolution, as spirit men and spirit women. Let us manifest this destiny.

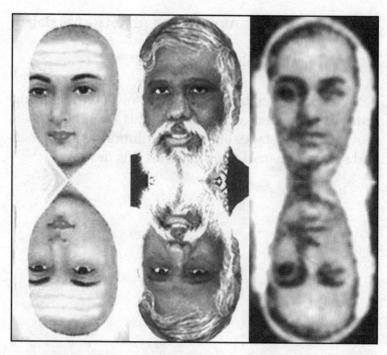

Ramalingam　　　　**Siva Baba**　　　**Ramalingam (Vallalar)**
(Vallalar)

Courtesy of Siva Baba

Siva Baba knows that he is the reincarnation of Ramalingam and Agastyar. These past lifetimes have also been confirmed by Ahtun Re, the spirit guide channeled by Kevin Ryerson, who has demonstrated an ability to make accurate past life matches. Siva Baba supports the reincarnation research that is being presented in this book.

Siva Baba has close connections with the soul of Shakespeare and with Wayne Dyer, who dedicated "Manifest Your Destiny" to Baba.

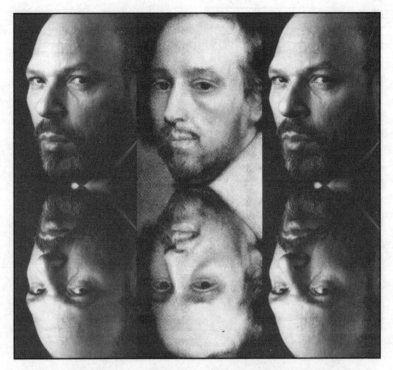

August Wilson   **William Shakespeare**   **August Wilson**

Reincarnation research shows that people can reincarnate very
quickly, within a matter of months or a few years. As such,
Shakespeare has likely had several lifetimes since he died in 1616.
Shakespeare recently reincarnated as August Wilson, who has been
called an "American Shakespeare," who has won two Pulitzer Prizes
and who has just had a Broadway theatre named after him in New
York.

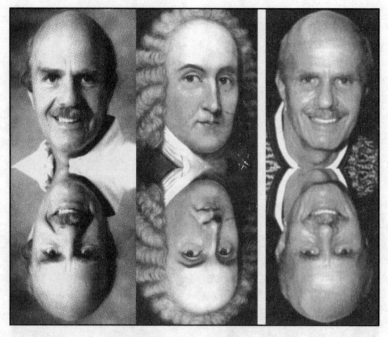

Wayne Dyer **Jonathan Edwards** **Wayne Dyer**

Courtesy of Wayne Dyer   Courtesy of Wayne Dyer

BIBLIOGRAPHY

Chapter 1

2. Sylvia Cranston, *Reincarnation, The Phoenix Fire Mystery*, Theosophical University Press, Pasadena, 1998, p. 128.
3. Joseph Head and S. L. Cranston, *Reincarnation, and East–West Anthology*, The Theosophical Publishing House, 1961, p. 35-39.
4. Ibid., p. 39–42.
5. Sylvia Cranston, *Reincarnation, The Phoenix Fire Mystery*, Theosophical University Press, Pasadena, 1998, p. 156–160.
6. Flavius Josephus, *Antiquities of the Jews*, Book 18, Chapter 1, No. 3.
7. Flavius Josephus, *Jewish War, Book 3*, Chapter 8, No. 5.
8. *Zohar*, Vol. II, fol. 99.
9. Sylvia Cranston, *Reincarnation, The Phoenix Fire Mystery*, Theosophical University Press, Pasadena, 1998, p. 132–133.
10. Joseph Head and S. L. Cranston, *Reincarnation, and East–West Anthology*, The Theosophical Publishing House, 1961, p. 56.
11. Ibid., p. 56.
12. *Quran*, Sura 2, The Cow, Verse 28.
13. *Quran*, Sura 11, Rome, Verse 38., from *The Essential Koran*, by Thomas Cleary, Harper, San Francisco, 1993, p. 89.
14. *Quran*, Sura 6, Cattle, Verse 95., from *The Essential Koran*, by Thomas Cleary, p. 56.
15. Joseph Head and S. L. Cranston, *Reincarnation, and East–West Anthology*, The Theosophical Publishing House, 1961, p. 57.
16. *Quran*, Sura 2, The Cow, Verse 287, from *The Essential Koran*, by Thomas Cleary, p. 18.
17. *Quran*, Sura 3, The Family of Imraan, Verse 30., from *The Essential Koran*, by Thomas Cleary, p. 22.
18. *Quran*, Sura 21, The Prophet, Verse 47, from *The Essential Koran*, by Thomas Cleary, p. 81.
19. *Quran*, Sura 36, Ya Sin, Verse 12, from *The Essential Koran*, by Thomas Cleary, p. 111.
20. *Quran*, Sura 5, The Table, Verse 69, from *The Essential Koran*, by Thomas Cleary, p. 49.
21. *Quran*, Sura 5, The Table, Verse 171, from *The Essential Koran*, by Thomas Cleary, p. 42.
22. Jeffrey Mishlove, *Roots of Consciousness*, Council Oak Books, Tulsa, Oklahoma, 1993, p. 191.
23. Joseph Head and S. L. Cranston, *Reincarnation, and East–West Anthology*, The Theosophical Publishing House, 1961, p. 39.

Chapter 2

1. Tom Shroder, *Old Souls*, Fireside/Simon and Schuster, NY, NY, 2001, p. 81.
2. Ibid, p. 81.
3. Ibid, p. 82.
4. Ibid, p. 74.
5. Ibid, p. 50.
6. Ibid, p. 50.
7. Ibid, p. 74.
8. Ian Stevenson, *Where Reincarnation and Biology Intersect*, Praeger, Westport, Connecticut, 1997, p. 168.

Chapter 3

Barbro Karlen, *And the Wolves Howled*, Clairview Books, United Kingdom, 2000

Chapter 4

1. Robert Snow, *Looking for Carroll Beckwith*, Daybreak/Rodale Books, Emmaus, Pennsylvania, 1999, p. 12–13.
2. Ibid., p. 79–84.
3. Ibid., p. 89.

Chapter 5

1. Courtesy of Jeffrey Keene.
2. Courtesy of Jeffrey Keene.
3. Courtesy of Jeffrey Keene.
4. John B. Gordon, *Remembrances of the Civil War*, p. 147–148.
5. Courtesy of Jeffrey Keene.
10. Courtesy of Jeffrey Keene.

Chapter 6

John Elliotson narrative courtesy of Norm Shealy, in a personal correspondence to the author

Chapter 7

Narratives courtesy of Wayne Peterson, in a personal correspondence to the author

Chapter 8

Quotation regarding media dubbing Alexandra Nechita as a "Petite Picasso" taken from the website: www.nechita.info/

Chapter 9

1. Charles H. Parkhurst, *My Forty Years in New York*, MacMillian, New York, NY, 1923, p. 20.
2. Ibid, p. 20.
3. John Greenleaf Whittier, *The Singer*, reprinted in: Mary Clemmer Ames, *Alice and Phoebe Cary*, Hurd and Houghton, New York, NY, 1873, p. 27.
4. Mary Clemmer Ames, *Alice and Phoebe Cary*, Hurd and Houghton, New York, NY, 1873, p. 93.
5. Quote provided by Penney Peirce from an Alice Cary website, source not identified.
6. Quote provided by Penney Peirce from a Charles Parkhurst website, source not identified.
7. Penney Peirce, *The Intuitive Way*, Beyond Words Publishing, Hillsboro, OR, 1997, p. 10.
8. Charles H. Parkhurst, *My Forty Years in New York*, p. 230.
9. Penney Peirce, from personal unpublished journal.
10. *The Ladies' Repository*, Sept. 1855, "Literary Women of America; Number VI, Some Notice of the Writing Genius of Alice Cary," editor, Rev. D. W. Clark.
11. Charles H. Parkhurst, *A Thanksgiving Message from Dr. Parkhurst, the Foremost Patriotic Preacher in America,*" Amherst Library.
12. Penney Peirce, *The Intuitive Way*, Beyond Words Publishing, Hillsboro, OR, 1997, p. 82.
13. From "God is Love, " by Alice Cary, reprinted in: Mary Clemmer Ames, *Alice and Phoebe Cary*, p. 263.

14. National Cyclopedia of American Biography, Vol 1, White and Co., p. 535.

Chapter 11

2. L. H. Butterfield, *Diary and Autobiography of John Adams, Volume 2*, The Belknap Press, Harvard University Press, 1961, p. 82–83.
3. Clifford K. Shipton, *Biographical Sketches of Those Who Attended Harvard College, Sibley's Harvard Graduates, Vol. XIV, 1756–1760*, Massachusetts Historical Society, Boston, 1968, p. 113.
4. Ibid., p. 116.
5. Ibid.
6. Ibid.
7. Ibid., p. 119.
8. Ibid., p. 120.
9. Ibid., p. 112.
10. Ibid.
11. Ibid., p. 116.

Chapter 12

1. George Athan Billias, *George Washington's Generals and Opponents*, Da Capo Press, New York, NY, p. 88.
2. Ibid., p. 90.
3. Ibid., p. 83.
4. Ibid., p. 97.
5. Ibid., p. 293.
6. Ibid., p. 303.
7. Ibid.

Chapter 13

1. Catherine Drinker Bowen, *Miracle at Philadelphia*, Book-of-the-Month Club/New York, NY/Little, Brown and Company, Boston, MA, 1966, p. 56.
2. Ibid.
3. George Mair, *Oprah Winfrey: The Real Story*, Carol Publishing Group, Secaucus, NJ, 1996, p. 12.
4. Ibid., p. 29.
5. Clarence L. Ver Steeg, *Robert Morris, Revolutionary Financier*, University of Pennsylvania Press, 1954, p. 174.
6. Ibid.
7. George Mair, *Oprah Winfrey: The Real Story*, p. 30.
8. Kermit L. Hall, *The Oxford Companion to the Supreme Court of the United States*, Oxford University Press, New York, NY, 1992, p. 932.
9. George Mair, *Oprah Winfrey: The Real Story*, p. 30.
10. Ibid., p. 48.
11. Ibid.
12. Ibid., p. 127.
13. Robert G. Ferris and Richard E. Morris, *The Signers of the Declaration of Independence*, Interpretive Publications, Flagstaff, AZ, 1982, p. 147.

Chapter 15

1. Jean Burton, *Heyday of a Wizard*, Warner Paperback Library, Undated, p. 24.
2. Ibid., p. 16.
3. Uri Geller, *My Story*, Praeger Publishers, New York, 1975, p. 188.
4. Ibid., p. 211.
5. Jean Burton, *Heyday of a Wizard*, p. 22–23.
6. Ibid, p. 17.
7. Uri Geller, *My Story*, p. 267–275.
8. Uri Geller, *My Story*, p. 239.
9. Uri Geller, *My Story*, p. 81.
10. Jean Burton, *Heyday of a Wizard*, p. 69.

11. Uri Geller, *My Story, p.* 11.
12. Ibid., p. 45–46.
13. Ibid, p. 241.
14. Ibid, p. 20.
15. Jean Burton, *Heyday of a Wizard*, p. 121.
16. Uri Geller, *My Story*, 173–174.
17. Jean Burton, *Heyday of a Wizard*, p. 39.
18. Uri Geller, *My Story*, p. 59.
19. Ibid., p. 61.
20. Jean Burton, *Heyday of a Wizard*, p. 100.
21. Gordon Stein, *The Sorcerer of Kings*, Prometheus Books, Buffalo, New York, 1993, p. 81.
22. Uri Geller, *My Story*, p. 30.
23. Ibid., p. 260.
24. Ibid.. p. 21.
25. Jean Burton, *Heyday of a Wizard*, p. 135.
26. Jean Burton, *Heyday of a Wizard*, p. 189–190.
27. Uri Geller, *My Story*, p. 142.

Chapter 18

1. APJ Abdul Kalam with Arun Tiwari, *Wings of Fire*, University Press (India) Private Limited, Hyderguda, Hyderabad , India, 1999, p. 6
2. Ibid, p. 24
3. Ibid, p. 32
4. Ibid, p. 15
5. Ibid, p. 17
6. Lewin B. Bowring, *Rulers of India: Haidar Ali and Tipu Sultan*, Oxford at the Clarendon Press, Oxford, England, 1899, p. 26

7. Ibid, p. 110
8. Ibid, p. 151
9. Ibid, p. 110

Chapter 19

1. G. W. Forrest, *A History Of The Indian Mutiny, Reviewed and Illustrated from Original Documents*, W. Black Blackwood, London, 1904-12, p. 404
2. Ibid, p. 409
3. Ibid, p. 419
4. Ibid, p.464
5. Ibid, p. 40

Chapter 21

1. Biswadeep Ghosh, *Hall of Fame: Shah Rukh Khan*, Magna Publishing Company, 2004, p. 46

Chapter 22

1. James Cross Giblin, *Good Brother, Bad Brother*, Clarion Books, New York, 2005, p. 7
2. Ibid, 44
3. Bhawanana Somaaya, *Amitabh Bachchan: The Legend*, Macmillan India LTD, New Delhi, India, 1999, p. 269
4. Giblin, p. 76
5. Ibid, p. 117
6. Ibid, p.127
7. Ibid, p. 171
8. Ibid, p. 211

INDEX

ABOUT THE AUTHOR

Walter Semkiw, MD, MPH

Walter is a medical doctor and the author of the *Return of the Revolutionaries: The Case for Reincarnation and Soul Groups Reunited.* He is also on the Board of Directors of the International Association for Regression Research and Therapies (IARRT) and the Intuition Network. Walter has founded the Institute for the Integration of Science, Intuition and Spirit (IISIS), which is dedicated to researching reincarnation and related phenomena scientifically. IISIS serves as a resource to archive, study and publish reincarnation cases. In addition, avenues to prove reincarnation though biochemical or biophysical means, such as DNA analysis, are being explored.

www.johnadam.net
walter@johnadam.net

ABBE FARIA

The Master Hypnotist Who Charmed Napolean
by
Diogo M Fernandes

Abbe Faria was one of the pioneers of the scientific study of Hypnotism. Born on 31st May 1766, in Goa, this new biography will be brought out as a special centenary edition, shortly by Ritana Books.